The Death of the Nation
and the Future of the
Arab Revolution

The Death of the Nation and the Future of the Arab Revolution

Vijay Prashad

UNIVERSITY OF CALIFORNIA PRESS

University of California Press, one of the most distinguished university presses in the United States, enriches
lives around the world by advancing scholarship in the
humanities, social sciences, and natural sciences. Its
activities are supported by the UC Press Foundation and
by philanthropic contributions from individuals and
institutions. For more information, visit www.ucpress.edu.

University of California Press
Oakland, California

Library of Congress Cataloging-in-Publication Data

Names: Prashad, Vijay, author.
Title: The death of the nation and the future of the Arab
    revolution / Vijay Prashad.
Description: Oakland, California : University of
    California Press, [2016] | Includes index.
Identifiers: LCCN 2016015686 | ISBN 978-0-520-29325-0
    (cloth : alk. paper) | ISBN 978-0-520-29326-7 (pbk. : alk.
    paper) | ISBN 978-0-520-96643-7 (ebook)
Subjects: LCSH: Middle East—Politics and government—
    21st century. | Arab Spring, 2010- | Islam and
    politics—Middle East. | IS (Organization)
Classification: LCC DS63.123 .P73 2016 | DDC 956.05/4—dc23
LC record available at http://lccn.loc.gov/2016015686

Manufactured in the United States of America

25   24   23   22   21   20   19   18   17   16
10   9   8   7   6   5   4   3   2   1

*For Soni Prashad, this book of catastrophes
and hope—a book of life.*

CONTENTS

INTRODUCTION

Abu Bakr al-Baghdadi welcomed Ramadan in 2014 by declaring
the formation of the Caliphate, with him as the caliph—namely,
the successor of the Prophet Mohammed. It is the first return of
a caliphate since Kemal Atatürk's Turkish National Assembly
abolished it in 1924. Al-Baghdadi, the nom de guerre for the
leader of the Islamic State of Iraq and al-Sham (ISIS), announced
that borders inside the *dar al-Islam,* the world of Islam, are no
longer applicable. He made this announcement because his fighters had taken large swathes of territory in northern Syria and in
north-central Iraq, breathing down on Baghdad, the capital of
the Abbasid Caliphate (A.D. 750–1258).

Al-Baghdadi's declaration came after ISIS threatened to make
its presence felt outside the territory it now controls. Bomb blasts
in Beirut, Lebanon, hinted at ISIS's reach. Jordanian authorities
hastened to crack down on "sleeper cells" for ISIS as soon as
chatter on social media suggested that there would be a push into
Zarqa and Ma'an. Private Kuwaiti funding had helped ISIS in its
early stages, but now Kuwait hinted that it, too, is worried that

ISIS cells might strike the oil-rich emirate. When ISIS took the Jordan–Syria border posts, Saudi Arabia went into high alert.

Many of those associated with the rebellion in Syria had suggested that ISIS was egged on by the government of Bashar al-Assad to allow his preferred framing of the Syrian war—that his is a war against terrorism and not against a civic rebellion. While it is true that Assad's government released a number of extremists in 2011, there is no evidence to suggest that he created ISIS. ISIS is a product of the U.S. war on Iraq, having been formed first as al-Qaeda in Iraq by the Jordanian militant Abu Musab al-Zarqawi. Deeply sectarian politics—namely, an anti-Shia agenda—characterized al-Qaeda in this region. Funded by private Gulf Arab money, ISIS entered the Syrian war in 2012 as Jabhat al-Nusra (the Support Front). It certainly turned a civic rebellion into a terrorist war. Political support from the West and logistical support from Turkey and the Gulf Arab states allowed it to thrive in Syria. It became a hub for international extremism, with veterans from Afghanistan and Chechnya flocking to al-Baghdadi's band of fellows. By 2014, ISIS held two major Iraqi cities (Ramadi and Fallujah) and two Syrian cities (Raqqa and Deir ez Zor). By the end of the year, ISIS would seize Mosul—the second major city in Iraq, and later Palmyra, a historical city on the fringe of the Syrian desert.

The West has been consistently naive in its public assessment of events in West Asia. The belief that the Arab Spring could be understood simply as a fight between freedom and tyranny—concepts adopted from the Cold War—befuddled the United States over Syria. There was a refusal to accept that the civic rebellion of 2011 had morphed quite decisively by late 2012 into a much more dangerous conflict, with the radical extremists in the ascendancy. It is of course true, as I saw in Syria firsthand, that the actual fighters in the extremist groups are a ragtag bunch with no special commitment to this or that ideology. They are anti-Assad, and they joined Jabhat al-Nusra or Ahrar ash-Sham because that was the group at hand with arms and logistical means. Jabhat al-Nusra is in the orbit of al-Qaeda, while Ahrar ash-Sham (Free Men of Syria)—funded by Qatar and Turkey— bears all the marks of extremism. Nevertheless, the fighters did fight for these groups, giving them the upper hand against the West's preferred, but anemic, Free Syrian Army. ISIS's break- through in Iraq has inspired some of these men to its formations in Syria. They wanted to be part of the excitement.

The West's backing of the rebellion provided cover for Tur- key's more enthusiastic approach to it. Intoxicated by the possibil- ity of what Turkey's foreign minister, Ahmet Davutoğlu, favored as "neo-Ottomanism," the Turkish government called for the removal of Assad and the emergence of a pro-Istanbul govern- ment in Damascus. Turkey opened its borders to the "rat line" of international extremism, with planeloads of fighters from Chech- nya, Libya, and Tunisia flying into Turkey to cross into Syria to fight for ISIS and its offshoots. ISIS spat in Turkey's salt. ISIS struck Turkey in 2013 with car bombs and abductions, suggesting to Ankara that its policy has endangered its citizens. In March 2014, the governor of Hatay Province, Celattin Lekesiz, called upon the government to create a new policy to "prevent the illegal crossing of militants to Syria." It was met with silence.

An ISIS billboard in Mosul depicts the flags of the states in the region. All are crossed out as being traitorous regimes. Only the ISIS black flag stands as a sentinel for justice. Among the regimes to be overthrown is the Kingdom of Saudi Arabia. Saudi Arabia has used its vast wealth to influence the region, and to outsource its own problems with extremism. In 1962, the kingdom created the World Muslim League as an instrument against secular Arab nationalism and Communism. Twenty years later, the war in Afghanistan provided the opportunity for the kingdom to export its own disaffected youth (including Osama bin Laden) to fight the Afghan Communists rather than its own royal family. The 1979 takeover of the Mecca mosque by extremists was an indication of the threat of such youth. Saudi policy, however, did not save the kingdom. Al-Qaeda, the product of this policy, threatened and attacked the kingdom. But few lessons were learned.

Saudi policy vis-à-vis Syria and Iraq repeats the Afghan story. Funds and political support for extremists in the region came from the kingdom and its Gulf allies. Saudi Arabia tried to stop its youth from going to these wars—a perilous mistake that it had made with Afghanistan. It was too late. They had already encouraged chaos—whether in Iraq, Syria, or Egypt, the latter poisoned by harsh repression after the promise of the Tahrir uprising. The Arab world, flush with hope in 2011, is now drowning in a counterrevolution financed by petrodollars. Saudi Arabia's response to the rise of ISIS is disingenuous. The kingdom feigns outrage, tells the Iraqis that it does not want to get involved, says that it wants to raise an army to fight in Syria. "We are asked what can be done," wrote its ambassador to the United Kingdom, Prince Mohammed bin Nawaf. "At the moment, we wait, we watch and we pray." The fact is that both the West and the Gulf Arabs *are* doing more. They finance the extremist rebels in Syria, and they see the Assad government as an obstacle to peace in the region. Both the West and the Gulf Arabs suggest that the terrorism that they dislike against themselves is acceptable for others. The history of their policies also suggests that Western and Gulf Arab intervention leads inexorably to the creation of police states (as in Egypt) and terrorist emirates. A lack of basic commitment to people's movements—anchored in unions and in civic groups—will always lead to such diabolical outcomes.

Meanwhile, sectarian lines are being hardened in the region. The battle now does not revisit the ancient fight at Karbala—the battle in A.D. 680 that created the fissure between the camp of the Umayyads (the Sunni) and the camp of Hussein (the Shia). This is not an age-old sectarian conflict that runs over the course of centuries. It is a modern one, over ideas of republicanism and monarchy, Iranian influence and Saudi influence. Shadows of sectarianism do shroud the battle of ordinary people who are frustrated by the lack of opportunities for them, and by the lack of a future for their children. Society's fissures do not disturb the rational world of political discourse. In fact, the needle of motion is the other way around. It is political division that lifted the scab of difference and acrimony off the skin of society. What motivates these political fights are less the petty prejudices of sect and more the grander ambitions of regional control. Al-Baghdadi has announced that his vision is much greater than that of the Saudi king or the government in Tehran. He wants to command a religion, not just a region. By such delusions are great societies destroyed.

The Death of a Nation and the Future of the Arab Revolution is a reporter's guidebook, not a scholar's treatise. It traces the philosophy of regime change as it manifests itself on the ground, from the devastation of Iraq to the ravaging of Libya. "Regime change," in this book, is not merely conducted by armed action, but is also driven by policies of economic hardship pushed by the International Monetary Fund (IMF) and World Bank as well as by sociopolitical agendas that encourage sectarianism and stifle human development. Taking a wide look at the concept of regime change on the ground reveals that not only did this approach operate in Iraq (2003) and Libya (2011), but it also operated in Egypt (2013), and it goes on in Syria. It takes a hundred years to build a state. It takes an afternoon to destroy it.

Four Arab countries have been laid waste over the past fifteen years—Iraq, Libya, Syria, and Yemen. One Arab country— Egypt—has been silenced and its people's dreams revoked. Another Arab country—Palestine—has been prevented from making its historical appearance in the world. Regime-change theory is responsible for the destruction of the four states—Iraq, Libya, Syria, and Yemen. Regardless of the high intentions of their authors, regime-change policies have outcomes that are horrendous. Massive bombardment—the preferred contemporary method of regime change—destroys infrastructure and institutions. Vindictive occupations isolate sections of the population that are seen to have been beneficiaries of the overthrown regime. Inflamed sectarianism tears society apart. The endgame is chaos, not democracy.

The Death of a Nation is an argument about the slow political death of the idea of Arab nationalism in the fires of sectarian war and chaos that runs from Iraq to Libya, from Yemen to Palestine. But it is also about the Arab revolution, which—despite all appearances of futility—remains alive and well in the hearts of the Arab masses. They want something better, something other than endless war and occupation—a condition that produces a neurological uncertainty. Other dreams incubate here and there. "They wait," wrote the Palestinian poet Mahmoud Darwish, "and waiting is steadfastness and a stand."[1]

CHAPTER ONE

Obituary of the Arab Spring

Arab children,
Spring rain,
Corn ears of the future,
You are the generation
That will overcome defeat.

Nizar Qabbani, "Hawamish 'ala
daftar al-naksah" (Footnotes to the
book of the setback), 1967

Popular rebellions reflect the urges of a people, but the people are themselves not always capable of victory. If the structure of social order in a particular formation is weakened by war or by economic turmoil, the popular rebellions might be able to move history forward. Even here, the record shows that unless there is an organized force that is ready to seize the day, historical motion can falter. Older, dominant social classes that have a monopoly over violence hastily enter the fray to their advantage. Human history is littered with failed uprisings. They are the norm. Success is the exception. But neither failure nor success holds back the frequency of revolts. These are in the nature of human desire: the march toward freedom.

Slogans defined the air of 2011—*Khubz wa-ma' wa-Ben Ali la* ("We can live on bread and water, but no more Ben Ali") and *Yasqut, yasqut hukm al-'askar* ("Down, down with military rule"). Enthusiasm was the order of things in North Africa. Men and women, young and old, from various social classes, descended onto the squares of towns and cities to say: enough. Decades of futility had burdened their history. Intellectuals in Tunisia dusted off copies of the poetry books of Abu al-Qasim al-Shabbi (1909–34), singing "To the Tyrants of the World" to a new tune,

> You've taken off heads of people and the flowers of hope; and watered the cure of the sand with blood and tears until it was drunk.
> The blood's river will sweep you away and you will be burned by the fiery storm.

In Egypt, a young folk singer, Ramy Essam, held his guitar tightly in Cairo's Tahrir Square to sing, "We are united, we demand one thing: Leave, leave, leave." That word—*leave* (or *irhal*)—came from a chant to a song. It defined the ambition of the people: they wanted the departure of the tyrants.

So they fell. Tunisia's Ben Ali went first, followed by Egypt's Hosni Mubarak. Ben Ali and his family went to Saudi Arabia. Mubarak went to his seaside home in Sharm al-Sheikh. Both moved to towns on the Red Sea. Courts found both of them guilty—although as events soured in Egypt, Mubarak would be forgiven. Not so Ben Ali, who still lives under the protection of the Saudis in Jeddah.

Matters began to get complex. Saudi Arabia's legions snuffed its own disgruntled population with jail sentences and handouts, and then entered Bahrain to crush its Pearl Monument encampment. NATO's jets fired up to bomb Libya and bring the force of imperial arms into the uprisings. Proxy armies and money of the old order entered both Libya and Syria, changing the mood of the Arab Spring from jubilation to trepidation.[1] The Syrian poet Adunis, whose flinty (and Orientalist) comments on the rebellion disturbed his reputation, captured the grave pall that fell over the region by the time Libya and Syria entered the frame. In *al-Hayat,* one of the leading daily pan-Arab newspapers (31 March 2011), Adunis wrote, "A politics led in the name of religion by a cart pulled by two horses—heaven and hell—is necessarily a violent and exclusionary politics." He continued mournfully, "The present in some of its explosions is copying the events of the past with modern instruments."[2] At the time Adunis was pilloried for his pessimism.

Five years on, obituaries of the Arab Spring have now begun to emerge. The general sense is of futility: What was the point of the uprising if the outcome is worse than the situation that existed? Mass social change is rarely predictable. No people rise up with the expectation that they will fail. That is why the opening of every mass struggle is deeply inspirational. It is also the case that each mass struggle results in a new order that is not capable of its original spark. Sitting in his Turkish exile in 1930, Leon Trotsky wrote his magisterial *History of the Russian Revolution.* Thirteen years had elapsed since the 1917 October Revolution. The revolution was already being derided. "Capitalism," Trotsky wrote in his conclusion, "required a hundred years to elevate science and technique to the heights and plunge humanity into the hell of war and crisis. To socialism its enemies allow only fifteen years to create and furnish a terrestrial paradise. We took no such obligation upon ourselves. We never set these dates. The process of vast transformation must be measured by an adequate scale."[3]

How to measure the Arab Spring that began in 2011? In Tunisia and Egypt, mass political action certainly deposed unpopular leaders, but it was not able to transform the regimes. Figureheads went, but the tentacles of elite power remained intact. The highest expectation of these revolts was that they would inaugurate an epoch of democratic governance for these two countries. In other words, Tunisia and Egypt would have experienced a bourgeois revolution.

Much was expected of Egypt, but these expectations were exaggerated. Mubarak left on 11 February 2011. Two years later, on 3 July 2013, the military conducted a coup against the elected government of Mohammed Morsi of the Muslim Brotherhood. Apart from the Muslim Brotherhood, few other parties had a link with sections of the people. This was not the métier of the liberals. They were professionals who had little political contact with the masses. Hatred of the Muslim Brotherhood's suffocating agenda had thrown the liberals into a convoluted alliance with the military by 2013. One of the most uncomfortable facts of recent Egyptian history is that more people came out onto the streets on 30 June 2013, to oppose the government of the Muslim Brotherhood, than in 2011 in Tahrir Square. All kinds of people took to the streets that day: Salafis alongside liberals, reactionaries alongside revolutionaries. The liberal stalwart Mohamed ElBaradei said that the military "will just come back to stabilize. And then we will start all over again." This was naive. The military dismissed the political process, began its campaign of imprisonment of dissent, and portrayed itself as the inheritors of Gamal Abdel Nasser and stability. Tensions in the Sinai Peninsula over the rise of Islamist radicalism and the emergence of chaos in Libya provided the military's new leader, Abdel Fattah el-Sisi, with a raison d'être. But tension in the Sinai began in 2010, predating both the Tahrir uprising and the emergence of the Brotherhood to power. If anything, the emergence of terrorist cells signals the failure of the military rather than its necessity. Human-rights groups are unable to give an accurate figure for those who are in prison under spurious charges and for those who have been killed in clashes and mass executions. The current government's own definitions of imprisonment and murder do not allow for ease of calculation. Everyone whom the government does not like, it seems, is now a terrorist. It is the term of art for *dissenter.*

Even celebrations of Tahrir are forbidden on 25 January. On the fourth anniversary of Tahrir, in 2015, the security services killed twenty-three people, including the poet and socialist Shaimaa al-Sabbagh, who was shot with flowers in her hands. Thousands came to bury her. The fifth anniversary—in 2016—was silent. The military came out to hand out flowers. They now claim the day.

Threats to the bourgeois turn in Tunisia came from all directions—the old order eager to reappear without Ben Ali, the IMF wanting cuts in the budget, extremist groups incubating in the slums of Tunis. What saved Tunisia was its trade union, the Union Générale Tunisienne du Travail (UGTT), which claims 20 percent of the country's population as its members. It is the most representative civil society organization in the country, although it went through decades of somnolence. When the new, post–Ben Ali period in Tunisia seemed to be on the verge of falling apart, the UGTT dragged to the table its historical enemy, the employers' association, and its allies in the human-rights field to draw up a roadmap for the country. That roadmap, created by these social forces, handcuffed the political parties into a dialogue that led to the new constitution. It was the Tunisian working class, therefore, that created the basis for stability in the new Tunisia. It is this working class that won the Nobel Peace Prize for 2016. The classical gesture of the Nobel Committee would have been to honor the two main political luminaries: Rached Ghannouchi, of the Ennahda party; and Beji Caid Essebsi, of the Nidaa Tounes party. After all, when Ben Ali fled the country, it was the Ennahda—largely in exile and part of the Muslim Brotherhood current—that seized the political opportunity. But the old order did not fall easily. Beji Caid Essebsi had been appointed the interim prime minister. Essebsi is the perpetual survivor. He was a close associate of Habib Bourguiba, Tunisia's main leader in the anticolonial struggle and then its first president. When Ben Ali overthrew Bourguiba in 1987, Essebsi threw his lot in with the younger generation. During the Arab Spring, Essebsi again corralled sections of the Tunisian elite out of its allegiance to Ben Ali and threw in his lot with the future to become interim prime minister. Between the Ennahda leadership and Essebsi a modus vivendi was established, despite great rancor. After elections in October 2011, Essebsi handed over power to the Ennahda candidate, Moncef Marzouki. Three years later, Essebsi's Nidaa Tounes (Tunisia's Call), a secular front, defeated Marzouki, giving Essebsi the presidency. If the Nobel had been awarded in the conventional way, the prize would have gone to the leadership of Ennahda and Essebsi for the peaceful transition from the reign of Ben Ali to the new dispensation based on the 2014 constitution. But that would not have captured the essence of what happened in Tunisia.

When matters seemed bleak in 2013, it was not the political parties that broke the mold and aligned themselves to a peaceful path. The UGTT took up that historical task—drawing in the employers' association and the two human-rights groups to form the Quartet. Danger stalked their approach. Two important left leaders fell to assassins' bullets in 2013. Chokri Belaid, of the Democratic Patriots' Movement, was shot dead on 6 February, and Mohammed Brahimi, of the Popular Front, was assassinated on 25 July. The Revolution of Freedom and Dignity seemed to be moving into perilous waters. Anything could have happened. Strikes and protests were met with violence. Tunisia was on the knife's edge. It was at this point that the Quartet's maneuver was essential. As the representatives of society, the Quartet forced the political parties to come to the table. Ghannouchi's Ennahda party had been accused of being behind the assassinations. This was the summer when the Muslim Brotherhood was removed from power by a Western-backed military coup in Egypt. Ennahda, which is allied to the Egyptian Muslim Brotherhood, was at a disadvantage. It also needed a way out. The forces led by Essebsi, some of the old regime, knew that they could not crack down on the workers in the streets and on Ennahda. The army did not move on their behalf as it did against Morsi. Tunisia required a compromise. That is what the Quartet delivered. Absent that, Tunisia might have gone down the road of Egypt. It was saved from that travesty.

Tunisia's respite could very well be temporary. Behind the veneer of the Nobel lies a grave reality. A high debt overhang and frustration in the gullies of the small towns and cities provoked Essebsi in early 2016 to suggest that ISIS is in the shadows. On the Tunisian side of the Libyan border, battles are common between security forces and ISIS (as well as various other outfits). The town of Ben Guerdane was caught in such a battle in March 2016. But oxygen for Tunisia's economy—as a respite for its security threats—was not forthcoming. The policy space for Tunisia is narrow, with little imaginativeness from the World Bank, the IMF, and the commercial lenders. They are unwilling to countenance a massive investment to shore up this fledgling democracy.⁴ For now, the multilateral agencies look the other way as Tunisia increases its public-sector employment and funnels higher wages to these workers. A proper exit from the shadows is not available. The vortex of instability remains open.

Tunisia established a constitutional democracy, although its political class—with some new faces—does not have the political wherewithal to solve some of the pressing problems of the population—namely, jobs for the burgeoning youth. Egypt has drifted back into the arms of the military.

SULTANS OF ARABIA

Freedom is an elusive idea. Ravages of history have produced institutions that favor the elite, who are resilient in the ways of metamorphosis. During antifeudal movements, petty royalty threw off their regal garb, donned the suits of the bourgeoisie, and took their places at the front of the new order. The great Arab nationalist revolutions of the twentieth century—from Egypt to Libya—rid the region of monarchs, but failed to deepen the roots of popular democracy. They roused the people, but often asked them to stand behind the military. Green uniforms stood in as sentinels of revolution. The actual revolutionaries—labor and peasant organizers, communists—went to prison. The colonels and captains seized their rhetoric.

In one redoubt of the region—the Arabian Island (*al-jazira al-arabiyya*)—monarchy fashioned itself as an ally of the gunboats of the West. It had no roots in the desert. It was a purely modern invention—1820 for the al-Khalifa dynasty of Bahrain, and 1932 for the al-Saud dynasty of Arabia. The West decided—early—that the defense of the Arab monarchs was tantamount to self-preservation. Much of this had to do with oil. The Carter

Doctrine of 1980—to protect the Saudi monarchy—merely put into legalese what had been common policy till then. It was the nail in the coffin of freedom for the Arab lands. The West, with its superior firepower, backed the Arab monarchies, flush with petrodollars, against the will of the Arab people, from Morocco to Iraq. The founding of the World Muslim League in 1962— with complete U.S. support—suggested to the Arab lands that secular nationalism and socialism were anathema—that the hand on the tiller of Arab history had to be Saudi. Saudi Arabia and the West—unlikely partners—exported Saudi Arabia's version of Islam (Wahabbism) and the West's paranoia about Communist intervention across the region. Prisons opened up for the Left, and Saudi-funded mosques threw their doors open for the adherents. This sets in concrete the social formation of the Arab lands.

Long before the Arab Spring came Arab nationalism—the ideology that the Arab people must create their own destiny outside the confines of Western control. The contours of Arab nationalism were wide—mostly secular, often socialist, typically with a resounding emphasis on the "Arab people." The early Arab nationalism—rooted in the Nahda (Awakening) of the nineteenth century and made manifest in the Arab Congress of 1913—was initially elitist and chauvinist. An echo of that old chauvinist Arab nationalism can be heard from Saudi Arabia today when it speaks of "Arab solidarity" (particularly against Iran). Grandees of the Ottoman administration with talents frustrated by the preferences toward the Turks sought their own national project—with themselves as the main beneficiaries, and with the peasants (*fellahin*) as political cannon fodder. People like Rida Pasha al-Rikabi, Izzat Darwazeh, Shukri al-Quwatli, and Saad Zaghlul Pasha held the reins of this movement. Their

nationalism whipped from the widest Arab canvas to their
localities—whether Egypt for Saad Zaghlul Pasha or Syria for
Rida Pasha al-Rikabi. That both were pashas—the title of a
high-ranking Ottoman official—says a great deal about their
social position and their ambitions.[5]

Gamal Abdel Nasser and his military associates, after the 1952
overthrow of King Farouk's monarchy, seized this mantle of Arab
nationalism. It would then sweep through Iraq, which overthrew
the monarchy of King Faisal II in 1958, and into Libya, which overthrew King Idriss in 1969. Nasser, Brigadier Abd al-Karim Qasim
of Iraq, and Colonel Muammar Qaddafi of Libya wore uniforms,
but they were not initially defined by them. Arab nationalism was
greater than the men who became its icons. It was an ineffable sensibility for self-rule and for an end to Western intervention (including the colonization of Palestine by Israel). Grand images of Arab
efflorescence spread from city to countryside; boldness had arrived
in the region. Nasser's speeches traveled the region through Sawt
al-Arab, the Voice of the Arabs radio, interspersed with the revolutionary poems sung by Abdel Wahab and Umm Kulthum and long
paeans to the revolutionary Algerians, Yemenis, and Palestinians.[6]
Pan-Arabism was the revolt of the common Arab people (*al sha'ab
al 'arab*). Linkage of Arab nationalism to the Third World Project
at the Bandung Conference (1955), in the Afro-Asian People's Solidarity Organization (founded in 1958), and in the Non-Aligned
Movement (founded in 1961) sharpened its anti-imperialism. Antipathy to monarchies and imperialism became its ethos. Support for
Arab nationalists across the region became axiomatic. Nasser put
resources into the Yemeni civil war and encouraged the union
between Egypt and Syria. But there were limits to this Arab
nationalism. It distrusted Communists, whom it threw into prison.
It could not fathom non-Arab minorities—particularly the Kurds,

whose national aspirations ran counter to the Arab nationalism prevalent in Iraq and Syria during the 1950s and 1960s. (It did not help that Jalal Talabani pushed the Kurdish Democratic Party in Syria to change its name to the more provocative Democratic Party of Kurdistan—announcing the name of the country rather than merely the population.)[7] Arab nationalism could not contain all the energy of nationalism, with older animosities between Iraq and Egypt—say—coming in the way of true unity. Antipathy to Zionism and to imperialism drew them together, even as other fissures kept them apart.

When Egypt took control of the Suez Canal in 1956, the Israelis, British, and French invaded the country. Although the United States brokered the withdrawal of this intervention, U.S. President Eisenhower nonetheless felt that Nasser "embodies the emotional demands of the people of the area for independence and for 'slapping the White Man down.'" This was not said with approval. Later, Eisenhower suggested that the "underlying Arab thinking"—which desired independence—was rooted in "violence, emotion and ignorance."[8] Arab nationalism had to be opposed. It was in this endeavor that the United States found its major political allies in the region—not the secular nationalist forces, but the decrepit monarchies of Saudi Arabia and Iran. When the flavor of Third World nationalism came to Iran in 1951 through the unlikely patrician Mohammed Mosaddegh, it had to be removed. Mosaddegh's attempt to get the Iranian people a fair deal for their oil was scandalous to Washington and its oil barons. A CIA and British intelligence coup removed Mosaddegh and returned the shah—a mediocre man—to the Peacock Throne. "It was a day that should never have ended," wrote a CIA internal report. "For it carried with it such a sense of excitement, of satisfaction and of jubilation that it is doubtful whether any other can come up to it."[9] The message across the Persian Gulf to the Saudi royal family was clear: if the United States would go to such lengths to return the shah to his throne, the Saudis need not fear the urges of the people. During the Mosaddegh period, as oil flow from Iran seemed less certain, the United States shifted its gaze to the Arabian Peninsula. By 1953, the United States had become a major purchaser of oil from Saudi Arabia. Not only did the CIA coup settle the anxiety in the palaces of the Saudis, but the purchases of oil from the peninsula suggested American dependence.[10] All this was underlined by 1954, when the U.S. ambassador to Saudi Arabia wrote to his handlers in Washington that the special friendship between the United States and ARAMCO (the Saudi oil company) was "the most important single American interest on the face of the earth outside the US."[11] The Eisenhower Doctrine provided material support to any state in the region threatened by Communism. This meant, effectively, that the monarchies would be protected against any threat to their existence. The United States, then, became the protector of monarchy in West Asia. It casts its nuclear umbrella above them.

The blow to the growing Arab nationalism came not directly from either the West or the Saudis. It came from the defeat of the Arab armies in the 1967 "battle of destiny" (*al-Ma'raka al-Masiriya*) against Israel. That broke the spirit of Arab possibilities. Nasser resigned his post. A million people went out to Tahrir Square in Cairo to ask him to rescind his resignation. He did, but he was a broken man (much like his friend Nehru after the India-China war of 1962). Nasser died in 1970. (Nehru died in 1964.)[12] The defeat corroded the confidence of the leaders at about the same time that their economies went into a tailspin. Huge expenditure for defense was a poor stewardship of the social wealth. It meant debt to foreign commercial banks. In 1973, Nasser's successor, Anwar Sadat, started the *infitah* (openness) policy of inviting private—including foreign—investment in Egypt. Nasser's confidant Mohamed Heikal described the changes in Egypt with a wry play on language—the era of *thawra* (revolution) had been supplanted by the era of *tharwa* (fortune). No doubt the old socialist journalist had a sneer as his hand flourished the word for "fortune"—concentrated with increasing volume at the top of the class structure.[13] The decade that followed saw more and more states governed by Arab nationalism find themselves in economic crisis and foreign debt and then, after 1979, catapulted into the Third World debt crisis.[14] The exuberance of the Palestinian fedayeen gave Arab nationalism a boost in a time of great gloom. Even the Palestinian defeats—in Jordan in 1970 and Lebanon in 1982—did not diminish the role it played for an otherwise rendered Arab nationalism. It is no wonder that it was networks that organized on behalf of the first and second Palestinian intifadas of 1987 and 2000, respectively, that created the groundwork for the Arab Spring of 2010–11.

From the standpoint of the West and its regional allies until the 1980s, anti-Communism and anti–Arab nationalism defined their narrative of events in the region. The states governed by Arab nationalism typically remained governed by one party or a small coterie, although they promised to take care of the basic needs of their populations. Surrender political power, they seemed to say, and we shall provide you with lives of reasonable dignity. With the economic crisis that opened up in the 1980s and 1990s, the basis for social goods began to evaporate, and access to basic goods through the private sector became more and more expensive. These states—once the providers of a social floor—now became merely mechanisms of repression and cronyism. It was easy, therefore, for the West to pivot from its language of anti-Communism to one of "democracy promotion." Saddam Hussein was the poster child of the autocrat by the 1990s. It did not matter that he was a close ally of the United States and the Gulf Arabs in the previous decade. His break with the Gulf Arabs revoked his privileges. With Communism no longer a threat in the 1990s, the West painted Iraq as the modular "rogue state." Syria and Libya were not far behind. The undemocratic Gulf Arab monarchies and the security state in Egypt were insulated for being U.S. allies. Ideology was all very well. More important than that was the maintenance of the old pillars of stability in the region—Saudi Arabia and Israel, with Egypt bought off with an annual $1 billion payment to pledge peace with Israel.

After Nasserism, the next threat to the Saudi-Western order came from the Iranian Revolution of 1979. The World Muslim League and its ancillary groups had made the argument that secular nationalism and socialism were anti-Islamic. The Iranian Revolution now arrived in the region and proposed the existence of an Islamic republic. Iran directly threatened the ideological claims made by the Gulf Arab monarchies. It was this challenge that had to be routed—initially by Iraq's failed invasion and long war (1980–88). Iran held fast against both the Saudi-backed attempts and the U.S. attempts at destabilization.

AMERICA'S WAR, IRAN'S VICTORY

When U.S. President George W. Bush prosecuted his war against Afghanistan and Iraq in 2001–03, he delivered a major geopolitical victory to Iran. Two of Iran's historic adversaries— Saddam Hussein's Ba'ath Party and the Taliban—fell by the wayside as Iran's allies—the Iraqi Dawa Party and the forces of

Ismail Khan of Herat—took center stage. America fought the war; Iran won it. Iran stretched its influence to the Mediterranean Sea and to the Hindu Kush. It rattled the doors of the Saudi palaces and of the White House.

Attempts to hem in Iran came immediately. The U.S. Congress passed the 2003 Syria Accountability Act, which was premised on breaking Iran's ties to Damascus and through there to Beirut and Palestine. The Damascus airport provided Iran with the main resupply route for the Lebanese political and military force Hezbollah and the Palestinian political and military force Hamas. Israel's war against Lebanon in 2006 was the next feint—this time targeting Hezbollah, who have close ties to Iran. The nuclear-sanctions regime that began in 2006 pushed hard against Iran's geopolitical allies and its own economy. Israel's threats against Iran and the assassination of Iranian scientists as well as the Western strike on Iran's computer system (Stuxnet worm) provided the next blow. None of these succeeded. Iran continued to find trading partners among the assertive Global South—China certainly, but also India.[15] By the turn of the decade, it had become clear that Iran was not going to bow easily to Western pressure and return to its isolation. It had become a regional power, and that was that.

The Arab Spring allowed Iran a wider role than had previously been possible. Iranian diplomats traveled the region to suggest that this was less an *Arab* Spring and more an *Islamic* Spring. It was, for them, a sequel to what they began to call the "Iranian Spring" of 1979. Iran's leadership made noises about new alliances with the new governments, which seemed—at first—as if they would have less of a prone relationship with the West. The post-Mubarak regime in Egypt allowed Iranian warships to cross the Suez Canal, and Egypt's President Mohammed Morsi visited Tehran—

both firsts since 1979. The dynamic of the Arab Spring—fought over between the regional powers (Turkey, Iran, and the Gulf monarchies)—seemed in doubt. Turkey's Recep Tayyip Erdoğan traveled to Cairo in September 2011 to claim the uprising for his neo-Ottoman foreign policy. But in fact, Erdoğan's party—the Justice and Development Party (AKP)—and the Qatari government had close ties to the Muslim Brotherhood. They had already begun to funnel money and assistance to their fraternal parties in North Africa. This rankled Saudi Arabia and the United Arab Emirates—both of whom did not want to see either the Iranians or the Brotherhood in the saddle. Morsi's dance with Tehran showed that the Muslim Brotherhood was not a serious bulwark against Iran. The Saudis and the Emiratis went alone.

In the early days of the crisis in Libya in 2011, at the most hopeful point of the Arab Spring, a senior Saudi diplomat told me scornfully that it would come to nothing. The Saudis feared—more than anything—that the waves of enthusiasm would cross into their kingdom and threaten their dispensation. The endangered Gulf Arab monarchies went on the rampage to protect their order. Breathing fire, the Saudi, Emirati, and Turkish proxies caused havoc in Syria and Libya, as Saudi money bankrolled the coup by General Sisi in Egypt and opened a new war against Yemen. Qatar—tail between its legs—retreated from its position of adversary, as Turkey spiraled out of control with its war against the Kurds. The West backed the Saudis fully, although it was wary of the Saudi initiative in Syria. Disagreement over Syria did not prevent the Saudis from prosecuting their own game there—largely through their proxy Jaysh al-Islam and others. It was not enough to push back against Iran itself to make Syria into a geopolitical struggle. The Saudi and Gulf Arab temperament is geared toward bringing sectarianism to the table. In 2009, UAE Crown Prince Mohammed Zayed al-Nahyan told a U.S. official that Iran had established "emirates in south Lebanon and Gaza, sleeper emirates in Kuwait, Bahrain, the Eastern Province of Saudi Arabia, and the mother of all emirates in Southern Iraq."[16] That same year, UAE Foreign Minister Sheikh Abdullah bin Zayed said that Saudi Arabia fears that the new Pakistani president, Asif Ali Zardari, "is Shia, thus creating Saudi concern of a Shia triangle in the region between Iran, the Maliki government in Iraq and Pakistan under Zardari."[17] Here is the hallucinatory spirit of the Gulf. Anti-Iran morphed rapidly into anti-Shia rhetoric and practice. It is how Saudi proxies have operated in Syria and in Iraq and why Saudi Arabia began its endless war in Yemen. It is why the Saudi regime executed the Shia cleric Sheikh Nimr Baqr al-Nimr on 2 January 2016. These are provocations along sectarian lines. They are what the Saudis know.

DEFEATS

The Arab Spring was defeated neither in the byways of Tahrir Square nor in the souk of Aleppo. It was defeated roundly in the palaces of Riyadh, Doha, and Ankara as well as in Washington, Paris, Tehran, and Moscow. From there came the petrodollars and arms to scuttle the ambitions of the people. Tunisia was saved because it has a strong trade union. Otherwise the Saudis and Erdoğan's regime—with Western support of various enthusiasms—have laid waste to the Arab world. What began as great hope has now reached a point of great disappointment. Embers of the future remain burning—but only here and there.

On a September day in 2013, the novelist and journalist Sahar Mandour and I are sitting in the outdoor section of Beirut's

T-Marbouta—the restaurant and café that gathers Beirut's intellectuals and artists. Mandour is the editor of the Palestine supplement of *as-Safir,* one of the Arab world's fine newspapers. We are talking about the war in Syria and the political morbidity in Egypt. But as we sit here in Lebanon, other premonitions hang over us. Almost a million Syrian refugees had already come to Lebanon. That number would only grow in the years that followed. On the pavements of Hamra, outside the café, young Syrian children—refugees in Beirut—earned meager amounts of money selling flowers (girls) or polishing shoes (boys). The Lebanese state has been weakened by the long civil war (1975–90), the Israeli occupation (1982–2000), and the constant threat of the return of both. "There is always that shadow," says Mandour.[18] A former chief of police in Beirut during the civil war tells me that the civil war never ended; it is merely now "at halftime." Like many Lebanese writers, Mandour cannot escape from the civil war. She writes of the mundane existence of ordinary Beirutis who struggle to find their place in the moral and sexual economy of our age. Her novel *32,* for instance, is about five young women whose transit to adulthood is blocked by various anxieties—each one rooted in the legacies of the civil war but refracted in the present.[19]

We are not talking about Lebanon alone. We are talking about the region and the sense of gloom that has descended with the dampening of the Tahrir dynamic. Mandour's father is Egyptian and her mother is Lebanese. One eye is focused on Cairo, the other on the Levant. Around the time that we sat in that café, Sahar wrote a surreal essay on Egypt's revolution and its stasis. She quotes a song sung by Umm Kulthum, and then writes, "Yesterday was love. Yesterday was also the break-up. And today is but one moment in a succession of stories which were born and grew out of another point in time, and which will continue on into other points in time." This is cryptic. But it anticipates this: "For hope, like despair, is but a passing emotion in the flood of human life."[20] Over her coffee, she bemoans the complexity of our time. "During the lead up to the U.S. invasion of Iraq in 2003," she says, "we took a clear position against war and against dictatorships: *la li-al-harb la-al-dictatoriyat*. Today, no such simple slogan is possible. That slogan is old. We need new positions, new slogans. We need to find our way out of the confusion of today." The general mood among intellectuals of Mandour's generation, those who came of political age with the Bush war on Iraq, is somber and introspective. The "confusion of today" is the best description of the situation. It is where the Arab Spring has brought them. They are nonetheless eager to go elsewhere. Somewhere beyond the obituary, to what comes next.

CHAPTER TWO

The State of the Arab Revolutions

You can't capture half a city and call it a revolution.
Elias Khoury, 2013

No question that the uprisings of 2011 have had a decisive impact on the Arab world. Leaders overthrown in Tunisia and Egypt, a regime destroyed in Libya, monarchies nervous in the Gulf, and deadly wars bleeding Syria and Yemen. The scale of these changes was not predictable a decade ago, when the carapace of the neoliberal security state, exemplified by the Mubarak regime in Egypt, held fast. Concentration was on the devastation wrought by the destruction of Iraq. The brazenness of the imperialist thrust not only petrified the leaders in the Arab states, who hastened to collaborate with the United States, but also threw a blanket of gloom over the population. What could be possible if their own harsh regimes became subcontractors of the United States, in a world increasingly unipolar and prone before imperialism? The year 2011 changed all this. It was—as the European Union's President Herman Van Rompuy put it—"the strongest answer to the fatuous hate and blind fanaticism of the 9/11 crimes."[1] Those who took to the squares and the streets seemed to say: *we are not terrorists, but are people who want to live in dignity.* Even the defeat of 2011 has not returned the region to the status quo. Memories cannot be arrested. Nor can the imagination.

FORCES

Beneath the ground of the Mubaraks and the Ben Alis, around the corner from their Mukhabarat (intelligence service) offices, grew a crafty resistance. It came in many forms, some overlapping, often antagonistic to each other:

The most obvious oppositional force was political Islam (*al-harakât al-islamiyya al-siyassiyya*).[2] It emerged in the 1920s as part of a global movement to draw Islamic resources toward the anticolonial struggle. The Muslim Brotherhood, founded in 1928, was not only a reaction to what it saw as westernization, but also crucially an attempt to provide modern institutional goods (medical care, education) to the vast mass of Egyptians who had been left out of the modernization of their country.[3] It was this double nature of political Islam that distinguishes it from the more reactionary (backward-looking) forms of Islamism, such as Saudi Wahhabism. The sources of contemporary political Islam are many, deriving their strength from the writings of such varied contemporaries as Sayyid Maududi (1903–79) and Sayyid Qutb (1906–66). Qutb's theory that political Islam must first go after the "nearer enemy"—namely, the new states of the Arab world—because they are impious (*kufr*) before going after the "further enemy," the imperialist bloc, made their forces a target of internal repression. The West also detested the "nearer enemy," which allowed the Muslim Brotherhood to be an ally of Western intelligence. The Brotherhood was, as a British intelligence officer noted in 1971, a "handy weapon."[4] Killings by the "nearer enemy," including that of Qutb in Egypt, pushed the leadership of political Islam into exile or underground and hastened a turn toward the armed road; a section of the Brotherhood in Egypt split off to form Islamic Jihad, one of the sources into al-Qaeda.

Inspired by the Iranian Revolution of 1979, funded by the Gulf monarchies that preferred that the "nearer enemy" be farther than their own emirates, and egged on by Western intelligence as a foil against the growth of the left or even liberalism, political Islam had a growth spurt in the 1980s. It is what enabled them in Algeria and, from a slightly different history, in Turkey to come close to political power and then be removed summarily by military force. In Algeria this led to a brutal civil war (1991–2000), while in Turkey the "postmodern coup" (1997) led the Welfare Party to a canny coalitional politics that resulted in the formation of the Justice and Development Party or AKP (2001), the current ruling party. The mass character of political Islam had to remain in the shadows, cosseted in the mosques, as its more public face morphed, with the exception of Turkey, into civil war or terrorism. In Syria, where political Islam had been severely repressed, its leadership lived abroad, and it had only a marginal presence in half of Syria's governorates.[5] An ill-fated attempt at political power—driven by the gun—in the 1970s ended for the Syrian Brotherhood in the ash heap of Hama. The Syrian Brotherhood was the only Muslim Brotherhood group of any capacity in West Asia. It was crushed by 1982 and never recovered. If in North Africa the Brotherhood continued to exist in the shadows, in the Levant it lost its ambitions: in Lebanon the Islamic Group formed an electoral alliance with the right-wing Future Movement, while in Jordan the Islamic Action Front sat in parliament until it had a rift with the king over its protests in 2011. Egypt's

Muslim Brotherhood kept apart from other currents in the 2000s, when protests developed against Mubarak's desire to win reelection and against the imperialist wars in Iraq and Palestine. In 2005, the Brotherhood descended on Ramsis Square, near Tahrir Square, in the thousands. The repression against the Brotherhood was sharp. But they did not disappear. The advantage of political Islam was that it had a dedicated cadre, a presence through the mosques in the everyday lives of considerable sections of the population and, because of this, the ability to throw itself into political activity. While the union hall and the political offices could be easily shuttered, who would question meetings in mosques?

The second most powerful force in the Arab world was the groundswell of young people whose frustration with the suffocating regimes came on a variety of axes—angered at the lack of employment options, frustrated with the lack of political opportunities, and dulled by the social stultification of the national security regimes. But the youth who seemed to be on the streets in large numbers might have less to do with their own demographic pressures and more to do with the simple fact that in North Africa the population is largely young.[6] There are class fissures that divide these young people, certainly, and these would require much more clear analysis.[7] What united them was that they were city people; few of the youth in the rural areas (except perhaps in sections of Syria) had their sensibility. This idea of "youth" and the "young" is precisely an urban phenomenon. Various social identities among urban youth provided the platform for their politics—students, unemployed educated youth, slum youth with various degrees of education and employment. Nothing quite like it is visible in rural Egypt and Tunisia. Nonetheless, the "clean slate" sentiment among the urban youth needs to be acknowledged. Having participated in overthrowing Ben Ali and Mubarak, and then tangentially Qadd-afi, this section of the population felt an emerging sense that they would not wish to settle for anything short of a true transformation of the political dispensation.

These young people came not without political experience, as was clear in particular from Egypt.[8] During the course of the decade of imperialist aggression, it was these younger people who formed the bedrock of Egypt's main protest movements.[9] Their political training was, interestingly, provided by the opportunities afforded by left and Nasserite intellectuals who had formed the Egyptian Popular Committee in Solidarity with the Palestinian Intifada in 2002. In response to the Israeli occupation of Palestine, students across Egypt organized solidarity protests, including at Alexandria University, where the police shot and killed a twenty-year-old student, Mohammed El-Saqqa, during a demonstration on 9 April. (Almost three hundred students were injured during this Egyptian intifada.) An antiwar bloc grew out of this pro-intifada sentiment as the United States planned its war on Iraq. During 20 and 21 March 2003, about twenty thousand Egyptians took over Tahrir Square in protest after the United States began its operations in Iraq. The Mubarak regime banned demonstrations and arrested eight hundred people, including two members of parliament: Nasserite leader Hamdeen Sabahi and former Wafd Party member Mohamed Farid Hassanein. In October, the left-wing writer Sonallah Ibrahim, who went to receive the Novelist of the Year award from the Egyptian government, courageously said, "a government, in my opinion, does not possess the credibility to grant it," and walked out, leaving the prize on the table. The cries on the street reflected this sentiment: "Baghdad is Cairo, Jerusalem is Cairo," linking the pro-intifada and antiwar sentiments with struggles in Egypt, for "We want

Egypt to be free; life has become bitter." Out of these stands emerged Kefaya (Enough), a pillar of the 2011 Tahrir revolution, but formed in 2004 to prevent Mubarak and his son from running for the presidency. The "youth" that came to protest in 2011 had a decade-long experience in these struggles against the imperialism that had so confidently walked the Arab lands for the past several decades.

The youth were not detached from the Egyptian working class. Young people formed the 6 April Youth Movement in solidarity with the textile workers' strike of 6 April 2008. It is among this youth strand that new social ideas incubated. Traditional political formations often prey on sectarian differences or hasten back to standard forms of family power, whereas these newer social blocs are more generous to new ways of considering social life. This is an essential development that stands in stark contradiction to the suffocation of even the more moderate religious politics. These young people openly talked about new ways of to live life. In the first flush of Tahrir, militants from these movements formed the Revolutionary Youth Coalition (RYC), which took up residence in the square. "The 25 January Revolution," wrote the RYC in their first manifesto, "has cancelled the old social contract between the people and the regime."[10] These are brave words. It had been only three years since workers and young people saw each other tear down posters of Mubarak. A wall of fear had been broken. It was evident in the new political audacity, in the slogans and songs.

Across North Africa, in Tunisia, rumbles from among the youth came on mainly economic grounds. By 2010, a third of young Tunisians were unemployed. The unemployed earned themselves a label in Algeria and Tunisia—*hittistes*, those who lean against the wall. Some of these *hittistes*—graduates of Tunis

University—formed the Union of Unemployed Graduates in 2006. It should be pointed out that the Moroccan National Association of Unemployed University Graduates was created in 1991. It reflects the regional problem of educated-youth unemployment. Across the Global South, those with higher rates of education—particularly college degrees—face greater rates of unemployment than those with less education.[11] It is to the credit of the North African college youth, mainly urban dwellers, that they created platforms to organize their grievances. In the summer of 2008, youth protests took place simultaneously in Morocco, Algeria, and Tunisia—all over the issue of joblessness. They were met with harsh repression, and no answers. Tunisia's response to the problem was not to consider problems in the labor market, but—with World Bank assistance—to cut off public job guarantees.[12] Maya Jribi, leader of the Progressive Democratic Party, said in 2009, "In Tunisia, the youth have lost hope and prospects. The movement of Gafsa is a matter of the whole society."[13] What Jribi referred to was the struggle of the miners working at the Compagnie des Phosphates de Gafsa. The phosphate miners—many of them young men—revolted in 2008. They drew the youth of the cities, in small numbers, to their struggle. The state arrested workers, threw them into unjust legal proceedings, and watched as sympathy developed among sections of the public. Corruption in the circles of Ben Ali had corroded the system. It saw the people turn away from the state, and sent many of them to prison. Nothing else was available.

The third strand—related to the Gafsa struggles—is far more diffused and less identified by the mainstream media, although in the long run this is perhaps the most important dynamic: the flickers of political protest from the remnants of the organized working class and from the marginal slumlands.[14] The revival of working-class politics came alongside a dramatic decline in living standards in the Arab world, particularly as the price of bread rose due to instability in the world wheat market in the years before 2011. Mubarak's neoliberal reforms of 2004 ushered in the business-man's government of Ahmed Nazif.[15] Almost two million workers joined a strike wave that opened up that year and escalated to the monumental textile strikes of 2006 (notably at Mahallah's Misr Spinning and Weaving, with twenty-five thousand workers) and the strikes of the municipal tax collectors in 2007 (ten thousand workers went on a sit-in in Cairo's streets and formed the Inde-pendent General Union of Real Estate Tax Authority Workers). A walk through the massive Ghazl al-Mahalla plants gives one a sense not only of their history of militancy but also of their role in Egyptian politics. These factories have not been economically self-sufficient for many years, and nonetheless they have been able to insist on their continuation. No attempt to close down these plants has worked. There is something of Egyptian nationalism wrapped up in the workers of Mahalla. Their major strike of 6 April 2008 gave confidence to the rest of the country. They were, in many ways, the authors of the Tahrir dynamic. Two workers believe that because it was a worker-led struggle, it had more revo-lutionary content than the Tahrir uprising. "6 April 2008 was a revolution by all means," says Kamal el-Fayoumi, a worker at the factory. "All of Mahalla's residents came out against Mubarak. If a few more major cities like Suez or Alexandria rose up with us, the Mubarak regime would've fallen then and there." His fellow worker and militant Karim el-Beheiry agrees. "6 April 2008 wasn't an uprising," he says. "It was the real revolution."[16]

In Tunisia, that same year, the phosphate workers of Gafsa con-ducted their brave and lengthy protest.[17] Harsh working condi-tions in the phosphate mines and lowered wages in a time of cuts in social services defined the life of the workers. As the company "restructured," unemployment in the area rose to 38 percent. But this was not the spur to protest. It came from the announcement of an employment competition by the company, who had now earned a reputation for selling jobs rather than hiring the most qualified candidates. Hunger strikes and sit-ins came alongside the blocking of rail lines that carry the phosphate from this region near the Algerian border to the ports. Students from nearby towns joined the workers by blocking main roads with burning tires and by throwing brickbats at the police. The main unions did not throw their lot in with the strike, nor did the main intellectuals derive national implications for this local event. But the consequences of the strike lingered, particularly among workers and students across the country who saw it as a flash of inspiration.

The heft of the organized working class should not be under-estimated, nor should it be exaggerated—because right next to these workers stand the apparently disorganized residents of the slumlands, whose livelihood had been equally constrained. Cities of the Global South are catalyzed by overwhelming rural-to-urban migration and therefore by the emergence of permanent slum-like housing developments. These migrants rarely enter the organized employment sector; instead, they work for subcontrac-tors, become petty entrepreneurs, work as domestic servants, and so on. For them, politics is not often concentrated at their point of employment, where they work in small groups, often within disci-plinary systems that threaten them with abjectness if they as much as object to the tone of voice of their supervisors. Union growth in these new economic areas is constrained, and economic protests are therefore few and far between.[18] What is far more pos-sible is in their place of habitation. Here they are concentrated demographically and they have clear issues to fight for—namely, access to water and electricity, prices of foodstuffs, and security for their families.[19] If these workers seem unfamiliar with the landscape of "organized politics," they are not disorganized. They are connected to each other through networks of street and neighborhood, of kith and kin, of the Ultras football clubs of the al-Ahly and Zamalek and Zabaleen rag pickers' collectives. Women in these streets are linked to each other as they combine their efforts to bring basic necessities into their homes. These linkages are crucial, since they form an infrastructural web of connections that become political when the need arises. Here political Islam plays a role, largely because of the presence of the mosque networks inside the slumlands. It helps with the distribution of some necessary goods. But the price it asks is exorbitant—namely, obedience to its orders. The slumland is libertarian in its ethic, unwilling to bend fully to the dictates of the middle class that dominates the Brotherhood's mosques. The Brotherhood has a shallow analysis of capitalist pressures and few answers to the deeper questions about social deprivation. It cannot answer the fundamental questions, nor will it allow the behavior of the poor to remain outside its bourgeois pieties.

The politics of the slums is no less important than the politics of the factory. Indeed, these two forces were the unrecognized mass base of the Arab revival of 2011—but they had no organized electoral platform to allow their demographic strength to translate into legislative power. Out of the stumbles of Egypt's socialist parties emerged—in 2014—the Bread and Freedom Party (Eish we Horria), which has a presence in most of the governorates. It will require years to make its presence felt in a substantial way. On 4 March 2014, Eish we Horria launched its campaign on behalf of slum dwellers—a sign that it recognizes the nature of the new working-class politics. In Tunisia, the assassination of the left leader Chokri Belaid in 2013 muted the Popular Front dynamic, which will possibly still reemerge as the carrier of this possibility. Between the rubble and the rebel has to emerge the future.

The West favors the secular liberals, who have only a meager mass base. These are often sections of the bourgeoisie and the salariat who have links to the West either through college education or through their own economic activity, who have accepted the view that there is no alternative to Western hegemony (although they might speak out against depredations of human rights by Western governments through their imperialist wars), and who believe that one result of this hegemony is that free-market economic policy linked to a human-rights agenda is the most credible path forward for their countries. These liberal parties have lost credibility on both the economic and political fronts. As well, liberalism in the Global South is compromised by the ease with which it abjures its human-rights agenda when the state begins to go after Islamists, for example, whom the liberals see as fair game for state repression; this was most obvious after the ouster of Morsi in 2013. Liberalism is also weakened by its adherence to IMF-style policies that are known generally to sharpen inequality—one of the main complaints of the mass of people in the Global South. Despite the fact that these are people who champion legal and legislative agendas, they seem quite comfortable with the religion of free markets, which often undemocratically constrain the lives of the masses. Their standard-bearers find it easier to come to power on the back end of a tank (as Mahmud Jibril did in Libya in 2011 and as Hazem al-Beblawi did in Egypt in 2013) than in the electoral field, where they simply do not have the organization or the ideology to motivate the millions. In Egypt, the secular liberals were able to assert themselves into the center of the National

Salvation Front, a platform set up to oppose the Morsi constitutional process in 2012 that includes the liberals. Key liberal members of the National Salvation Front, such as Mohamed ElBaradei, Ziad Bahaa-Eldin, Laila Rashed Iskander, Durriyah Sharaft Aldin, and Maha el-Rabat joined al-Beblawi's government—which meant they went along with the overthrow of the admittedly increasingly authoritarian Morsi government and joined hands with the admittedly authoritarian military command. The debate over whether the overthrow of Morsi was a coup or not (like Turkey in 1960 or Chile in 1973) is of grave importance to the United States and the Egyptian military ($1.3 billion per year is on the line), and to the liberals, who would not like the military aspect to overshadow the mass struggles against Morsi. Certainly it was the mass struggles and a strike by global capital that rattled the Muslim Brotherhood's cage, but it was the military that affected the transfer of power. The liberals were provided with few alternatives but to join the new regime, which is a short-term advantage but has the medium-term problem of legitimacy over its claims for democracy.

Struggles of a mass character develop out of the interplay between economic feints (as in strikes) and political protests (as in the antiwar or pro-intifada struggles) as well as out of a slow transformation of the social terrain where the legitimacy of the ruler is eroded. There is no way to predict when the constrained struggles (this strike, that demonstration) explode from their marginality to become a major social force. It is in this transformation that the element of spontaneity appears. When that explosion takes place, and when the protest becomes a social force in its own right, people with no role in the smaller struggles are drawn to join in. The cautious and prudent tendency of sections of the popular classes is thrown to the wayside as a new romantic sentiment comes over the protest. Fear of joining a protest dissipates, and an enthusiasm grows to be part of a new historical dynamic. It is in this environment of the "mass strike," as Rosa Luxemburg put it, that typically apolitical people begin to flood the streets, against the old regime but not clearly in favor of anything else.[20] Revolts become revolutionary when the apolitical sections join the struggle—a point that can be neither properly calibrated nor properly encouraged. This is the element of mysticism in political struggle. It is what happened on the avenues of Tunis and in Cairo's Tahrir Square.

This is a thumbnail sketch of some of the political forces unleashed by at least a decade of political unrest.[21] Within the conjuncture of 2011–12, these forces inhaled their own power and potential and exhaled to overthrow leaders. But their exhalation was not sufficient to knock down the entire regime in one blow. States are not built on their head alone, but grow deep roots that are often as hard to identify as they are to unearth. Old social classes with insurance ties to all political branches find themselves standing upright regardless of who takes power, as long as it is not the working class and its working-poor ally. The bourgeoisie is intimately linked to the military through family ties and through close business arrangements, and it is the bourgeoisie as well that has been able to incorporate itself into the moderate (elite) sections of political Islam. Its interests are held intact despite the transformation. The bourgeoisie's view of the world is helped along by its intellectual and political allies on the international stage (the bankers, the IMF, the ratings agencies, and of course the governments of the North and the Gulf Arab monarchies). They urge the new regimes to follow older policies properly poured into new concepts to sweeten them for political consumption. It is this sense of the intractable nature of change that gives rise to concepts such as the "deep state" and the "shadow state"—ideas that indicate that there are unchanging elements that maintain power regardless of who is now in charge.[22]

BLOCKAGES

Gathering around the new regimes, aggravating their limitations, are forces of global capital and of Northern imperialism who have other objectives in mind than the needs of the Arab people. The revolts of 2011 rattled the United States, whose main pillars of stability—the Gulf Arab monarchies and Israel—had been threatened by the power shifts. The NATO-GCC [Gulf Cooperation Council] intervention in Libya allowed the North to foist its own social forces back onto the saddle of Arab history.[23] The popular unrest seemed likely to spread via Bahrain into the other Gulf monarchies, and the removal of Mubarak and the potential threats to Assad in Syria and King Abdullah II of Jordan would have encircled Israel with untested Islamic regimes. This had to be forestalled, which provided the urgency of the NATO intervention. Now the North could reestablish itself as the friend of freedom after the ignominy of seeing its allies (France's Ben Ali and the United States's Mubarak) being ousted. A cooptation of the rebels in Syria followed, although, now into its fifth year of fighting, that backing has not amounted to much tangible military support, and Syria continues to bleed. Via the IMF and through its military subvention, the United States has been able to reenter the everyday management of Egypt and Tunisia—despite the continued antipathy of the people to U.S. meddling (as the chants against U.S. Ambassador Anne Patterson in 2013 and the attacks on U.S. consular facilities in Libya and Egypt in

2012 establish). It is these imperialist maneuvers that enable the old social classes to comfort themselves about their immortality. Assertions of regional powers (Iran, Qatar, Saudi Arabia, and Turkey) hold the spotlight, but beneath them the old Northern capillaries of power reassert themselves. They are hard to manifest and to defeat.

These Northern capillaries of power whip through the multilateral agencies that have played a contradictory role in the Arab world. The United Nations has a mixed reputation in the region: on the one hand, its relief work in Palestine and assistance for refugees has been crucial and much respected; yet on the other hand, its political work—often seen to be in cahoots with the North (namely, in Iraq)—has been less than salutary.[24] The UN and its allied organizations have not adopted a theory of democracy, rights, and needs that differs from that of the North. The UN's Economic and Social Commission on West Asia has experimented with new ideas of decentralization, but these have not been given the attention they deserve.[25] One of the most important avenues for the creation of new categories and a new bank of information on the state of the Arab world was the creation (under United Nations Development Programme [UNDP] auspices) of the *Arab Human Development Report* in 2000. A decade of reports provided the basis to understand issues of political rights and women's rights in an Arab framework. Where these reports have not had their impact is on the programs developed by the new political initiatives, which often produce reactive documents rather than forward-thinking agendas for the region. Far more influential in the region than these more liberal agencies are of course the IMF and the World Bank, who, despite the immensity of the challenges and the density of the protests in the region, persist in pushing a neoliberal agenda on the population. An IMF working paper studies the turbulence of the Arab Spring and notes that the situation is bleak for the population. Nonetheless, it suggests the need to implement "a growth-friendly fiscal adjustment to reduce generalized subsides, bolster investment, and strengthen targeted social safety nets"— everything that the IMF has pushed for the past several decades.[26] Multilateral agencies, hamstrung by the hegemony of the IMF logic, are unable to offer the kind of pragmatic and bold agenda for the region that is necessary. Until they are able to shake off the IMF logic, their only contribution will be their collection of the data of suffering and the provision of much relief.

The World Bank returns to the field of battle with a new strategic plan named *Economic and Social Inclusion for Peace and Stability in the Middle East and North Africa* (2015).[27] While there is a much in the new document that is laudable—concentration on the refugee crisis and concern about the unemployment crisis—the broad strategy adopted again calls for private-enterprise-led growth. There is no political will by these multilateral organizations, which rely upon donor funds from the West, the Gulf Arabs, and the Japanese, to confront the role of international finance in the suffocation of public-policy possibilities in the Arab lands (as in the rest of the Global South). It is the curious way in which global finance has organized itself that poorer countries have to borrow capital at higher rates than richer countries and find it hard to constrain capital for long-term projects. Finance prefers the rate of return in highly speculative investments, such as in the commodities market (including for edible commodities)—whose turbulence unsettles producers in the Global South and adversely affected consumers. None of the main international agencies have the freedom to lift the burden of poverty from off the shoulders of the people in these parts of the world. Material realities in the Arab world sit heavily across the political hopes of the people.

Political Islam is incapable of challenging, and unwilling to challenge, these old social classes. It has links to them. It does not sufficiently grasp the enormity of the economic challenge that it has so cavalierly claimed it can solve. A precursor to this kind of dismissal of economics can be heard in Ayatollah Khomeini's quip "Economics is for donkeys"—although this was made before 1979, when the possibility of rule had not occurred to Khomeini. Between the sophisticated Ennahda party, led by Rached Ghannouchi, and the brasher, now-deposed presidency of the Brotherhood's Mohammed Morsi there is no difference in terms of their solicitude to the IMF and their inability to craft a pro-people alternative.[28] There is no social democratic agenda even: that of demanding an annulment or a radically renegotiated odious debt and crafting proposals for capital controls to harness foreign direct investment rather than allow it to run riot in the real-estate and financial sectors. It did not help Morsi's government that it chose to emphasize the creation of a sanitary social domain in Egypt rather than stand up for what the people wanted—a more democratic civil society and a more just economy. Social policies tinged with religious rhetoric had little place in a polity that was trying to find its way after a heroic popular expulsion of a long-standing authoritarian leader. Rather than lead the people against the "deep state," the Morsi government attacked the people only to weaken their "one hand" (Eid Wahda) and open themselves to the return of the military. It was a missed opportunity only because the Islamists had a narrow vision for their rule. They misread the situation and reversed the tide of history as a result.

Tunisia's ruling bloc—a combination of the old regime and the Islamists—took charge of an economy with great structural challenges. Afraid of the political consequences of failure, the governments expanded public-sector employment to eight hundred thousand, twice the pre-2011 level.[29] Wages for public-sector workers increased, eaten as it has been by inflation. Danger of implosion protects Tunisia's government from the pressures of global finance. Young people, economist Karen Pfeifer told me, see this as a "great disappointment." They face high unemployment, migrate to Europe to work, or join groups such as ISIS. Tunisia has the largest number of ISIS recruits—now three thousand—of all countries in the region. "Since the Bardo Museum attack in March 2015," says Pfeifer, "the ISIS fight has increasingly been waged in Tunisia, with fighters crossing back and forth over the porous border with Libya." In rural Tunisia, says Pfeifer, "self-mutilation, hunger strikes, and even suicides" have begun to define the landscape. "The press has been brought under stricter control to prevent reporting on this crisis," she points out, "and the country has been under martial law for months."[30]

An IMF study team left Tunis in March 2016, leaving behind the promise of a $2.8 billion loan over four years. This came to bolster the hemorrhaging Tunisian exchequer, although the IMF insisted that the government's main goals should be "promoting private-sector development and modernizing the public sector." Tunisia is insulated partly from financial pressure largely because it is the only post–Arab Spring state to suggest a transition to democratic governance. If finance puts tighter screws on Tunisia, the tender sores that Pfeifer sees will open up virulently.

The spectacular fall of major Arab leaders in 2011 created impatience among the population that resembles the short attention spans demanded by our present technologies (not the least of which is the news cycle of television). But revolutionary waves work at a different cycle. They do not work in the short term alone. The Mexican Revolution, for instance, opened in 1910 and lasted for two decades. Only when Lazardo Cardenas took power in 1934 did the dust settle. The Soviet Revolution opened in 1917, but did not find its feet (and then only barely) before 1928. The overthrow of the autocratic government occurs in the short term, the consolidation of the new regime takes place in the medium term, and then the economic and cultural changes required to set up a new dispensation take place in the long term. The Arab Spring, strictly speaking, was the first phase of the short term. The region poised to enter the medium phase, where the fights to establish new governmental authorities that would be loyal to the spirit of the Arab Spring took place. Now, five years later, the ledger is unbalanced. History oscillates between a return to the time before 2010 and to the edge of the next moment. The overthrow of Morsi in 2013 and the tumult in Tunisia show that the region has slipped deeply. But this is not an abject return to 2010. Something else has been inaugurated. The totality of the Arab Revolution is a "civilizational" uprising, an energetic thrust by very large sections of the population against the dispensation that they have had to live under: a two-headed force, with one head representing neoliberal economic policies and the other the security state. It was an uprising for a political voice, certainly, but not for a political voice alone. This was a revolutionary process against economic deprivation and political suffocation—with electoralism only a tactic on a long road to a genuine sense of participation in a more horizontal social life. The memory of that upsurge makes an irreversible slip backward impossible.

RETURN TO THE SQUARE

One Sunday in February 2014, I walked across the 6 October Bridge, crossing the well-mannered Nile River, thinking of a different emotion—a more formidable sensibility—and walked down to Tahrir Square, El Midan. Along the road I passed young men from upper Egypt, dressed in black, standing behind small metal barriers, armed and bored, smiling when you smile at them—the human face of the military. They are now in charge, having substituted themselves for the popular rebellion of the past three years. Nevertheless, the graffiti on the walls near Tahrir, along Mohamed Mahmoud Street, hinted at other things. In 2011, the police killed fifty people in one memorable encounter on that street. Protesters returned on the first anniversary of that massacre, only to die once more; among the dead this time was sixteen-year-old Gaber Salah Gaber, or Jika. In 2013, a Cairo court sent First Lieutenant Mahmoud El-Shinnawy to prison for three years. The "eye sniper" was convicted of shooting deliberately into the eyes of protesters. "Glory to the Unknown," says one drawing. It is the sign of the continued upsurge.

These drawings are the most public reminder of the inspirational protests of Egypt's Arab Spring. Tahrir Square itself is quiet. The previous night, I watched on YouTube Jehane Noujaim's Oscar-nominated documentary *The Square*. It is the first Egyptian film to be nominated for an Oscar. (It did not win.) Noujaim put the film up on the Internet so that as many people as possible could view it. The film is heady, following individuals such as the actor Khalid Abdalla (*The Kite Runner*) and the singer Ramy Essam as they become part of the crowd. The Muslim Brotherhood comes off as a caricature, betraying the liberal worldview of the filmmakers. Noujaim retells the excitement of the mass protests, depicting fairly graphically the crackdown by the security forces and the resilience of the people. *The Square* is a film about protests. It rarely warns us of the difficult politics that underlies Egyptian society. In one corner stand the people and in another Mubarak and his establishment; the exhilaration would dissipate if the contradictions among the people were allowed to be truly grasped, and it would dampen further if the granite block of the establishment were on full display. Other films, such as Ibrahim el-Batout's *Winter of Discontent* (*El sheita elli fat*) and Ahmad Abdalla's *Rags and Tatters* (*Fars wa-gata*), take us into the heart of the security establishment. They warn us that Tahrir is an opening, not an ending. Ahmed Hassan, the narrator of Noujaim's movie, suggests as much. He tells us that the mass upsurge in Egypt cannot be reduced to this or that political accomplishment; it has produced a new way to see the world.

Ahmed Hassan's insight can be found elsewhere. The rock band Cairokee and the singer Aida el Ayouby produced a haunting song in late 2011 called "Ya el Midan." It opens with Aida el Ayouby's melancholy voice, "Oh Square! Where have you been?" and then describes the wide range of people who filled it, "the ones who gave up and the brave ones, the ones who scream, and the silent ones." Listening to this song makes one wistful for the mass demonstrations, but then there is the enduring lesson: "There is no going back, our voice is heard, and dreaming is no longer prohibited."

As I walked away from the square, an elderly woman sold me a facsimile of the identity card of Field Marshal Abdel Fattah El-Sisi. It has his particulars and then his profession: Savior of Egypt. Since July 2013 when the Egyptian military removed Mohammed Morsi from the presidency, debates have torn apart families, friends, and political parties. A friend tells me she is afraid to broach the subject with her son, who has very strong views on what happened on 3 July when the military took charge. Good and decent people sit on both sides of the debate. One side is clear that what the military did was a coup since it entered the political process to depose a legitimately elected head of government. Others say that although this might be true technically, it fails to meet a much more important test. Morsi, they say, had become undemocratic. It is an intractable debate, now made mute by military power.

During the first elections after the removal of Mubarak, two candidates remained in the second round—Ahmed Shafik, a die-hard member of the old regime (known in Egypt as the *foloul,* or "remnants"), and the Muslim Brotherhood's Morsi, by default the representative of the Tahrir dynamic. Morsi won the election with a small margin, 51 percent of the vote. Much of the support for him came from those who would not in good conscience be able to vote for his opponent. That would have been like voting Mubarak back to power. Once in office, however, Morsi did not govern as the winner of a complex and narrow mandate. To inoculate himself from the "remnants of the regime," he adopted wide-ranging powers. He then proceeded to push the Muslim Brotherhood's agenda on matters of family life and public order, against his liberal allies. Protests against Morsi's policies were met with violence that mimicked the high point of the bloodshed during 2011, with Mohamed Mahmoud Street as a focal point of the continued struggle. In 2012, young people from the working-class areas of Cairo took to the streets alongside workers, liberals, and other disenchanted people. A twelve-year-old street child on Mohamed Mahmoud Street told the anthropologist Mayssoun Sukarieh, "Last year Egypt was one hand, and now we are divided."[31]

The military was able to draw upon this disenchantment to move against Morsi. The immediate spur, a senior retired military officer told me, occurred when Morsi went to the Cairo Stadium on 15 June 2013 and spoke alongside Salafi clerics such as

Mohamed Abdel-Maksoud and Mohamed al-Arifi, the former fulminating against those who had protested against the Brotherhood government and the latter calling for death to the Shias and using the most sectarian language to describe the conflict in Syria. Morsi went on to announce that he would break relations with the Syrian government and would welcome extremists to travel from Egypt to that war. A week later, a mob entered the village of Abu Musallim in Greater Cairo and lynched four Shias, including the cleric Sheikh Hassan Shehata. Shias make up about 1 per cent of Egypt's population. This was a war of hatred unleashed by the Brotherhood. It was, the officer recalled, the final straw for the military. It moved against Morsi as soon as possible. Egypt's military claimed to be drawn into the conflict because of a call from the Tamarod (Rebellion) movement that had organized mass demonstrations against Morsi. El-Sisi played the movement cleverly: he asked the activists to call the people to the streets to give him a legitimate mandate to crack down on the Brotherhood, which is precisely what happened. It is how the liberals walked directly into the arms of the military. Because they have no mass base, they cannot fight the Islamists themselves; they must fight them from the barracks.

El-Sisi captured the empty space. He sent in his armed forces to imprison the Brotherhood and anyone who threatened him. Men with beards found themselves under threat. On 14 August 2013, Egyptian security forces cleared out the Brotherhood's encampment at Rabaa Square, killing at least 817 people if not over 1,000. Human Rights Watch called it "Egypt's Tiananmen Square."[32] The Brotherhood has weathered storms before. It will take refuge in the professional unions, where it has always been strong—organizations of engineers, lawyers, journalists, and doctors. Revolution took it by surprise. It is not in its personality, since it is mainly a middle-class group that has piety as its main plank.[33] Mosques beckon, as does their charity work. The flood will seek to drown them, but they have ready-made arks at hand.

El-Sisi's crackdown came alongside a process to chill the press into sanctification of his role in saving Egypt. Three fronts emerged as if from nowhere: A Nation's Demand, El-Sisi for President, and Kamel Gemilak ("Complete Your Kindness"). These campaigns gathered millions of signatures asking the general, then field marshal, to lead the country. It was to be an election by acclamation.

Cafes in the triangle made by the neighborhoods of Zamalek, Garden City, and Dokki buzz with frustration and anticipation. Something surely must happen. Tahrir could not have brightened up life and so quickly left Egyptians in the dark once more. A new media project—Mada Masr—has its office in an old art deco building in Garden City. It takes in the complexity of this moment in Egypt and tries to make sense of it for itself. Many of the posts on its website read more like the voice of a journalist trying to understand a moving political field than of a news reporter casually putting together the news of the day. There is a cryptic tone to its headlines: "Elections Law Will Immunize Presidential Results" and "He Who Has Lost Something Does Not Give It." The latter story is by a young journalist, Passant Rabie, who tracks the dissatisfaction among the police for the task they have been set by the military. An anonymous police officer tells Rabie: "Every regime that comes into power uses the police force to rid it of all their opponents. Every regime politicizes us."[34]

These are hard times for the press in Egypt. As we spoke in Mada Masr's office, the government held Al Jazeera reporters in prison, accusing them of conspiring with the Brotherhood. A courageous blogger, Alaa Abd El-Fattah, has been in prison since November 2013 for calling for a demonstration against the new constitution. Mada Masr's editor, Lina Attalah, tells me that space for dissent in Egypt has never been very wide, but over the past few months "the little dissidence left for websites and individual journalists is met with prosecutions and arrests." Eventually, because of international pressure, the Al Jazeera reporters went free. Alaa Abd El-Fattah is still in prison. So are scores of other journalists, artists, and intellectuals.

El-Sisi looked at the emergent workers' movement and felt pressured to co-opt sections of it. The popular labor leader Kamal Abu Eita, of the Egyptian Real Estate Tax Authority Union, went into the government set up by El-Sisi after Morsi's ouster. He held the post of Minister of Manpower. Eita used his position to push unsuccessfully for a higher minimum wage. Mada Masr's opinion editor, Dina Hussein, tells me: "There is talk that the decision to increase the minimum wage was behind the [February 2014] ousting of the government of [Hazem] al-Beblawi due to uncertainty on how such a policy would be financed."[35] Eita had also used his pulpit to attack the strike wave that continues in the belt of large textile mills in Mahalla. But Eita was disposable. He was fired in 2014, and then accused of embezzlement (together with his successor Nahed el-Ashry). Egypt's unemployment rate is near 14 percent, with a staggering 69 percent of the unemployed between the ages of fifteen and twenty-nine. (These figures are based on government data.) Prices continue to rise, and despite infusions of capital from Saudi Arabia, the public finances are in a mess. This has set in motion labor unrest from Alexandria's bus drivers to Kafr el-Sheikh's pharmacists.[36]

Workers played a crucial, but underappreciated, role in the Tahrir dynamic. Their unions did not always serve them well.

The only sanctioned left Nasserite party, Tagammu, had joined the streets, and its activists linked with those of other small socialist groups to form the Socialist People's Alliance Party in 2011. During the tumultuous period of 2013, the Socialist Alliance backed the military and lost the most vibrant organizers, who went on to form, in November, the Bread and Freedom (Eish we Horria) Party. Its Cairo secretary, Akram Ismail Mohamed, tells me that his party wants to do more than put out press releases and articulate a purist political line. Such practices have short-circuited the Egyptian Left. Akram Ismail Mohamed is eager for mass contact, and tells me that Eish we Horria has activists in many of the twenty-seven governorates, even in upper Egypt, which is otherwise cut off from Cairo. Campaigns against torture and alongside the workers' struggles will draw together popular linkages. Eish we Horria's Mona Ezzat goes further, taking her party into the fight for housing for slum dwellers. It will take considerable time to draw the unions and the people's organizations into "one hand," the symbol of unity during the Tahrir uprising. As of now, the divides in Egypt run deep. Bridges are being built, but construction is slow.

Libya's descent into what appears to be permanent civil war threatens the borders of its neighbors—namely, Egypt and Tunisia. Terror attacks in Tunisia and in Egypt put fear in the hearts of ordinary people. In Egypt, El-Sisi has mounted the charger of antiterrorism and cracked down harshly on the Sinai Peninsula and elsewhere. Terrorists provide the alibi for a convenient crackdown against *every* kind of dissent. A glance across the border at Libya sends a chill across the region, with few people eager for that kind of future. The destruction of Libya pushes a feeling of depoliticization. Who would want to risk a protest if the outcome is chaos?

At Cairo University, the students ask, "How do you remain optimistic?" That question itself is the answer. By asking it, the students and Egyptians in general indicate that they want to be optimistic. Or they could look across the way to Tunisia, where the protests of the unemployed in 2015 went from the western Kasserine province to the main avenues of Tunis, the mining area of Gafsa, and Sidi Bouzid, the town that started the Arab Spring. Thousands of people—many of them young—gathered to reclaim the energy of 2010 and renew their demands for betterment of life. What is the point of an uprising, they suggested, if there is no improvement in their existence? Unemployment rates are high and frustration is wide. The general unemployment rate is 15.2 percent, but the rate for youth (37.6 percent) and recent graduates (62.3 percent) is alarming. Another suicide—this by Ridha Yahyaoui—catalyzed the protests. Tunisia's prime minister, Habib Essid, cautioned patience. Essid is of the old guard. "Solutions exist, but patience and optimism are needed," he said. What solutions exist is not clear. Essid and his colleagues warned that if the protests continue, chaos will be sown and ISIS from Libya will sneak across the border. Some people agree with his fears. Others did not heed it. The protests continued. The trade unions and the unions of the unemployed joined together to fight. They await a new project for Tunisia, if not for the entire Arab region. If the old regimes seemed incapable of solving the problems of the present, what political forces today have answers to the current challenges? That is what the students mean when they ask about optimism. Optimism is not merely an attitude to the world. It is a stance that emerges when one has a compelling reason to feel like the future will be bright. Groups like Eish we Horria have the imagination to answer the questions. But they have no power. At least not yet.

Tunisia's Beji Caid Essebsi said, in February 2016, "The region is marching towards the abyss."[37] It is a bleak assessment from a sitting president. He is depressed by the Saudi bombing of Yemen. It is the final straw. But it is not the only one. A pall hangs over Egypt. Politics raised on a pedestal at Tahrir Square has crashed down. A wall of Saudi and U.S. money surrounds Heliopolis Palace.

CHAPTER THREE

The Anatomy of the Islamic State

Our enemies did not cross our borders
They crept through our weakness like ants.

Nizar Qabbani, "Hawamesh 'ala daftar
al-naksah" (Footnotes to the book of the
setback), 1967

THIS IS GOING TO BE LIKE SYRIA

The execution of Western journalists and aid workers in north-ern Syria and a threat to the U.S. allies in Iraqi Kurdistan in the summer of 2014 brought ISIS onto the concern list of the West, and subsequently to the world. That ISIS had already seized the Iraqi cities of Fallujah and Ramadi and the Syrian cities of Raqqa and Deir es-Zor almost a year beforehand had not sent up the amber light of caution. Iraq and Syria had been seriously threat-ened by ISIS, which had captured land that straddles the two countries and had been in control of the Omar and Tanak oil fields in eastern Syria as well as the Qayyara fields near Mosul in Iraq, from where it had begun to accumulate its revenues. In Jan-uary 2014, two ambassadors from Western European countries told me at a breakfast in Beirut that my reports had greatly exaggerated the influence of ISIS. They wanted to maintain the view that the Syrian civil war was between the forces of freedom (the rebels) and authoritarianism (the Syrian government). That Cold War–derived framework had not been applicable to Syria at least since early 2012, when dangerous forces had inserted themselves into the emergent chaos. By 2014, those powers had seriously threatened not only Damascus but the entire region—from the borders of Iran to the borders of Saudi Arabia. As his fighters spread themselves across this land, the leader of ISIS, Abu Bakr al-Baghdadi, did something audacious: he anointed himself the Caliph of Islam and dropped the geographical limitation to his organization. The Islamic State was born, with its caliph a former Iraqi military man in his forties.

No doubt ISIS is a menace to regional stability. Nor is there any doubt that ISIS is a serious threat to the people who live under its dominion. But the threats to the region are not authored solely by ISIS, nor, by any metric, could an analysis of its threats ignore the history of imperialism in the region. The temptation to measure the brutality of ISIS against the history of Islam is a great error. Certainly, ISIS takes its own inspiration from that history—one that stretches back to the revelations of *al-Quran* and in the political battles that caused the great schisms inside the world of Islam. But the emergence of ISIS cannot be understood as part of religious or religiopolitical history.[1] Nothing in the soil of Syria or Iraq suggested its emergence prior to the massive attack on Iraq by the United States and its allies in 2003, and prior to the slow and deadly civil war in Syria since 2011. Al-Baghdadi might seek to crown himself in the legacy of the caliphates, but his own existence is premised not so much on divine history as on the history of imperialism in West Asia.

Nor is ISIS alone. It entered Syria in January 2012 from Iraq to provide support against the government of Bashar al-Assad and some elements of the Free Syrian Army (such as in the 2012 fight over Menagh Air Base, near Aleppo). Its proxy was called Jabhat al-Nusra (the Support Front). For a while, both ISIS and al-Nusra worked together. Then, as al-Baghdadi's ambitions increased, the leader of al-Nusra broke off and pledged his allegiance to al-Qaeda. Other extremist fighters poured into Syria, forming proxy armies of regional powers and drawing in detachments of local rebels. Saudi Arabia's Jaysh al-Islam operated around Damascus, while Ahrar ash-Sham—backed by Qatar and Turkey—held fast in northwestern Syria. Along the Turkish border, various other Turkish proxies—some of them drawing support from the Turkmen population in Syria—grew in strength. Small bands of fighters, disassociated from any major project, sought to ally themselves with one or more proxy platforms of the regional powers. They came with imposing religious names—La Ilaha Ila Allah Battalion (There is No God but Allah Battalion)—or with grand historical names—Nour al-Din al-Zenki Brigade (named for a twelfth-century ruler of Aleppo)—or indeed with names as memorials to fallen comrades—Martyrs of Jabal al-Zawiya (a reference to Jabal al-Zawiya, a rural area southwest of Aleppo; even this group would soon have greater ambitions and rename itself Martyrs of Syria Brigade). The local and minor groups of fighters sought the larger platforms because they had access to logistics— guns and money—as well as to the glue of ideology.[2] Each week in the early years of the conflict, small groups of these fighters— ragtag in appearance—would stand before the standards of the larger platforms and pledge their allegiance to them and their leadership. Videos of these events would surface on YouTube, and agglomerations of fighters would confront either each other or the

Syrian army and its allied militias. Many of these groups did not wear extremism on their sleeves, although their central figures often came straight from the most orthodox mosques; for instance, Nour al-Din al-Zenki Brigade's leader, Sheikh Tawfiq Shahabuddin, was integrated into the Salafi networks that emerged from Saudi Arabia and the Gulf.[3]

Whatever the Syrian revolt had been in the early months of 2011, by the end of the year few close observers could say with a straight face that extremism had not defined the essence of the rebellion.[4] The difference between Jaysh al-Islam and ISIS is narrow. Their virulent sectarianism is almost identical, but so, too, is their brutality. There is no question that the forms of violence mirror those used by the Syrian government, whose artillery and air force have a tendency to indiscriminately bomb civilian areas. Casualty rates among civilians rose astronomically—so much so that within two years of the conflict, the United Nations stopped counting the numbers of dead. The morgues could not be trusted. After two hundred thousand, the count ended. But these numbers included the fighters on all sides. An assessment by the Damascus-based Syrian Centre for Policy Research suggested that by early 2016 the number of dead had crept up to 470,000.[5] Death, displacement, and imprisonment set the terms for Syria. Between the hammer and the anvil, Syria's population continues to suffer.

But so, too, does the population of Iraq. A United Nations study found that from January to October 2015 almost nineteen thousand civilians were killed, with more than thirty-six thousand injured and one million displaced. "The violence suffered by civilians remains staggering," noted the report.[6] Disputes abound about the actual count of the dead. One study, from October 2013, suggests that the casualty count from 2003 is about half a million dead.[7] Even the authors of this study recognize that it is an undercount.

They were able to survey only a limited part of Iraq and could not talk to those who had fled the country. A *Lancet* study from 2006 had already suggested that the death toll in Iraq had exceeded 655,000—before the turmoil that followed after 2006.[8] A study by Physicians for Social Responsibility proposes that a more accurate figure would be far in excess of one million dead between 2003 and the present.[9] These deaths came after the brutalities of the U.S. occupation in Abu Ghraib, in the battles of Fallujah, and in the manner in which U.S. troops attacked Iraqi civilians to break the insurgency.[10] Records from interrogations of marines who killed twenty-four Iraqi civilians, including a seventy-six-year-old man in a wheelchair, in the town of Haditha in Anbar Province in 2005, show us how mundane was the cruelty. The marines shot them at close range. When the marines reported what they had done, Chief Warrant Officer K.R. Norwood recorded the deaths as routine. Later, when he was interrogated, Norwood said, "I meant, it wasn't remarkable, based off of the area. I wouldn't say remarkable, sir."[11] Major General Steve Johnson, who commanded U.S. troops in Anbar, said that this was "a cost of doing business." The range of violence—whether of the U.S. occupation or the insurgency or later ISIS—shares the same quality of viciousness and ordinariness.

In 2010, former U.S. Ambassador Joe Wilson went to Iraq to have a close look at the problems faced by the U.S. government as its occupation spilled into its eighth year. Wilson had been in the U.S. embassy in Baghdad in the lead-up to the Gulf War of 1991. He knew Iraq well. In a confidential email to U.S. Secretary of State Hillary Clinton, Ambassador Wilson wrote, "My trip to Baghdad has left me slack jawed. I have struggled to find the correct historical analogy to describe a vibrant, historically important Middle Eastern city being slowly bled to death." He says that Berlin and Dresden are not a good analogy because they were not "subjected to seven years of occupation that included ethnic cleansing, segregation of people by religious identity, and untold violence perpetuated upon them by both military and private security services." By the latter two he meant the U.S. military and the U.S.-hired security services, such as Blackwater.[12] Ambassador Wilson's observations about the virulence of the U.S. soldiers in Iraq are scathing:

> The soldiers I saw on [the U.S. military base at the Baghdad airport] are not infused with the commitment to help Iraqis help themselves. I scoured the PX for t-shirts for my kids to memorialize my trip but was hard put to find any that were not horribly bellicose or racist in nature. Shirts with mushroom clouds conveyed the Baghdad weather as 32,000 degrees and partly cloudy. Others referred to Arabs as camel jockeys and those were the least offensive. Were I the commander, those shirts would not be on the shelves as they convey adolescent macho Pastor Terry Jones attitudes. The service people don't see themselves there to bring peace, light, joy or even democracy to Iraq. They are there to kill the "camel jockeys."

Pastor Terry Jones, from Florida, had threatened to burn a Quran in public to send a message against Islam. This was the mood that Ambassador Wilson saw among the troops. "I think we all need a slap in the face," he wrote, "to remember what hell we have wrought in Iraq and what the consequences of stupid wars can be."[13] One of the consequences is ISIS.

ISIS is rooted in hatred for those who are *kuffar,* non-Muslims. It manifests this hatred not in terms of the West, but in terms of Iraqis and Syrians who follow Shiism or Christianity or who belong to small communities such as the Yazidis of Ninevah Province (Iraq). The mountainous areas of northern Iraq—

Mount Sinjar and Mount Zawa, for example—contain small communities that have over the centuries cultivated complex social foundations. They have drawn from major religious traditions and formed their own customs based on their own interpretation. The Yazidis, for instance, draw their social and religious resources from old Mesopotamian traditions and Iranian influences (including parts of Zoroastrianism), with the magnificent Melek Taus (Peacock Angel) at the center of their religion. When Saddam Hussein's close confidant Tariq Aziz came to India, he told the press gaggle that he was a Chaldean Christian. I remember being shocked by that, since I had thought of the Chaldeans as an ancient people like the now-extinct Nabataeans of Petra or the Circassians of Syria. (The former no longer exist, but the latter do.) ISIS despises this complex cultural ecology of Iraq, and targeted these people with special venom. A UN report documents mass executions, the sale of Yazidi women as sex slaves, and other abominations. But it also suggests that in some localities, people have paid ISIS a tax and made their accommodations with the group.[14] Haifa Hazan (age forty-nine) watched the ISIS fighters on the day in 2014 that they took Mosul, the heart of Ninevah Province. "This is going to be like Syria," she worried.[15] In Syria, ISIS and other extremists rampaged through Christian towns, such as Ma'loula and Mahardah. Their reputation had made its way back from Syria. What had begun in Iraq had swung, pendulum-like, to Syria and now whiplashed back.

From where did this nightmare arise?

EMERGENCE OF EXTREMISM

Two generations ago, the Communist movement made serious gains in the swathe of land that runs from North Africa into

West Asia. Sudan boasted the largest Communist party in Africa, and Iraq had the most numerous party in West Asia. These parties had a substantial influence in their countries, with a leftward tilt of the dial after the 1958 coup that overthrew a British-appointed monarchy in Iraq and after the Communist-led 1969 coup in Sudan. Creative Communist actions came alongside innovative Marxist analyses of the regional developments from Lebanon's Mahdi Amel and Sudan's Abdel Khaliq Mahjub. It is precisely what sent important Islamist thinkers to study Marxism and Communism, with an assessment of volume 1 of Marx's *Capital* by the Iraqi cleric Muhammad Baqir al-Sadr in his *Iqtisaduna* (Our economy, 1960) and with a sympathetic repudiation of Marxism by the Iranian sociologist Ali Shariati in his *Insan, Islam va Marxism* (Man, Islam and Marxism, 1974).[16] It is no surprise that both al-Sadr and Shariati came to Marxism from their deep Shiite assessment of Islam and the Muslim world; the social base of the Communist cadre in Iraq and Lebanon came from the workers who hailed from Shia communities.[17] Al-Sadr's movement organized itself around the principles of a cadre party, drawing from Bolshevism its organizational architecture as well as elements of what Shariati called Islamic socialism. The idea of a classless society—*nizam i-tawhidi*—appealed to the workers, as it did to these intellectuals. Adoption of socialism's idioms allowed this branch of political Islam to appear neither reactionary nor lethargic. Out of these initiatives—and the assassination of Marxist intellectuals and Communist leaders—come Lebanon's Hezbollah and the Sadr movement in Iraq.

Arab nationalism, which had taken an antagonistic position against colonialism and imperialism, might have developed alliances with its nations' domestic Communist parties against the theocrats. But this was not to be. The Communists endangered the status quo as they produced struggles against the tendency of Arab nationalism to favor the domestic bourgeoisie against the needs and demands of the peasants and workers. It was this internal critique that led Arab nationalism to typically have a strained relationship with Communism; both Egypt's Gamal Abdel Nasser and Iraq's Saddam Hussein filled their prisons with Communist activists and Marxist thinkers.[18] Arab nationalism of the Ba'ath (Renaissance) variety had a deep antipathy to Marxism and Communism. The intellectual founder of the Ba'ath movement, Michel 'Aflaq, wrote in his *Fikratuna* (Our idea, 1948) that Marxism was alien to the Arabs. In 1958, 'Aflaq came to Baghdad from Damascus, Syria, to tell the new regime (backed by the Communists) that the Ba'ath represent "the Arab spirit against materialist Communism. Communism is Western and alien to everything Arab." Faced with Communist dissent for his plans to unite Egypt and Syria, Nasser went to Damascus in 1959 and accused Communists of being "foreign agents who neither believe in the liberty of their land or their nation, but only do the bidding of outsiders." Arab Communists felt compelled to follow the Soviet Union's recognition of Israel in 1948, cutting them off from the mood of great anger and sorrow at the Palestinian *Naqba* (Catastrophe). It took a decade for the Communists to rebuke that recognition, but by then the damage had been done. Association with the Soviet recognition of Israel undermined the principled critique of Arab nationalism by the Communists.[19] When the Syrian Communists declined to accept the United Arab Republic, they were pilloried as agents of Zionism. A combination of the carrot (Nasser's adoption of the language of socialism) and the stick (Nasser's imprisonment of the Communists) would lead the Egyptian Communist Party to liquidate itself in 1965. The hegemony of Marxism and the slow growth of Communism in this zone were not eternal. By the 1980s, Communist movements in the area would be wiped out, and Marxism would be relegated to the universities (if that). In its place would come not Arab nationalism, which had its own problems with the Communists, but various forms of theocracy.

None of the lessons of Shariati or al-Sadr would influence anxieties in the Arabian Peninsula. The sultans of Arabia feared the Communists who had inserted themselves in the outer reaches of the peninsula. Inklings of Communist rebellion in Iraq and Lebanon in 1958 as well as the growth of Communism in Sudan came alongside the fiery secular nationalism of Nasser. Strike activity in the eastern part of Saudi Arabia among oil workers threatened the kingdom's treasury. In 1953, the U.S. embassy in Saudi Arabia worried that "Communist involvement in a manner and degree not now ascertainable is a distinct possibility."[20] U.S. embassy spies worried about "Red stimulation," something that bothered the kingdom. A combination of Arab nationalism and Communism threatened the sultans and their U.S. backers. In 1956, adoring crowds greeted Nasser when he visited Saudi Arabia's oil lands in Dhahran; but when King Faisal went to the same town that year he was met with demonstrations. Civil society had to be molded away from these secular icons. The kingdom summoned god to the task.

In 1962, the Saudi regime created the World Muslim League (Rabita al-Alam al-Islami), the WML.[21] The reason was communicated to the U.S. government by Saudi Prince (soon to be King) Faisal's brother-in-law Kamal Adham; the U.S. embassy note summarized it simply: "The Saudis feel that Islam forms a significant bulwark against communism."[22] Inside Saudi Arabia, the prince proposed a list of reforms, most of which were far too vague to mean anything (to "raise the nation's social level"). One reform, though, number five, had real meaning—to propagate Islam. The Committee for the Propagation of Virtue and the Elimination of Sin sent out its religious police, the *mutawiyin* (the pious), on the instructions of the royal family to maintain order. They were keen to condemn both folklore and rationalism—apostasies of the past and the present. In the chamber of the *mutawiyin* lay files to traduce the secular nationalists and the Communists.[23]

The *mutawiyin* and their small religious cells provided comfort to the Saudi regime that order would be maintained inside their kingdom. The Eisenhower Doctrine of 1957 already provided a security umbrella around the kingdom, making it safe from external attack. Three years later, U.S. Treasury Secretary Robert Anderson said, "Middle East oil was as essential to mutual security as atomic warheads." The United States had come to rely upon Arabian oil for its newly expanding carbon-based social order.[24] Saudi intelligence and its military forces had provoked uprisings in Oman and in Yemen to push petty claims for land— but found that in both of these venues, the Communists had asserted themselves. The Dhofar uprising in Oman was contained (and then defeated in 1976), but in South Yemen the Communists were able to seize power. Insulation came through the buffer state of North Yemen, but this was not sufficient. Saudi Arabia would continue to try to overthrow the Marxist government in South Yemen, financing one jihad after the other to cleanse the peninsula of the red vermin.[25]

The WML played only a modest role here. Its work was elsewhere. The WML fought to "combat the serious plots by which the enemies of Islam are trying to draw Muslims away from their religion and to destroy their unity and brotherhood." The main targets were nationalism (Nasser's influence) and Communism.

The idea that these antimonarchical ideologies were anti-Muslim (and anti-Arab) had to be pushed hard; it meant that to be Arab is to be tribal and Muslim, the two pillars of the Saudi ideology. WML missionaries went after Muslims in the Communist bloc and in the lands of the newly assertive postcolonial states. No WML project took its missionaries into the capitalist lands, where Muslims suffered forms of discrimination and found their faith under attack. WML had an explicit political agenda, and not a theological one. It was to uproot the menace of Communism and secular nationalism.

Cold War allegiances played a hefty role in the creation of the Organization of Islamic Cooperation (OIC) in 1969. It was designed to directly provide a counterweight to the more left-leaning Non-Aligned Movement (NAM), created in 1961. The OIC's main countries were all pro-U.S. in their orientation: Morocco, Saudi Arabia, and Pakistan. Pakistan at this time was the state with the largest number of Muslims. (It would lose this standing when Bangladesh won its independence in 1971.) Intellectual leadership of the OIC came from the Pakistani scholar Sayyid Abu-Ala Mawdudi, who had become very influential as well in the WML. The general thrust of the OIC was to undermine the NAM, whose founders— Egypt, India, Indonesia—were seen not only as geopolitical enemies of the pro-West bloc, but also as regional adversaries (Nasser's Egypt against Saudi Arabia, India against Pakistan). It was this alliance that deployed Pakistani pilots to Saudi Arabia's war against Yemen in 1969 and again in 1979 against the fears of an Iranian invasion. Pakistani troops have routinely patrolled Saudi Arabia's northern border. This relationship sent Pakistani troops—under the command of Brigadier Zia ul-Haq—to defend King Hussein in Jordan and attack the Palestinian Liberation Organization in 1970 (Black September).

Fortune favored the sultans. Petrodollars flooded the Arabian Peninsula. Muslim Brotherhood professionals exiled by the Arab nationalist regimes in the 1960s and 1970s brought their technical skills to develop the kingdom and the emirates. They—along with economic migrants from South Asia—converted the peninsula into a technocratic landscape. Qatari poet Maryam Ahmad al-Subaiey wrote of "this army that builds our country," which "remains invisible beneath the burning sun."[26] Every third resident in Saudi Arabia is a non-Saudi worker. The indentured workers, reduced to sweat, have no rights in the Gulf. Democracy for them is a distant dream.[27] Among their lot came Muhammed Qutb, younger brother of Muslim Brotherhood ideologue Sayyid Qutb, who had been executed by the Egyptian state in 1966. The incipient antimonarchism of the Muslim Brothers frightened the Saudis. Worried that the money and the amenities as well as the influence of the Brothers would create a call for political change, King Faisal passed an order in 1971 to deepen social control through the religious police, and to dole out the oil wealth as patronage, not as income. The "ruler's sword and his gold," said the writer Abdelrahman Munif, would set the terms of engagement for the region. Either take one or the other. "The Arab oil has corrupted the Arab condition," he wrote, "not only in the oil lands, but in the Arab world as a whole."[28] What threat came from the Muslim Brothers had been squashed. It would later assert itself not as an internal problem but as a geopolitical one, as the Muslim Brotherhood's main patrons—Turkey and Qatar—would pose regional challenges to Saudi Arabia.

The idea of the "jihad" had older resonances. But in the twentieth century, the Saudis, the West, and the Pakistanis sequestered the concept in the 1970s to tackle the growth of secular nationalism and Communism in Afghanistan. Saudi money and Western logistical support helped sections of the Pakistani intelligence world and military craft a new resistance to the government in Kabul. Pakistan's governor of the North-West Frontier Province—Major General Naseerullah Babar—reached into Kabul University and made a connection with a professor, Burhanuddin Rabbani. Rabbani had studied in Cairo's al-Azhar, where he encountered the works of Sayyid Qutb, whom he translated into Persian. Rabbani introduced Major General Babar to his two prized students— Gulbuddin Hekmatyar and Ahmed Shah Massoud.[29] Hekmatyar had made his name in the engineering school by throwing acid in the faces of unveiled female students. These were nasty men, who had little mass support. Babar's assistance, which would be enhanced soon by Saudi money and U.S. logistical support, would enhance their stature and allow these men to become "leaders." They would draw the vocabulary for their anti-Communist endeavors from a new lexicon: not for them the term *fedayeen*— the secular term of art made popular by the Palestinians—but *mujahideen*—drawn from the well of Islamic theology to mean the one who does jihad. It was the Afghanistan adventure that *produced* the entire "jihad" dynamic. In Pakistan, the government held back on funding health and education (as per IMF dictates), allowing Gulf Arab money to enter and, in many places, to push the Saudi worldview with a militant edge. *Jihad* was reduced from its multiple meanings (including struggle to become a better person) to war against the Soviets, and then reduced even more to defense of Islam. Marginal characters in Afghan history suddenly became the new "freedom fighters" (as Ronald Reagan called them) of the region. The line from Babar's creation—with Saudi and U.S. assistance—to the mayhem in Iraq, Syria, and Libya is unbroken.

CONTRADICTIONS INSIDE ISLAM

The Iranian Revolution of 1979 posed a serious threat to the regime in Saudi Arabia on three counts. First, a Muslim monarch (the shah) had been overthrown. The Iranians dug deep into the well of Islamic thought to create an alternative model of Islamic governance—*Vilayat-e Faqih* (the Guardianship of the Jurists). This was not the nationalism of Nasserism and the Ba'ath, both decidedly secular. The Iranians had created an *Islamic* form of republicanism. A Muslim polity, they claimed, no longer required a monarchy. Second, the Iranians developed modern institutions, staffed by both men and women, and allowed for elections to a parliament—despite the fact that the clerics controlled the list of those who could run for election (prohibiting the Communist, liberal and Kurdish parties from participation). All this was anathema in Saudi Arabia. Third, the Iranian Revolution enlivened the intellectual and political boldness of Lebanon's Muhammad Husayn Fadlallah (and Musa al-Sadr) to move a political agenda along Shia lines—which would eventually, in the context of the Lebanese Civil War, create Hezbollah (the Army of God). It also provided a new discourse for already restive workers of the oil regions of Saudi Arabia—many of whom happened to be Shia. The Iranian Revolution's example provoked an uprising in Qatif in late 1979 under the standard of the Organization for the Promotion of the Islamic Revolution in the Arabian Peninsula, led by Hassan al-Saffar, alongside the Communists. That this was the oil land of Arabia terrified the monarchy. It had to be crushed, as it was.

It should be pointed out that almost a decade earlier—in 1970—Hafez al-Assad and his coterie of officers seized power in Damascus through a military coup.[30] Assad, who came from an Alawi family, nonetheless did not seize power and rule as an Alawite. He was a Ba'ath man first and foremost, and his regime drew in people of all kinds of social backgrounds. There was no threat to Saudi Arabia on religious lines.[31] Saudi Arabia and Syria wrestled from the 1970s onward. Sometimes they embraced as allies; at other times they attempted to throttle each other. Antipathy between Syria and Saudi Arabia would arise during and after the 1982 Hama massacre—when the Syrians went after the Muslim Brotherhood. Saudi Arabia carried no special feelings for the Brotherhood, whose bourgeois pieties did not appeal to the princes. From 1980 to 1988, Assad reached out to Tehran to cement an alliance against Saddam Hussein's regime, which was at war with Iran and which—despite being a fraternal Ba'ath regime—Assad despised. Saudi Arabia attempted to undermine the ties between Iran and Syria—by subterfuge but also by diplomacy. At the 2009 Arab League summit, Saudi Arabia's King Abdullah reached out to Bashar al-Assad, hoping that the son would be pliable. That honeymoon lasted two years, till 18 January 2011, when Saudi foreign minister Prince Saud al-Faisal said that the king had "washed his hands" of the relationship. Having washed his hands, the king sent in his close adviser—Prince Bandar bin Sultan—to run the armed operation against Assad.

Regional aspirations anchor the relationship between Iran, Saudi Arabia, and Syria. Religion is on the surface. It is not the essence. It should also be pointed out that there was little antipathy between the sultans of Arabia and the king of Iran—despite the different social bases of their monarchies. What united them was the color of their blood. That artery would be severed with the Iranian revolution. Much the same obfuscation lies in understanding the relationship between Saudi Arabia and Syria. Saudi Arabia expressed its anger at the links between Damascus and

Iran, which the Saudis framed in sectarian rather than political lines (because in Saudi eyes, Alawis and Shiites are both followers of Ali, and therefore—in its severest gesture—apostates).

Danger came into the heart of the kingdom when Juhayman al-Otaybi's al-Jamaa al-Salafiyya al-Muhtasiba (Salafi Group that Commands Right and Forbids Wrong) seized the Grand Mosque in Mecca in November 1979. Al-Otaybi was closely linked to the influential cleric Mohammed Abdullah al-Qahtani, who claimed to be the Mahdi. The Saudi regime crushed this uprising, beheaded the ringleaders, and suppressed this affront to its authority.

Not long after, the Saudi regime used its massive oil wealth to fashion answers to these two pressing problems: the Islamic Republic of Iran and the internal growth of true believers in the ways of the *salaf* (ancestors). It egged on a sectarian war—prosecuted by Iraq—against Iran, and it exported its disgruntled male youth toward jihad in distant lands as cannon fodder for Western wars.

On 5 August 1980, Iraq's Saddam Hussein came to Riyadh, sat with the king and his cabinet, and—for a price—pledged to contain Iran.[32] The pious that would come for the hajj in October worried the king's cabinet; any return to the instability of Qatif and al-Qahtani had to be avoided. Saddam Hussein's vast armies invaded Iran in September—using Saudi airspace when it was of use, and drawing liberally from the Saudi coffers ($1 billion per month in the early years of the war). The Saudis closely coordinated with the Kuwaitis to increase their oil production to offset any reduction from Iran and Iraq, and to raise funds to pay Iraq for its services to Arabia. Saudi aircraft patrolled the Persian Gulf and the Gulf of Oman. The scared little emirates along the waters (Bahrain, Kuwait, Oman, Qatar, and the UAE) hastily joined Saudi Arabia in the Gulf Coopera-tion Council, set up in February 1981 at the urging of the British and French. They had nothing to worry about. U.S. President Jimmy Carter articulated the Carter Doctrine, which—in essence—pledged to protect the royal families of Arabia. All of them came under a nuclear blanket as the U.S. warships parked in bases from Bahrain to Jebel Ali (UAE). In February 1982, a secret Saudi–American Military Committee was formed; the next month, the U.S. Pentagon noted, "Whatever the circum-stances, we should be prepared to introduce American forces into the region should it appear [that our] security of access to the Persian Gulf oil is threatened."[33] Based on the 1979 Carter Doctrine—the security of Saudi Arabia is equivalent to the security of the United States—the Pentagon had already drawn up plans for swift action.

To deal with the unrest of the true believers within, the Sau-dis hastily opened a pipeline to Afghanistan to embroil these men in the jihad against the Soviets. The Palestinian scholar Abdullah Azzam delivered a fatwa after the Soviets entered Afghanistan in December 1979: "Defense of the Muslim Lands, the First Obligation after Faith." Azzam called upon Muslims to come to the defense of Afghanistan, a call that was welcomed by Pakistani intelligence. (General Hamid Gul was waiting to receive the "first Islamic international brigade" with open arms.) General Gul would work closely with Abdul Rasul Sayyaf, an Afghan cleric and fighter who was trusted by the Saudi royal family and became their key conduit into Afghanistan. Sayyaf's Islamic Union for the Liberation of Afghanistan became the main receptacle for the Afghan Arabs who brought their frustra-tions with the king overseas to Afghanistan. Among them would be Osama Bin Laden.

By 1988, both pillars of Saudi strategy began to shake.

An exhausted Iraq sued for peace with Iran, and then turned to the Gulf Arabs for help with the recovery of its economy. A fight with Kuwait over oil revenues ran through 1989 and into the summer of 1990—when Saddam Hussein sent in his armies to sack Kuwait in order to recover payment for his services against Iran. This was the trigger for U.S. military action against Saddam Hussein, a close ally through the 1980s. This would become Gulf War I, and lead seamlessly into the long, drawn-out sanctions regime that lasted till Gulf War II in 2003 and the U.S. occupation of Iraq. In other words, Iraq would be in the maw of U.S. power from 1991 onward. Iran, on the other hand, went into a period of introspection. Khomeini died in 1989. Then, as the regime built up the infrastructure of the country as well as its military, the reformists emerged. Mohammad Khatami's Islamic Iran Participation Front and Akbar Hashemi Rafsanjani's Agents of Construction of Iran would provide the country with a new debate about the relationship between the state and society. Khatami would win the election in 1997 and become president, opening the door to what might have become a far less theocratic order. What did occur in Iran was that debates around social norms and political power did open up and continue to foster challenges to the political order (as was evident in the aftermath of the 2009 elections and in the election in 2013 of Hassan Rouhani to the presidency). The parameters of Iranian politics would remain between moderates and reformers on one side and hardliners on the other; liberal, leftist, and Kurdish parties remain outside the bounds.

The Soviets, meanwhile, withdrew from Afghanistan. Abdullah Azzam wrote an influential essay asking for the maintenance of a "pioneering vanguard" of fighters who would be the base (*qaeda*) for the Muslim world. More and more disaffected Muslims, frustrated with their lives in Arabia or in the other parts of the world, would turn up at the camps set up with Saudi money and Pakistani intelligence assistance. Inside Afghanistan festered the most dangerous and uncompromising tendencies of extremism. After the Soviets withdrew in 1989, the U.S.-Pakistani-Saudi warlords went on a rampage. More people died from 1989 to 1996—the era of these warlords—than during the decade of the Soviet intervention. It was in the trenches of this brutal war that Bin Laden would form al-Qaeda in 1989 and then develop its strength. Its tentacles would reach out from Afghanistan toward the home countries of its membership. Worried that the Saudi monarch would allow U.S. troops into Arabia to eject Saddam Hussein's army, Bin Laden recommended that these al-Qaeda fighters do the job instead. The holy lands should not be soiled by foreign troops, Bin Laden told the king, who smirked and laughed at the overblown folly of Bin Laden. The king's refusal set Bin Laden onto a course of permanent war against both the near enemy (the Arab leaders) and the far enemy (the United States). 9/11 was born in that refusal.

One of the temptations of analysis is to reduce these complex geopolitical and regional dynamics into theological categories—as if this were all a battle of Sunni and Shia, the schism that opens up in the seventh century among the believers. Of course, for the deeply pious who believe that the Shia and other "schismatic sects" are heretics, this is precisely how the tension between Iran and Saudi Arabia appears. Many fighters who join sectarian militias of one side or the other might view this battle as a defense of the faith. Hezbollah fighters go into battle in Syria with the view that they must protect the Damascus shrine of Imam Ali's oldest daughter, Zaynab, with the chant "*Labayki ya Zaynab*" ("We are with you, Zaynab"); although they also go because they are deeply disciplined, and they believe that their task is to defend Lebanon from those who would like to annihilate them. In the same way, the extremists that swim along the current of al-Qaeda see the Shia as *kafirs* (infidels) who must be put to the sword; hence these extremists are often called *takfiris*—those who seek out the infidels to kill. However real the Sunni–Shia divide is, it does not drive the political turmoil in the region.[34] The author of that is a cold war between Iran and Saudi Arabia, egged on by the West and Israel, that is rooted in ideas of political legitimacy and regional control. In 2006, the political officer at the U.S. embassy in Damascus, William Roebuck, wrote a note on how to combat Iranian influence in Syria. The most important section in the cable, which was sent to the U.S. State Department, is called "Play on Sunni Fears of Iranian Influence."

> There are fears in Syria that the Iranians are active in both Shia proselytizing and conversion of, mostly poor, Sunnis. Though often exaggerated, such fears reflect an element of the Sunni community in Syria that is increasingly upset by and focused on the spread of Iranian influence in their country through activities ranging from mosque construction to business. Both the local Egyptian and Saudi missions here, (as well as prominent Syrian Sunni religious leaders), are giving increasingly attention to the matter and we should coordinate more closely with their governments on ways to better publicize and focus regional attention to the issue.[35]

Stunningly, Roebuck wrote that despite the fact that these fears are "often exaggerated," the U.S. government should coordinate with Egypt and Saudi Arabia to fan the flames of sectarianism. The entire cable is filled with advice for regime change—creating splits in the military, advising the Gulf Arabs to stop investing in Syria, building up anxiety in the population about the economy, thereby creating the means to deprive the regime of any support.

Roebuck's cable is not new. It mirrors a cable from September 1979 written by the U.S. ambassador, Talcott Seelye, born in Beirut and a highly regarded Arabist in the U.S. State Department. Seelye, like Roebuck more than three decades later, accepted that evidence of sectarianism is hard to find. In a cabinet of thirty-five ministers, there were only three Alawites, and in the Ba'ath Regional Command there were only seven Alawites among the twenty-one members. "It becomes irrelevant whether Alawites have in fact assumed a disproportionate share of power or not," he wrote. "The important thing is that that they are perceived to have done so by the majority Sunnis and in this case perception is more important than reality." Seelye was cautious about regime change against Syria at that time: "It would be a task of considerable difficulty to oust [Hafez al-Assad] in light of the military elements backing him up. Nevertheless, there are various scenarios by which the regime could be brought down. An obvious one would be the assassination of Assad."[36] Assad will not fall, Seelye wrote in 1979, but "we are inclined to the view that his days are numbered." He did not fall. But his son came into the crosshairs of the U.S. government in the 2000s.

To reduce the cold war between Saudi Arabia and Iran to sectarianism is to miss the longer history of machinations in West Asia—which include the cloak-and-dagger role of the West.

IRAQ'S LONG NIGHT

In January 2014, a line of white Toyota trucks stood in the center of Ramadi, one of the main cities of Iraq's Anbar Province.

Young men stood around, most of them in the uniform of twentieth-century jihad: bushy beards are common, and so are various kinds of cloth to cover their faces during their desert transit. Many are dressed in black, the ninjas of al-Hamad, the Great Syrian Desert. These fighters of ISIS, shrugging off the January air, were prepared to drive into Syria to carry forward their goal of unifying the Arab lands under an ISIS caliphate that would run from the borders of Iran to the Mediterranean Sea. The men are excited. Arabic is the lingua franca, but there are also the tongues of international jihad—Chechen, Serbo-Croatian, French, and English. Among the latter, the accents range from Australian to British. Theirs is an adventure. These men exude little fear. It is hard to imagine that they will be shot at in a few hours as they cross the Syrian border, targeted by the Kurdish YPG (People's Protection Units) along the road toward the northern Syrian town of Raqqa—the ISIS capital. It is not hard, on the other hand, to picture them shooting back. These are hardened fighters. Guns seem integral to their swagger.

Between January and June 2014, ISIS fighters swept across north-central Iraq and northern Syria.[37] Iraq's Anbar Province fell to their guns early in the year, with the two most important cities (Ramadi and Fallujah) substantially in their hands. U.S. military hardware rushed to the threadbare Iraqi army to no avail. ISIS came under threat in Syria, where its allies such as Jabhat al-Nusra joined with the Free Syrian Army to expel it from its positions in northern Syria. The war of al-Qaeda against al-Qaeda in Syria moved ISIS fighters back to Iraq. It became the base for its 2014 assault on the cities along the River Tigris in Iraq. June was the breakthrough month, with ISIS and its allies seizing Iraq's second largest city, Mosul; much of Nineveh Province; the city of Tikrit (hometown of Saddam Hussein); and several smaller towns including Tal Afar, where al-Qaeda in Iraq was born in 2004. ISIS moved northward toward Baqubah. By the end of June, Baghdad had been surrounded. Al-Qaeda, which had no roots in Iraq prior to the U.S. invasion in 2003, seemed poised to take this great Arab city.

How did it come to this—that Iraq would begin to resemble Afghanistan in the midst of its own torturous and unending turmoil?

"Heritage," writes the Iraqi writer Haifa Zangana, "is a coffin we are forced to carry on our shoulders, then asked to run with on unfamiliar, rugged land."[38] Zangana, who had done her time in the prisons of Saddam Hussein's regime, had little nostalgia for a time before the U.S. attack of 1991, the sanctions regime that followed, the U.S. attack of 2003, and the U.S. occupation that came after that. Nor had the Iraqi intellectual Khair el-din Hasseb, of Beirut's Center for Arab Unity Studies. He, too, had been in the prisons of the Ba'ath. But when I asked him what had allowed Iraq to slide so deeply into the night, he said, "Not only did the American occupation change the regime. It destroyed the Iraqi state itself."[39]

When it suited him, U.S. President George W. Bush donned the mantle of freedom with the promise to vanquish authoritarianism in West Asia and North Africa. But, in fact, Bush's messianic dream was far more modest. In 2003, he had no desire to topple the sultans of Arabia or the dictatorships of Tunisia, Libya, Egypt, or Syria. They were all safe. He had already sent "unlawful enemy combatants" for "enhanced interrogation" to the "black sites," from Tripoli (Libya) to Damascus (Syria). Bush's eyes were focused on Saddam Hussein's Iraq. His war of aggression against that country and then the violation of the responsibility of an occupying power afterward created immense chaos in the region.

Operation Rapid Dominance (Shock and Awe) in 2003 broke the
back of the Iraqi state, destroying its already weakened infrastructure and making a mockery of its command and control
security establishment. Once it seized Iraq, the United States
cashiered any state employee with a Ba'ath party affiliation (de-
Ba'athification); the military lost its officer corps, the police its
leadership. Ten million Iraqis—half the population—were
affected by this mass dismissal.[40] Saddam Hussein had called his
last stand Ma'rakat al-Hawasim, the Defining Battle. The term
hawasim became used across Baghdad, at least, to refer to anything cut-price or stolen. This was an adulterated battle.

The Iraqi army gave way before the aerial assault, allowing
the U.S. forces to enter Baghdad in record time. They would
have been in the city faster had their transport vehicles not been
held up by a sandstorm. Iraqi troops shed their uniforms and
vanished to their hometowns. Their careers had known only
war and privation. From 1980—the war against Iran—to 2003,
war had been a regular feature of their lives. By the 2003 invasion, Iraq's army had been broken, and its society had been
squeezed of resilience. It was a walkover for the United States.

No people give up without a fight. Saddam Hussein had
recruited his crack detachments from the cities of the Tigris
such as Mosul and Tikrit. Some of those who threw off their
uniforms now fashioned themselves as "Fedayeen Saddam" and
began to attack U.S. positions. They would be joined in the
insurgency by others from the main cities of Anbar Province,
the cities along the Tigris, and towns such as al Souira, the
home of Saddam Hussein's deputy Izzat Ibrahim al-Duri. In
Diyala Province, east of Mosul, and in towns south of Baghdad,
al-Duri's detachments formed the Army of the Men of the Order
of the Naqshbandi (JRTN), drawing in frustrated Ba'athists and

soldiers ejected by the U.S. occupation (whose de-Ba'athification policy left many professional bureaucrats and soldiers without a job, and therefore able to turn their skills over to al-Duri). The JRTN are nominally Sufis, although Sufism in Iraq does not share the heterodoxy that one used to see among the Sufis of Syria (and of course South Asia). This Naqshbandi Army formed part of the Supreme Command for Jihad and Liberation—marked no longer by secular Ba'athism but by a strange mutation of Islamic Ba'athism. Al-Duri read the tea leaves well. Anbar Province became home to extremist organizations that unfurled new banners—al-Ansar al-Islam, Aseeb ahl el-Iraq, al-Jaish al-Islami fil-Iraq, Jaish al-Mujahideen, Jaish Muhammad, Jam'at al-Tawhid wal-Jihad, Jam'at Ansar al-Sunna. A strange mix of "Salafi nationalists" and "Islamist Ba'athists" emerged to combat the U.S. occupation, and in different degrees to incubate ideas of theocracy and global extremism.

Rural Iraq had relied heavily on subsidies from the oil rents. In August 2003, the U.S. occupation—driven by neoliberal fantasies—cut the agricultural subsidies. Rural Iraq went into distress. Protests in Diyala Province, in eastern Iraq, morphed from the grievances of farmers into anti-occupation insurgency. By cutting the lifeline for these farmers and further, making them buy seeds from U.S. agrobusiness firms, the occupation delivered the farmers to various strands of the insurgency. When al-Qaeda came to Iraq in 2006, its leadership chose Diyala Province as the first possible Islamic state. It was the base for attacks on Baghdad, largely conducted by peasants who saw their livelihood stolen from them. By 2007, Diyala's capital, Baqubah, was in the hands of al-Qaeda. "Baqubah is a symbol of resistance," said Saad Adnan, a farmer. The "Americans will be kicked out by the mujahedin."[41] They lasted a year before being removed by the

United States, after which the fighters decamped to Anbar and sought out another set of disgruntled farmers.

U.S. military commanders found themselves on the back foot. Dogged Iraqi fighters along the Tigris, in Anbar Province (Ramadi and Fallujah mainly), and in large parts of Baghdad seemed hell-bent upon the liberation of their country. Grotesque human-rights violations in Abu Ghraib prison during the early phase of the insurgency show how frustrated the U.S. intelligence officials became: they could not learn enough to break the back of what was fated to become a full-scale uprising against the occupation. When Muqtada al-Sadr's largely Shia Mahdi Army sent supplies to the mainly Sunni city of Fallujah and when Sadr City's Shia popula-tion donated blood for the Fallujah fighters in solidarity, this indi-cated that the uprising might be rooted in a reconstructed Iraqi nationalism.[42] Journalist Tony Karon noted that the insurrection of Fallujah and Sadr, combined with the harsh U.S. response, "has even had an iconic nation-building effect, as the plight of the besieged city [Fallujah] has become an anti-American rallying point across Iraq's traditional Sunni–Shia divide."[43] Portraits of Sadr could be seen in the hands of protestors in the largely Sunni towns of Anbar Province. Sadr began to be compared with Syed Hassan Nasrallah, the leader of Hezbollah, who had been called the new Nasser after Israel's withdrawal from Lebanon in 2000. Such unity of the Iraqis posed a serious threat to U.S. war aims. U.S. money sloshed around from one sectarian group to another, seeking fissures between Shia and Sunni that could be easily exploited. The potential of a reconstructed Iraqi nationalism was smothered in the sectarian war that was harnessed by the occupa-tion in 2006–07.

The U.S. occupation and the emergence of sectarianism oxygenated the growth of al-Qaeda in Iraq. It was unthinkable during the twentieth century that the ideology of Wahhabism would find fertile soil in Iraq. Iraqi society had embraced its complexity during the period of Arab nationalism, adopting secular ideas for its political world at the same time that it incubated deeply held religious traditions in its society. Now with the insurgency under way, al-Qaeda operatives led by the Jordanian militant Abu Musab al-Zarqawi entered Iraq and set up an organization in Tal Afar. They would be known locally as "the Saudis of Iraq."[44] Brutal anti-Shia violence marked their entry, with Osama bin Laden cautioning al-Zarqawi to be more moderate. Al-Zarqawi's brutality set the tone for al-Qaeda, and later for the creation of the Islamic State of Iraq (*Dawlat al-'Iraq al-Islamiyah*) in 2006. ISI was formed at the zenith of Iraqi sectarianism, with its new insurgents swearing an oath not only to free Iraq from U.S. occupation but also to crack down on the Shia population. In a letter to Abu al-Abbas (deputy of Abu Abdallah al-Shafi'i, leader of the Iraqi militant group Jund al-Islam) in 2007, bin Laden worried about the continuing violence in Iraq. He hoped that the random acts of violence by al-Qaeda against Iraqis were not policy but an error and that the senior leadership would hold the perpetrators accountable. "This thing happens a lot in the fields of jihad," he wrote. But he was not sure. Even bin Laden, leader of al-Qaeda, worried that the Islamic State of Iraq would spiral out of control into the nadir of violence of its own making. His worry was not for the violence itself, but for its possible outcome. "Suppose that al-Qaeda is defeated in Iraq," he wrote. "[I]t will without a doubt be a catastrophe."[45]

Iraq's politics since 2007 have been mired in sectarianism. Nouri al-Maliki, Iraq's prime minister since 2006, spoke expansively about Iraqi unity, but the reality was worse. To quell the insurgency, the United States financed Sunni tribal leaders in the

"Sunni Awakening," drawing fighters from the Islamic State of Iraq to their side in what became a war against al-Sadr's Mahdi Army. These fighters had no investment in al-Maliki's Iraqi unity or in the U.S. project. The Awakening was an opportunity to get U.S. funds, equipment, and training to go after their own adversaries. When U.S. funds dried up, these fighters went back to ISI and its assorted allies. Sectarian violence reached horrific proportions in 2006–07. Not a month has gone by since then that the UN Assistance Mission for Iraq has not recorded at least a few hundred deaths as a result of this violence. The UN's special representative Nickolay Mladenov said in 2013, after a particularly bad month, "The level of indiscriminate violence in Iraq is unacceptable and I call on the Iraqi leaders to take the necessary steps to prevent terrorist groups to fuel the sectarian tensions, which contribute to weaken the social fabric of society." Al-Maliki had no agenda to address the root cause of sectarianism. He was not its sole author, but his policies certainly contributed to deepening the alienation of sections of the Sunni public.

Sectarianism, says Khair el-Din Haseeb of Beirut's Center for Arab Unity Studies, is new to Iraq. A glance backward at Iraq's history enlivens Haseeb, who points out that before the U.S. occupation—and despite its many problems—Iraq incubated an Arab nationalist project. From Iraq's independence in 1920 until 2003, sectarianism at the elite level was little known to Iraqis, he notes. Of the prime ministers who governed the country in those eighty years, eight were Shia and four were Kurds, and of the eighteen military chiefs, four were Kurdish officers. The majority of the Ba'ath members, he says, were Shia, not Sunni. On the "55 Most Wanted" cards circulated by the occupation, thirty-five people had Shia backgrounds. Residential segregation among the working class and the peasantry was certainly as common in

Iraq as elsewhere in the world. This is a measure of older histories that were frozen by lack of mobility in the modern era. But residential segregation did not define the consciousness of the people, who had—through educational and media systems as well as other nationalist institutions—forged a sense of being Iraqi. That heritage is now squandered. Sectarianism arrived full-blown through the political grammar enforced by the United States's Coalition Provisional Authority in 2003 and was enshrined in the 2004 constitution written for the Iraqis by the United States and its allies. The U.S. occupation and its Iraqi associates channeled reconstruction and oil contracts on the basis of sectarian affiliation and political loyalty (as indicated by a report from the U.S. embassy in Baghdad in 2007, published by *al-Mustaqbal al-Arabi*). Zaid al-Ali, who worked at the UN mission in Iraq from 2005 to 2010, concurs. A poll in February 2004 found that only 18 percent of the population wanted to live in either federal regions or independent sectarian states (Kurds, Shia, Sunni). The rest wanted unity. Al-Ali cites a note from John Agresto, senior adviser to the Iraqi office of higher education and scientific research in Baghdad from August 2003 to June 2004. Agresto noted that the Americans sought out "the loudest and most virulent factions" to empower; they "gather together the representatives of the most antagonistic factions and think that's a good democracy. We've done nothing to blur the lines separating people and everything to sharpen them." The model for Iraq, as far as Agresto recalls, was not American individual rights, but Lebanese sectarianism.[46]

Bomb blasts and sniper fire became normal in Baghdad. The Iraqi government notes that the number of car bombs in the past few years has increased from an average of ten a month to close to seventy a month. The bombs, many of them set by ISIS and its related outfits, target Shia and Christian areas as well as Sunni politicians who work with the government. The T-walls and Green Zone offer a measure of the dangers. Baghdadis talk of *min zaman* ("once upon a time"), the old days before the threats. Gunfire drowns out the stories of ordinary Iraqis, who built lives on a thread, or else fled inside or outside their country. Skirting the edges of battles, ordinary Iraqis live out their lives—raising children, teaching them, working, tending to relatives who have been maimed by bombs, making *maqluba* with less meat in it, and *shinina* with more water. Every family seems to have someone with a physical scar; everyone carries an emotional one. Iraqi friends, uneasy about talking openly, are fearful of nothing in particular but everything in general. Old leftists, who had borne the brunt of the Saddam Hussein regime, look back fondly on those years because at least the politics was straightforward. New organizers who grew up in a collapsed society look forward to a world that is just a dream for which no hopeful signs currently exist.

On 25 February 2011, some of these new organizers and the older lefties, men and women both, gathered at Baghdad's storied Tahrir Square, chanting, "*Illi ma ezoor al tahrir omra khasara*" ("Whoever is not at Tahrir Square is wasting their life"). The Iraqi government, with agreement from the United States, had already accused the protestors of being Ba'athists, terrorists, al-Qaeda. But they were nothing of the sort. These were people from the Union of the Unemployed of Iraq and the Communist Party, from the Organization of Women's Freedom in Iraq (OWFI), and from the youth protest movement known as "Where Are My Rights?" Yanar Mohammed, of the OWFI, said, "You cannot build democracy with a gun." New movements had emerged, rooted in their localities—the Popular Front to Save

Kirkuk, the Movement in Steadfast Basra to Liberate the South, the Iraqi Association of the Tribes of Southern and Central Iraq—and, on the national level, the Popular Movement to Save Iraq, and the Student and Youth Organization for a Free Iraq.[47] They called for an end to the U.S. occupation and sectarianism as well as the release of political prisoners. Assassinations and disappearances took care of many of those who dared take to the streets, including journalist and theater director Hadi al-Mahdi. On his Facebook page, just hours before his murder on 8 September 2011, he wrote, "I am sick of seeing our mothers beg in the streets and I am sick of news of politicians' gluttony and of their looting of Iraq's riches." The path of nonviolent resistance was blocked in 2011, and then sent backward when Iraqi security forces massacred peaceful protestors in Hawija in April 2013. After that massacre, ISIS scouts came into Hawija to recruit fighters. They said, "You tried the peaceful route. What did it bring you? Now come with us." ISIS was the natural child of the sanctions regime of the 1990s and the U.S. occupation of the 2000s, but also of the sectarian crackdown by the U.S.-fostered Iraqi government between 2011 and 2013. Iraq's has been a history written in blood, the sky dark with death, a nest of bones beneath.

Walls and pillars across Iraq were plastered with campaign posters for the 2014 parliamentary elections. Prime Minister Nouri al-Maliki's State of Law coalition seemed assured of victory. A confident al-Maliki threw relatively unknown people and political defectors (including Alia Nassif of Iraqiya) onto his electoral list. Informed observers in Baghdad told me that this would allow al-Maliki to control the newly elected lawmakers. It was a sign of his authority rather than his weakness. A possible fleeting sense that the electorate might abandon his list sent al-Maliki to seek emergency powers through a bill sent to Parliament on

4 April. That the generally enfeebled lawmakers did not accept the bill says a great deal about their courage. Newspapers affiliated with al-Maliki's party, such as *Almasalah* and *Darbonh,* smeared the reputation of well-regarded secular politicians such as Mithal al-Alusi and Hanaa Edwar, as the cleric Kadhem al-Haeri—close to al-Maliki—issued a fatwa on 30 March to caution against votes for secular candidates. A ghastly new personal status (*ja'fari*) law was hastened to Parliament to appeal to the worst kind of misogyny. It would overturn Law no. 188 (1959), which gives Iraqi women the greatest institutional freedoms in the Arab world. "The corrupt ruling alliance is desperate to pass this law," Iraqi writer Haifa Zangana told me. "It is an election ploy. In the absence of any real political program, the *Ja'fari* law becomes one of their main campaign issues."[48]

Opponents of al-Maliki, such as the Islamic Supreme Council of Iraq's Citizen Bloc, Saleh Muhamed al-Mutlaq's Iraqi National Democratic Front, and Osama al-Nujayfi's Mutahidun bloc, floundered to make inroads into his virtual monopoly of power. They tried to deny him his third term as prime minister through a term-limit law in January 2013. The judiciary overturned the opposition's bill eight months later, delivering al-Maliki the opportunity to run again. Nouri al-Maliki's bloc almost lost the 2010 parliamentary elections. The shock, says Iraqi lawyer Zaid al-Ali, drove al-Maliki and his allies into a deeply sectarian trench at the same time that his government began to fully control the military and security establishment. Al-Maliki argued that the prime minister should always be a Shia. His proxies suggested that despite blatant evidence of corruption and incompetence, at least al-Maliki and his allies "recognize that Ali is the Wali of God," as Shiekh Salah al-Tufayli put it in 2012. Absent Sunni allies, al-Maliki could not be confident of victory. Propitiously, the insurgency of al-Qaeda groups in Anbar Province brought many Sunni notables to al-Maliki's side. They feared ISIS more than al-Maliki's brand of sectarianism. During the May 2014 elections, over 60 percent of the eligible voters came to the polls and gave al-Maliki's bloc a third of the parliament's seats. He was easily elected to his third term as prime minister. In Anbar Province, meanwhile, his writ did not run. That was already ISIS territory. They had dug themselves into Ramadi and Fallujah, preparing for their thrust into Baghdad. When ISIS attacked Mosul, what surprised the population of Iraq was the collapse of their armed forces. It was not the attack that shocked people. It was their lack of defenses.

Iran's influence in Iraq came in the early years of the U.S. occupation, when the Dawa Party of al-Maliki took charge of the new institutions. The United States—antagonistic toward Iran—nonetheless relied upon Iranian-backed exiles to create some semblance of order. Close links to Iran could be discerned in the Islamic Supreme Council of Iraq, whose leader—Abd al-Aziz al-Hakim, who had lived in his Iranian exile for almost a quarter of a century—ran the Badr Brigade and controlled the Interior Ministry. Commercial ties yoked the two countries together, from oil deals to infrastructural connections. In November 2012, the Iranians began work on a fifteen-hundred-kilometer natural-gas pipeline to run from the South Pars fields in Asaluyeh (Iran) through Iraq to Syria. These commercial deals came alongside tightened security linkages, with Iranian military officials making routine trips to Iraq—most spectacularly the visit by the Iranian defense minister, General Ahmad Vahidi, to meet Iraq's defense minister, Saadoun al-Dulaimi, in late 2012. It was in this period that Iraq declined the U.S. request to prevent Iranian aircraft from overflying Iraq to resupply Syria during the war. The strong linkages between Tehran, Baghdad, and Damascus deepened in this period as each of these powers felt threatened by the Gulf Arabs and the West. Such regional fragmentation took on a sectarian cast, inflaming anxieties on the ground.

After its reelection, al-Maliki's government put up billboards across Baghdad to celebrate Iraqi unity and the strong central government. Evidence for both were lacking. ISIS had a firm grip on Anbar Province, and had seriously threatened the border posts to Syria—namely, at Rutbah and Qa'im. In Diyala and Ninevah provinces, ISIS deepened its older ties with deposed Ba'athists and cashiered Iraqi military officers and soldiers. Al-Baghdadi recognized that this alliance of ISIS with people like al-Duri of the Naqshbandi Army was crucial. It would allow ISIS to traffic in the old Ba'athist anger at the new Iraq. ISIS targeted the centers of the old "Sunni insurgency," pushing beyond Mosul to the cities along the River Tigris—from Tikrit to Samarra. By late June 2014, with Anbar and Ninevah provinces in ISIS hands and with Diyala Province threatened, ISIS held the northern entrances toward Baghdad. The billboards in Baghdad were a rebuke to the country—a joke in the summer sun as the sounds of gunfire and heavy artillery crept closer to the city.

Over a million Iraqis fled the zone held by ISIS. They left for good reason. ISIS hastened to put its social agenda in place—no pleasures of tobacco and music to be permitted, harsh pressure on religious minorities, and severe rules set in place for the social interactions of men and women.[49] Human Rights Watch verified that the summary executions of hundreds of Iraqi soldiers took place as ISIS took Mosul. The smell of blood and fear is part of their modus operandi. Al-Baghdadi's alliance with al-Duri's Ba'athists did not moderate their conduct. ISIS leaders are not interested in compromise. Victory is before them, either on earth or in heaven. An ISIS fighter in Mosul sat under a sign that read, "The Iraqi Army Is a Thorn in the Eyes of Terrorism." That army was weakened. In its place came various Shia militias, such as the Asa'ib Ahl al-Haq (AAH), a breakaway from al-Sadr's Mahdi Army and given a long license by al-Maliki. Its leader, Qayis Khazali, was expelled from the Mahdi Army because he is a loose cannon. His group has been active across the region, accused of supplanting the security services and being some of the most ruthless fighters around the shrine of Sayida Zainab in Damascus, Syria. Lebanon's Hezbollah fighters complain that the AAH fighters in Syria had to be taken in hand and trained to calm down. Iraq's senior Shia cleric, Ayatollah Ali Sistani, issued a fatwa calling upon "all able-bodied Iraqis" to defend Iraq from ISIS. He roused up the AAH and its offshoots. Ammar al-Hakim, leader of the Islamic Supreme Council of Iraq, shrugged off his clerical uniform and put on military fatigues. This is the character of the fight—deep into the sectarian trough, with Iranian advisers at every corner.

In February 2014, al-Sadr had warned that Iraq "is ruled by wolves, thirsty for blood, souls that are eager for wealth, leaving their nation in suffering, in fear, in water puddles, in dark night, lightened only by moonlight or a candle, swamped by assassinations based on differences or ridiculous disagreements." His loyal troops conducted a show of strength across Iraq on 21 June. They stood guard before Baghdad. Sistani echoed al-Sadr's interest in the revival of Iraqi nationalism; the first step was for a unity government to come to Baghdad. Al-Maliki stepped down. His dourness had run its course. In his place came another member of al-Maliki's Dawa Party, Haider al-Abadi. Al-Abadi had been the party's spokesperson. He is more jovial than al-Maliki. This is a change of the guard rather than a change of the order. The politics are fraught. These are fractured countries, broken by war. Syrians and Iraqis are prisoners in a burning prison. There are no easy, unbarred exits.

By late 2014, the United States began to bomb ISIS positions near Mosul. Hasty doses of money and supplies came from the West and Iran to bolster the Iraqi army and to give confidence to the Iraqi Kurdish Peshmerga. Ground operations along the Tigris and extending outward from the Iraqi Kurdish capital of Irbil took hold into 2015. The fighting was slow. Close air cover from the United States, training from U.S. and European troops, and logistical and strategic support from Iran provided the Iraqi forces—regular and irregular—with the heft to take back Ramadi in late 2015 and to begin to consider operations to recover Mosul. ISIS meanwhile continued to threaten Baghdad with suicide bombings and other threats. No one knows what it would take to uproot ISIS from northern Iraq. It does not help that there are reports of the displacement of Sunni Arabs from the towns recovered by the government.[50] Some of this can be attributed to anti-Kurdish propaganda—but not all of it. Such stories are going to merely turn more people into the arms of despair and anger.

Indications flash here and there of lingering Iraqi nationalism. Few point to the forty thousand Sunni Arabs who are part of the People's Mobilization (al-Hashd al-Shaabi) units—the militias, including the Badr Organization, Muqtada al-Sadr's Peace Companies, and Kata'ib Hezbollah, which have provided crucial support to the Iraqi army. When Turkish troops entered Iraq in late 2015, all strands of political opinion—from all denominational and ethnic groups—opposed the action on the grounds that Iraqi sovereignty must not be violated. This included Turkmen groups, who are being trained by the Turkish armed forces and fight within the People's Mobilization units.[51] Perhaps the clearest indication of residues of Iraqi nationalism came when Iraq's grand ayatollah, Ali al-Sistani, wrote a letter to Iran's supreme leader, Ayatollah Ali Khamenei.[52] The customary belief is to see Shiism as being the primary identity of the Iranian and Iraqi religious establishment (the *marjaiyya*). Al-Sistani worried in the letter about the increasing influence inside Iraq of Qassem Soleimani, the leader of the Iranian Revolutionary Guards Quds Force. Some of this had to do with anxiety among the Najaf clerics of Iraq that their influence over Baghdad was being usurped through Soleimani by the Qom clerics of Iran.[53] Whatever the reason, the pulse of Iraqi nationalism lingers both at the level of the elites and—certainly—among those who had been on the streets in 2011 as part of the popular mobilizations. It is from here that Iraq will have to be rebuilt.

In May 2016, thousands of supporters of al-Sadr occupied the Green Zone and the parliament. "Peacefully, peacefully" (*"Silmiyyah, silmiyyah"*), they chanted as the security forces tried to eject them. Corruption and privations exercised the crowd, who came to the area from the slums of Iraq. They have not shared in the oil wealth. Earlier in the year, al-Sadr had demanded that the regime of embezzlement end and that a more just system be put in its place. Parliament refused to go along with al-Sadr's demand. It was inevitable that the Sadrites would descend on the Green Zone. These are Shiites who had no fealty to Iran or to the leaders of the Dawa Party. The slums form their politics. They waved the Iraqi flag—the emblem of their hopes. A day after their occupation, they withdrew with the threat that if the regime of embezzlement remains, they will return.

The wrath of ISIS struck Baghdad on 11 May, when three massive car bombs killed over a hundred people. The strikes had specific targets—two largely Shia neighborhoods and a busy commercial street near Baghdad University. The peaceful path is not open to ISIS. But this does not mean that ordinary Iraqis blame only ISIS for this violence. Abu Muntadhar told Robert Spencer of Reuters, "The state is responsible for the bombings that hit civilians."[54] What could he mean by that? Certainly ISIS conducted the bombings. But the conditions that spawn ISIS are within the responsibility of the state. Those institutions created during the American occupation are frazzled with sectarianism. A path to reconstruct the basis of these institutions is necessary. It is what those who seized the Green Zone demanded.

THE DESTRUCTION OF SYRIA

A small village in the upper elevations of the borderlands between Syria and Lebanon awaits the slow drop in temperature. Jabhat al-Nusra fighters who had been stuck in these upper redoubts fear the winter. They are already cut off from their supply lines and hemmed in by the Syrian and Lebanese armies, as well as by Hezbollah's fierce determination to prevent their further movement into Lebanon's Bekka Valley. It is mid-October 2014, and alongside the road, just outside the village, sit six al-Nusra fighters. They are all young, in their early twenties. Each has long hair and a beard—a Jesus look that does not match the various guns that are near at hand. One of them, Mohammed, with a Kalashnikov in his lap, is Lebanese. He has a college degree and has been with al-Nusra for at least a year.

In early October, a week before this encounter, al-Nusra fighters who had been encircled in the Qalamoun Mountains along the Syrian–Lebanese border broke into Nabi Sbat, east of the Lebanese town of Baalbek. They clashed with Hezbollah fighters, who pushed them back into the hills. The sound of mortar fire and gun-fire shakes the valley. Hezbollah's checkpoints are hidden in the hillsides of this undefined border. More such clashes take place as these al-Nusra fighters try to reopen their supply lines. Hezbollah officials say they are confident that they will be able to protect the roadways that link the Bekka Valley, where the town of Baalbek is the jewel, to Beirut and the coastline. The occasional car bomb by al-Nusra targets the Beirut suburb of Dahieh—a majority Shia neighborhood. But the open war that is destroying Syria has not been able to leak into Lebanon. These al-Nusra fighters know it. It is what frustrates them.

Mohammed does not dispute Hezbollah's skilled ferocity. He says that the Hezbollah fighters are much more difficult to tackle than those of the Lebanese or Syrian armies. But the war has made this young man from a moderate family in the Akkar region wary. His eyes sparkle as he speaks, but there is already iron in his soul. "If I had a job," he tells me, "I would not do jihad." I ask him about al-Qaeda, the parent organization of Jabhat al-Nusra. He speaks idealistically, but is not versed in scripture or in the ideological squabbles between the jihadi groups. "I was trained in engineering," he says, as if in apology when I tell him that I am not only a journalist but also a college professor. What gets him going is not al-Qaeda or al-Nusra, the formal colors of his outfit. He is enamored of the battlefield successes of ISIS. Its sheer audacity impresses him. They care for nothing—not the borders or the old order. Mohammed likes this. It excites him.

Across the battlefields of America's War on Terror have emerged groups that speak for the youth—the Taliban (Stu-dents) and al-Shabaab (the Youth). In many parts of the Arab world, those under thirty make up close to three quarters of the total population. This "youth bulge" comes alongside a colossal failure to provide jobs for these young people—many of whom are not only unemployed, but also unemployable. There is no credible agenda to tackle this serious problem of joblessness. An International Labour Organization study from 2013 found that youth unemployment in the Arab world stands at 23 percent, compared with a world average of 14 percent.[55] If jobs do come, says Mohammad Pournik of the United Nations Development Fund, they are secured through bribes or favors (*wasta*). "The real issue is the need for jobs with social dignity," said Pournik, "rather than jobs that come at the expense of dignity." Groups such as al-Shabaab and al-Nusra attract young men whose dignity has been reduced in their failed search for a better life.

Mohammed thoughtfully answers my questions about al-Nusra, his family, and his future. He thinks that the money for al-Nusra comes from the Gulf. He is right. People like the Qatari national Khalifa Muhammed Turki al-Subaiy collected vast amounts of money that they handed over to conduits such as Ashraf Muhammad Yusuf Uthman Abd al-Salam, who was then in Syria with Jabhat al-Nusra. Mohammed will not tell me much about his family for fear that this will help the authorities identify him. But of his future he is measured. His expectations are minimal. A mediocre formal education in Lebanon's northern city of Tripoli came alongside the fulminations of a cleric in the city's many mosques. It is from the latter that he found his way in the world.

Five years into the war in Syria, the country remains a bare shadow of itself. Morticians have stopped counting the dead, and the United Nations has only estimates of the displaced (about half the population). The suffering is acute. It cannot be captured in numbers, although the Syrian Center for Policy Research in Damascus persists. Its studies are crucial windows into the destruction of Syria. Close to half of Syria's people have been dislodged by this war, many rushing across the border, but most taking shelter with friends and families within Syria itself. More than half the population is unemployed, with survival being found in the shadows of the destroyed cities and towns. Poverty rates are dangerously high: 85 percent are in poverty, while as many as 69 percent are in extreme poverty and over a third are in abject poverty. Life expectancy has dropped from seventy years in 2010 to fifty-five years in 2015—a full fifteen years lost. No economy can survive such a sustained and complex war. Syria, which once ranked among the states with relatively stable indicators, is now in free fall. But worse, the damage done to Syria has maimed it for decades to come. For instance, 45 percent of school-age children are not able to study. The center notes that this itself accounts for "a human capital debit of 24.5 million lost years"—a number that seems unbelievable.[56] An entire generation has been set aside. Syria, where the educational systems had once been the pride of the Arab world, now sees children oscillating between trauma and illiteracy. One gauge of the peril is the extreme step taken by Syrian refugees to flee the area, even to risk going to chaotic Libya, from which they chance the Mediterranean moat. Walking through Syrian refugee camps provides a sense both of the desolation and of the pure relief at human resilience; even the most scarred people try to plant flowers outside their UN tents.

The war itself is relatively dull; battles here and there threaten human lives and seem to make little progress. Fighters like Mohammed seem equal parts bored and ecstatic. No wonder the fighters take drugs such as Captagon, which gives them "chemical courage" and gets them out of ennui. The government of Bashar al-Assad, which the West, Turkey, and the Gulf Arabs thought would fall on several occasions, remains intact but deeply weakened. It continues to control most of the major population centers. Despite their antipathy to his government, Western journalists and diplomats feel safest in the government's realm. Fear saturates the zone of the rebels, whether the slowly depleting Free Syrian Army (FSA) or the various Islamist groups such as the al-Qaeda affiliate al-Nusra, the Saudi proxy Jaysh al-Islam, or ISIS. Kidnappings for ransom and for spectacular killings are the threat. There is no longer any reliable force that carries the "moderate" banner for the West. In September 2015, General Lloyd Austin of the U.S. Central Command told a U.S. congressional committee that there are perhaps "four or five" of the U.S.-trained forces intact in the field. Millions of dollars have been spent in vain. U.S.-trained fighters seem to flow into the extremist outfits, which are seen by them as more effective. The rebels lean largely toward extremism of one shape or form. In his elegiac account of the war, the journalist Charles Glass notes, "No one, apart from the undertaker, is winning."[57] The entrails of this war suggest little hope. Few signs of peace are visible. UN peace conferences in Geneva are either of no consequence or abandoned. Even exhaustion—which is the mood among many fighters—is not a guarantee of a cease-fire. The combatants resemble boxers in the final rounds of their championship bout, blinded by pain and fatigue, groping for a target on the body of the other; except that in this case, there are no rounds, no bells, no going the distance, since the war seems to stretch till infinity.

Was Syria fated to join the Arab Spring? Bashar al-Assad did not think so. He was confident that the wave would wash across North Africa and settle before it entered the Arab East. The southern city of Daraa was the epicenter of small-scale protests that faced vicious escalation from the local governor, Faysal Kalthum. Assad sacked Kalthum and asked a former agricultural minister, Adel Safar, to form a new government in Damascus. He made concessions to the Islamists by allowing teachers to wear the niqab (face veil) and by closing Syria's only casino (which had been opened in Damascus in January 2011). On 24 March, Assad's adviser Bouthaina Shaban called for the revival of the reform era of 2005. She said that living standards for state employees must be raised with wage increases and enhanced health insurance, that laws on the buying and selling of land in border areas must be relaxed, and that political reforms need to be immediately enacted. This latter would include the allowance for freer media, more political parties, and an end to the emergency laws (in place since 1963). The emergency laws were lifted and emergency court trails ended. These olive branches came in rapid succession. They would have been sufficient in another time, but this was the time of Tahrir; nothing less than the departure of the leader was going to be enough for the opposition and for the youth who had taken to the streets. Old redoubts of opposition—Hama in particular—turned out demonstrations. The retaliation was swift. On 1 July 2011, a fireman from Hama, Ibrahim Qashoush, sang at a public gathering, "Come on, Bashar, leave!" (*"Yallah Irhal ya Bashar"*). Four days later, it was said that his body had been fished out of the Orontes River, with his throat cut. Not long afterward, Qashoush emerged in Turkey. He was told to go underground, for—as he was told by the rebels—you are "worth more dead than alive."[58] The fog of deception settled heavily across Syria. In June, the Syrian government took diplomats to visit a mass grave in Jisr el-Shughour—where the bodies of Syrian soldiers lay buried. What had occasioned the executions was not clear. Had the protestors killed these soldiers, or had they been shot by others soldiers because they had mutinied? U.S. Ambassador Robert Ford went with a Syrian government delegation to visit the site. When he came under criticism for going with the government, the U.S. State Department said that he had merely gone to "see for himself the results of the Syrian government's brutality." The case had already been closed as far as Washington was concerned. It drew its line in the sand. Any massacre would be placed at the front door of the Assad regime.

Unlike Tunisia and Egypt, protests also began to appear on Syrian streets on behalf of the government. If the anti-Assad protesters chanted, "God, Syria, Freedom, and that's enough" ("*Allah, Suriya, huriyawa bas*"), the pro-Assad crowds chanted, "God, Syria, Bashar, and that's enough" ("*Allah, Suriya, Bashar wa bas*"). For every sign that echoed the Tunisian slogans for the removal of the leader, there was one that read, "We are all with you, Bashar" ("*Kullna ma'akya Bashar*").[59] The size of the antiregime demonstrations—but for in Hama—remained small compared with those in Egypt, and defections from the military did not come in significant numbers despite all the encouragement from Google, Al Jazeera, and the office of U.S. Secretary of State Hillary Clinton.[60] Few brigade commanders brought their entire brigades to the Free Syrian Army—as had taken place in Libya. The Libyan military had been broken by its ill-starred war against Chad in 1987. It was not comparable to the Syrian military, which was highly disciplined and trained. It was naive to believe that the Syrian Arab Army would collapse in the same way that the Libyan army did in 2011, or that the army would abandon the civilian leadership as it did in Egypt. None of these stories repeated themselves in Syria. Allegiance to the military did not come from sectarian feeling alone. Bashar al-Assad's chief of staff—till he was killed by the Free Syrian Army in 2012—was Dawoud Rajiha, who came from a Greek Orthodox family; he was succeeded by Fahd Jassem al-Freij, who comes from a Sunni Arab family from Hama. Assad maintained support among considerable sections of the population—certainly the bourgeoisie of Damascus and Aleppo, but also the urban middle class. He was correct in his assessment that the outcome in Tunisia and Egypt would not be repeated easily.

What provoked the outbreak? The story cannot begin in May 2011. It has a longer history. Out of Syria's colonial past emerged the one-party Arab regime—to protect Syria's integrity from the knives of Britain and France, and later the United States and Israel. But that one-party regime could not be sustained. Too many complex desires and aspirations had been suppressed by these regimes, whether in Egypt or Syria or Iraq. Popular discontent was legion. Each of these regimes, as we saw with Egypt, had a basic contract with the population: we will provide for your economic, social, and cultural needs as long as you leave the politics to us. By the 1990s, the contract frayed. These regimes turned to neoliberal policy frameworks that whittled at the welfare schemes and encouraged corruption. The beneficiaries of the new reforms, Charles Glass writes, "were newly privatized bankers, Bashar's cousins who obtained licenses to sell mobile phones, middlemen and brokers with urban educations and customs, not the newly landless trying without money or education to adapt to metropolitan life." [61] Even Assad's close adviser Bouthaina Shaban admitted by October 2011 that "Rami Makhlouf isn't the only one who made money in the past period," referring to the man who became a symbol of the corruption and whose name appeared prominently in the Panama Papers. "There are many people, big capitalists, who made a lot of money." [62] Shaban had a front-row seat for this, since her husband—Khalil Jawad—handled many of the business deals for the Assad family. The frustrations of the newly landless were compounded with the drought that hit the area around the Euphrates River. (In September 2010, the UN's special rapporteur on the right to food, Olivier de Schutter, said that as many as three million Syrians had been thrown into extreme poverty by the extreme weather.)[63] Dr. Bassam Barakat, an adviser to the Assad government, told journalist Reese Ehrlich of the neoliberal reforms, "The Syrian regime made a big mistake. We had an army of unemployed young people."[64] It was from among this army of the unemployed that the rebellion grew.

If the contract to provide basic needs was withdrawn, the other side of it—political suffocation—was not changed. The vocabulary of violence in the dungeons of Syria is highly developed, from the *dulab* (to be hung from a suspended tire and beaten) to the *bisat al-rih* (the flying carpet—namely, to hang the prisoner on a piece of wood and then beat him or apply electric shock treatment). Promises of a political opening came as early as 2001, but Bashar Assad dithered. Opponents went to prison or exile. Pressure for reform came from people who had sympathy for the problems of the one-party state. Why Assad did not accept their suggestions is clear. Crony capitalism—a condition familiar around the world—prefers less accountability, and so, less democracy. Those prisons came into use during the West's War on Terror, when the U.S. government outsourced incarceration and torture to Damascus. In February 2011, a month before the rising, the Syrian Association for Human Rights and the Arab Organization for Penal Reform published a report on prison overcrowding. Who was in prison? People like the former judge Haitham al-Maleh (age eighty), who was convicted by the Emergency Laws for "weakening national sentiment." His crime: calling for civil liberties. By 2015, al-Maleh said that he preferred living under ISIS to living under Assad.[65]

The Assad government was soured by al-Maleh's affiliations to the Brotherhood. But all those in prison did not come from this strand. Others came from the institutional Left. Riad al-Turk, former leader of the Syrian Communist Party; Aref Dalila, dean of the Faculty of Economics at Damascus University; and Maher Charif, a Palestinian Marxist and leader of the Palestinian Communist Party (formally Hizb al-Sha'b al-Filastini), went to prison. None had affinities with the West, and all rebuked the politics of the Brotherhood. They sought a less suffocating relationship between the state and society. That had to be denied. The *dulab* and the *bisat al-rih* came into action. These are the habits of power. The road to Damascus had only one lane; compromise was not a destination along it.

When the Syrian uprising morphed rapidly into a brutal war, the emir of ISIS—Abu Bakr al-Baghdadi—set up Jabhat al-Nusra (The Support Front) as the al-Qaeda front in that battle. Al-Nusra joined a variety of extremist groups that had already begun to suffocate the civil rebellion of 2011 and the anemic Free Syrian Army (made up of defectors from the Syrian armed forces). The extremists brought a tenacious energy to the fight. They did not need front lines and the heavy artillery required by the Soviet training received by the Syrian armed forces and their defectors. These were fighters who knew close combat and relied upon Toyota trucks to move swiftly across Syria's uneven topography. Al-Nusra made some rapid gains, first with orchestrated bombings in Syria's cities and then with seizure of territory (as in the eastern city of Deir ez-Zor in May 2012). The calling card of al-Qaeda's outfits consisted of conducting mass executions and exerting stiff sanctions for anything they deemed to be against their laws.

Revolutions, Glass writes, "produce surprising outcomes, and those who start them must be prepared for the unintended consequences of success as much as for failure."[66] It is the latter that began to stalk Syria. Syria, wrote the Irish journalist Patrick Seale, is the "mirror of rival interests."[67] That was in 1965. The phrase applies to the present. Not long after the protests began in May 2011, rival interests threw themselves into the struggle. They left little room for the Syrians themselves. Two Western ambassadors—Robert Ford of the United States and Eric Chevallier of France—went to an antigovernment demonstration in Hama on 7 July. Both were received with jubilation. The visits of Ambassadors Ford and Chevallier had a very significant effect. In Libya, the United States—egged on by France—used its air power through the North Atlantic Treaty Organization (NATO) to pulverize the forces of the Libyan army. It was the NATO attack that delivered Libya to the rebels. By July it was clear that absent such a bombing by the United States on the Syrian Arab Army, the rebels—even with Gulf Arab and Turkish support— would not succeed. The visit of Ambassadors Ford and Chevallier to the protests sent a strong message that U.S. and French airpower was forthcoming. That message lingered for years, despite the fact that it had become clear by the time of their visit that no UN authorization would be possible. As the Indian Ambassador to the UN at the time, Hardeep Singh Puri, told me on 18 February 2012, the Chinese and the Russians—backed by the Global South—would refuse to give the West a resolution for aerial bombardment of Syria after the Libyan fiasco.[68] Ambassadors Ford and Chevallier would have known that by July 2011. Yet, they—backed by Presidents Barack Obama and François Hollande—sent a message to the weak rebels that the West was going to assist them. This kind of moral intervention, with the promise of military intervention to come, provoked the intensification of the war and the refusal of any dialogue. No concessions from the regime would be sufficient to the opposition if it appeared that Western bombers were on the horizon. The promise of the bombers sent a signal to the regime that it was facing a battle of annihilation.

Short of a bombing raid, the United States—through the CIA—began to help the Saudis, led by Prince Bandar bin Sultan, buy arms in Eastern Europe and transfer them across a porous Turkish border to the proxy groups of Qatar, Saudi Arabia, and Turkey. This was an operation known as Timber Sycamore.[69] Exiled leadership of the Muslim Brotherhood began to be assertive. It had cells deep underground in Syria, but this was not going to be of any consequence. Demography goes against the Brotherhood in Syria, which had never had a presence—before 1982—in more than half the governorates of the country. Backed by Qatari and Turkish money and emboldened by Western enthusiasm to weaken Iranian influence in the region, the Brotherhood and groups far more extreme than it (such as Ahrar ash-Sham and Jabhat al-Nusra) appointed themselves as the opposition's leadership. Based in Turkey, they created the Supreme Military Council so that they could control—through the spigot of money—the armed operations on the ground. In mid-December 2012, one of the most prominent liberals in the Istanbul-based opposition—Dr. Kamal Labwani—said, "If the Americans want to recognize this Coalition, then they take the responsibility of putting the Muslim Brotherhood in power and all the consequences that entails."[70] When the United States displayed hesitation about supporting al-Qaeda-backed groups, the Brotherhood objected. Senior Brotherhood leader Mohammed Farouk Tayfour said that such a decision would be "too hasty." He was backed by secular opposition figures—such as the intellectual Yassin al-Haj Saleh—who said that divisions in the ranks would only advantage Assad. Tayfour and Saleh provided cover for these al-Qaeda groups, which would soon smother them. As Omar Dahi wrote, "More and more Syrians came to see the SNC and its Turkish and Gulf backers publicly embracing pluralism, while in fact facilitating the rise of fanatical forces, and minimizing or dismissing their crimes." He suggests that only a few people—such as Abd al-Aziz al-Khayyir and Haytham Manna—"were vociferous in warning of the corrosive impact of militarization, including the rising danger posed by *takfiri* groups."[71] For his pleas, Manna faced an orchestrated smear campaign on social media and in the press.

As one of the leaders of the Syrian opposition, Tayfour is seen by the West as "moderate" and reliable. But his history tells another story. Tayfour is now the deputy leader of the Syrian Muslim Brotherhood. He is from Hama, where he had been a leader of the Brotherhood's armed wing, the Combatant Vanguard (Attali'a el-Moukatillah). This group attacked the Aleppo Artillery School in 1979, opening up a war between the Muslim Brotherhood and the Syrian state that ended with the 1982 massacre by the state of tens of thousands of people in Tayfour's hometown of Hama.[72] The war between the Brotherhood and the Syrian state ran for three bloody years—including an assassination attempt against Hafez al-Assad in 1980. Tayfour and his comrades had some sympathy for the means deployed by al-Nusra. Even when the United States did put al-Nusra on the terrorism list, it continued to be seen as a legitimate ally by the various proxy armies and large sections of the opposition leadership as they fought against the Syrian state. Western governments saw Tayfour as part of the moderate opposition. His own unseemly history was irrelevant, and his reasonableness gave cover to worse elements who fashioned themselves as the rebels.

By October 2012, International Crisis Group found that "the presence of a powerful Salafi strand among Syria's rebels has become irrefutable."[73] Liwa al-Tawhid, the main force in Aleppo, worked closely with both Ahrar ash-Sham and Jabhat al-Nusra, as well as a host of other rebel formations. "Conditions were favourable," wrote the authors of the Crisis Group report. "The uprising was rooted in a social category ready made for Salafi preachers, the poor rural underclass that, over years, migrated to rough, impersonal urban settings far removed from its traditional support networks. And conditions ripened: as violence escalated, hopes for a quick resolution receded, and as alternative tendencies (proponents of dialogue; peaceful demonstrators; the exiled leadership; more moderate Islamists) proved their limitations, many naturally flocked to Salafist alternatives."[74] By early 2012, it had become impossible to imagine that a "moderate" force could emerge in these conditions.

Among the various extremist groups, one of the largest by 2012 was Ahrar ash-Sham, the leading section in the Islamic Front. Its principle leadership—including its charismatic leader, Hassan Abboud—was wiped out in 2014 in a huge suffocation bomb. Hassan Abboud, his successor Abu Jaber, and the current leader, Abu Yahia al-Hamawi, are all from the Ghab Plains of Syria in the rural hinterland of Hama. These are small-town and peasant men, part of the constituency that the Crisis Group report identified. Their political itineraries display their search for more hardened groups: Abu Jaber, for example, went from the Free Syrian Army to the al-Fajr Islamic Movement to Ahrar ash-Sham. Hassan Abboud was the protégé of Abu Khaled al-Suri, al-Qaeda's main representative in Syria. Money and logistical support from Qatar and Turkey have been essential for Ahrar. Rooted as it is in the Ghab Plains, it is driven by motivations that

are cultivated in Ankara and Doha. It was also given over to the
unseemly. Slogans of extreme violence appeared occasionally on
walls and on the lips of young fighters—"*Massihiyeh ala Beirut,
Alawiyeh ala Taboot*" ("Christians to Beirut, Alawis to the Coffin").
Zahran Alloush, backed by the Saudis, told his followers, "The
jihadists will wash the *rafida* from Greater Syria. They will wash
it forever, if Allah wills it." *Rafida* is a particularly heinous anti-
Shia slur. It began to define the character of the rebellion. "The
war has reached the stage at which many on both sides no longer
regard the other as human," wrote Charles Glass, "let alone as
citizens of a country in which all must coexist."[75] The Lebanese
writer Elias Khoury told me, "The rational outcome of Saudi
ideology is al-Qaeda. Saudis hate al-Qaeda because it turned on
them. But practically their politics lead to the thinking of al-
Qaeda."[76] The proxies of Saudi Arabia seemed indistinguishable
from the affiliates of al-Qaeda.

Yassin al-Haj Saleh, a Syrian dissident who had become an
important voice of the rebellion after sixteen years in Syrian prisons, went underground in 2011. He went to his native city of Raqqa,
which had fallen to ISIS in March 2013. In an open letter, "Fare-
well to Syria, for a while," written in October 2013, Saleh wrote
that his city had been taken over by "the specters of horror of our
childhood, the ghouls." The situation in Raqqa, Saleh wrote, was
deplorable. It was hard to watch "strangers oppress it and rule the
fates of its people, confiscating public property, destroying a
statue of Haroun al-Rashid or desecrating a church, taking people
into custody where they disappeared in their prisons." He fled
Syria for Turkey. In December 2013, Saleh's wife, Samira al-Khalil,
the well-regarded Communist, was abducted in Douma (near
Damascus) along with her comrades from the Violations Docu-
mentation Center—Razan Zeitouneh, Wael Hamada, and Nazem

al-Hammadi. The kidnapper was most likely Jaysh al-Islam, the Saudi proxy that the West still seemed to consider as a "moderate" army. The whereabouts of the four activists are unknown. Their fate is as uncertain as of that of the beloved priest of Deir Mar Musa al-Habashi in Nabk (north of Damascus), Paolo Dall'Oglio, who went to Raqqa in July 2013 to negotiate with ISIS. Early into the uprising, Father Paolo, whose instincts for freedom are immense, warned that the "fight for freedom" would be "transformed in a civil war, and this will create space for all kinds of extremisms and crimes against humanity and disasters."[77] That Father Paolo was kidnapped is known. Beyond that is silence.

Moutaman al-Baba and I are sitting in Beirut near the old Green Line that divided the city during its civil war. Al-Baba is a Syrian businessman in a hurry, who speaks with the credibility of a man with insider's knowledge who has moved away from his earlier commitments. In 2011, al-Baba financed the purchase of arms for the Syrian rebels near Damascus. He threw himself into the Syrian uprising with his money and his contacts. In early 2012, al-Baba wrote to UN–Arab League envoy Kofi Annan saying that people like al-Baba were ready to pay for the revolution. They wanted no Gulf Arab money to come into their fight. "We have a network to help and support people," he wrote. But the Gulf Arab money and influence swept into the rebellion, he admitted to me. Al-Baba soured on the endeavor. He fled Syria that summer. In November 2012, he published an essay called "Syria and the Raped Revolution." The revolution was over, he wrote. The extremists had taken it away from the Syrian people. Voices like that of al-Baba were not heard over the din. When he was with the revolt, the studios of al-Arabiya and the BBC welcomed him. When his views changed, he could not get on the air. His Syrian voice was no longer of interest.

Al-Baba has no faith in the creation of a "moderate" armed force. Events show him that it is impossible. The FSA, built mainly of defectors from the Syrian armed forces, is weak—weakened by attacks upon it not only from the Syrian army but also from the extremist forces. Its leader, Salim Idriss, had been the head of the Supreme Military Council in 2012, but the next year he was run out of his headquarters by the Islamic Front. He is now likely in Doha, Qatar. His successor—Abdullah al-Bashir—has been sidelined. By 2014, FSA officials were saying, "The leadership of the FSA is American."[78] Blocked from any major victory, squeezed by the much more fierce Islamist rebels and by the Syrian army, the FSA has gone in two directions—toward extortion and smuggling, and toward coordination with the Islamist rebels for territorial gains. The Americans pushed the FSA to form a new front—the Harakat al-Hazzm (Movement of Steadfastness). When it did not make any impact, it was dissolved into al-Jabha al-Sham (the Syrian Front). Not long after its formation in 2014, it was taken over by Ahrar ash-Sham's Abu Amr al-Harkoush. In Idlib, fighters formed al-Faylaq al-Khamis (The Fifth Legion), which they claimed is nationalist, with the Syrian flag on its materials rather than the pennants of jihad. But its leadership had been Islamist just before it decided to hide its beards under a balaclava. The most desperate attempt was made when the Obama team reached out to Saudi Arabia to create a "moderate" force with $500 million. It is a miserable proposition given the immoderate nature of the tutor. Saudi Arabia's own proxy in Syria is Jaysh al-Islam, led by Zahran Alloush (whose father, Abdullah, is a Syrian cleric in Saudi exile). Alloush's speeches bristled with sectarianism. Little wonder that on 11 December 2013, his fighters (along with al-Nusra) conducted a massacre of Alawites, Christians, Ismailis, and Druze near Adra

Workers' City (northeast of Damascus). Alloush was killed in late 2015. No moderate armed force is in evidence.

Endless cups of juice and plates of biscuits come between al-Baba and myself. We are talking about the barbarism that has taken hold of Syria since 2014. Al-Baba has six cell phones on the table before him. He wants to create a network against the encroachment of extremists into his beloved Syria. Al-Baba is not alone, and he knows it. There are many Syrians who are horrified by what has happened to their country. People like al-Baba do not see themselves as responsible for the emergence of the extremists. They wanted a more just and free Syria. The Syrian government had blocked the space for their ambitions. It was not capable of genuine reform, he felt. Into the breach came Gulf Arab money, pushed along by a naive West, suggests al-Baba. This is what ruined Syria.

My mind wanders to the al-Nusra fighters who are sitting on the side of road, polishing their Kalashnikovs. Their futures had been sidelined. They were not seeking democracy or human rights, or free markets. What they wanted was dignity. They have found something in this struggle, and will not so easily withdraw from it—aerial bombardment or not. But their ambitions are irrelevant. They are cannon fodder for regional rival interests.

The pipeline of funds that is familiar to the world of al-Qaeda—including individual donations from Gulf sheikhs—lubricated al-Nusra and the Islamic State. Hatred for Bashar al-Assad in the world of the Gulf Arabs was refracted through their political fear of Iran's influence in the region. ISIS fighters freely spoke of their support from Saudi Arabia, even as they maligned the kingdom for its corruption. In 2006, al-Zarqawi said enigmatically of his support, "While it was the poor citizens of Iraq who financed this struggle, I have the support of the richest people of earth." He could only have meant the Gulf Arabs. In 2011–12, the Saudi man in Turkey was the former journalist and chevalier of the Lebanese politician Saad Hariri—'Uqab Saqr. Caught on tape, Saqr said he was involved in funneling arms, including rockets, into northern Syria from Lebanon and Turkey. (Later Saqr would deny this, saying that he was actually sending only blankets and milk for babies, although sources on the ground verify that he was the courier for Saudi weapons.) On the tape, the rebels beg him, implore him to fill their arsenal. He is aloof and nasty. It is a window into the kind of operation that the Saudis ran in the early years. It was designed to build loyalty and dependence. They succeeded.

On 8 March 2014, before the Mosul blitzkrieg, Iraqi premier al-Maliki cautioned Saudi Arabia and Qatar to cease their support to ISIS. He would repeat these allegations in June. Both times the Saudi government feigned outrage. Both sides are correct. It is unlikely that official Saudi channels have financed ISIS (although the Saudis have directly supported Jaysh al-Islam and others, whose tenor is not so far from ISIS). Private Kuwaiti, Qatari, and Saudi funds are a more likely source. In early February 2016, Saudi spokesperson Major General Mansour al-Turki said that during the war in Afghanistan in the 1980s and 1990s, private individuals used the Saudi financial system to send billions of dollars to extremists who would become al-Qaeda. A secret U.S. State Department cable, written by Secretary of State Hillary Clinton, in 2009 captures the U.S. view of who was funding the extremists. Saudi Arabia, Clinton wrote, "remains a critical financial support base for al-Qaida, the Taliban, LeT [Lashkar-e-Tayyiba, based in Pakistan] and other terrorist groups." These groups "probably raise millions of dollars annually from Saudi sources, often during Hajj and Ramadan."[79]

Startup money for ISIS came from these very channels. Taxation regimes in Anbar Province (Iraq) helped ISIS; as they took territory in Syria, this taxation system was expanded. The spluttering oil fields of eastern Syria added to their coffers, as did their sale of stolen antiquities from both Syria and Iraq. Money never seemed to be a problem. The Toyota trucks always seemed to appear, new models with glistening white paint. Their media team had the best cameras, and their social-media team was always prepared to get their high-quality propaganda videos online. It was no surprise that ISIS would produce a glossy annual report that resembled that of any corporation or that it would launch a Twitter app.

Al-Nusra and ISIS had no problem in recruiting fighters. From 2011 onward, Assad has opened his prison doors to release many who had extremist backgrounds. The civic rebellion was overrun by these extremists, who were more adept at organization and armed struggle. These hardened men provided the backbone of Jabhat al-Nusra, ISIS, and other Islamist groups. On 21 July 2013, ISIS blew its way into the Abu Ghraib prison outside Baghdad and freed five hundred of their confederates. These prisoners were joined by extremists from across the world who heeded al-Baghdadi's call to come and create an emirate. When NATO became the air force for the rebels in Libya in 2011, Western intervention provided such battle-hardened veterans with a new confidence (and new equipment, including weaponry). The Turkish government looked the other way as these fighters of the Libyan Islamic Fighting Group and its offshoots took flights from Libya to Turkey's eastern city of Mardin. The airports at Mardin and Gaziantep began to resemble the airport of Peshawar in Pakistan at the high point of that jihad in the 1980s. These foreign fighters would go across the border to al-Hasakah and join ISIS and al-Nusra convoys that drifted in their safe zone between Aleppo, Raqqah, and Ramadi. Even when ISIS struck inside Turkey (such as in May 2013 in Reyhanli in Hatay), the Turkish government did not close down the channel. It remains open to this day.

When Assad seemed most weakened, his geopolitical allies came to his rescue. Iran brought in strategic planners, provided logistical and financial support, and asked Hezbollah to cross the border from Lebanon and bolster the flagging Syrian military. A senior Hezbollah official told me in 2013 that they entered Syria on existential grounds: their access to supplies from Iran is vital to the protection of Lebanon from Israeli threats. As we spoke just outside Beirut in the countryside, he would occasionally stop to alert me to the sounds of Israeli fighter jets, which routinely overfly the country. "It is this," he said with a dramatic flourish, "that motivates us to fight in Syria. We are not there to save the government. We are there to save ourselves." The combination of Iran and Hezbollah allowed the Syrian army to retake parts of the spinal cord that links Damascus to Aleppo. The Syrian military, trained in the East German method, uses heavy artillery against adversaries rather than close combat. This, and the indiscriminate use of barrel bombs, intensified the civilian casualties. Hezbollah fighters were dismayed by this method of warfare. They preferred close combat against their adversaries, which prevents threats to civilians. A combination of Syrian government forces and Hezbollah held off the onslaught from the extremists. It had become clear by 2013 that neither side would be able to win an outright victory. Syria was being bled.

The fog of geopolitics had made everything unclear. Syria was sidelined. The United Nations envoys (Kofi Annan, Lakhdar Brahimi, and Staffan de Mistura) tried to contain the escalation and bring together the major players toward a process.[80] In 2012, a small window opened when Egypt—under Morsi—formed the Syria Contact Group, which included regional adversaries: Iran, Saudi Arabia, and Turkey.[81] Before this could get going, the West and Russia scuttled it. They had bigger fish to fry. Qatar, Saudi Arabia, Turkey, and the West—through their Friends of Syria group—jockeyed for influence over the various iterations of the Syrian opposition—the Syrian National Council and the Syrian National Coalition. Fractiousness was their mode, as the various tussles between Qatar and Saudi Arabia or the Europeans and the Gulf Arabs broke any hope of common purpose. The Local Coordination Committees of Syria—an umbrella of local opposition groups inside Syria—stood opposed to al-Qaeda outfits, whereas both had an antagonistic relationship to the Istanbul-based and Paris-based oppositions. Meanwhile, the United States had its own complex games going, unclear whether it wanted al-Qaeda groups to dominate the agenda but then unwilling to be on the sidelines of the process. Israel's confusion mirrored that of the United States. It wanted Assad to be hit hard in order to hurt Iran and Hezbollah, its local adversary. On the other hand, it did not want Assad's regime to be fatally wounded since this would bring an al-Qaeda group to power in Damascus. Such an outcome was too unpredictable. For a long while in this war, it has seemed as if the West—and Israel—have been content to see Syria bleed and weaken. No outcome is desirable to them.

What united the fractious opposition groups, and their regional and Western allies, was the slogan "Assad Must Go." In fact, the Syrian Muslim Brotherhood—emboldened by its Turkish client— had suggested that peace would come after a "bullet is directed at Assad's head."[82] This was Ambassador Talcott Seelye's position in 1979 with regard to Assad's father. It was now the position of the opposition, including the West. Such a posture was a nonstarter with Damascus, and so with the Iranians, the Russians, and the Iraqis. They had other proposals. The opposition, whose precondition ("Assad Must Go") had become the basis of its unity, would not take any of the Damascus proposals seriously. Hope that the U.S. bombers would fire up continued to fuel the energy of the opposition. It was their only prospect.

Syria, Iraq, and Iran feared the games being played by the West and the Gulf Arabs. The release by WikiLeaks of a tranche of cables from the Saudi foreign ministry in June 2015 rattled the capitals. It showed how the Saudis had spent their considerable fortune maintaining an institutional apparatus to propagate their ideology in the region and to battle both Iranian influence and Shiism.[83] This tranche confirmed that older Saudi games through the World Muslim League had been reincarnated in the Supreme Council for Islamic Affairs. Space for trust deteriorated. It was going to be hard to rebuild.

Obama set red lines on chemical weapons but could not follow up on them. A major attack on 21 August 2013 in Ghouta, near Damascus, suggested that chemical weapons had been used against civilians. Debate about who fired the weapons remains open.[84] Circumstantial evidence suggested that the Assad army had fired these weapons. If so, Obama's red line had been tripped and his bombers should have come into action. When U.S. Secretary of State John Kerry met with Russian Foreign Minister Sergei Lavrov to discuss the killings, the latter put a proposal on the table that went along the grain of Obama's temperament. Lavrov proposed that the Organization for the Prohibition of Chemical Weapons (OPCW) and the United Nations would come into Syria and remove all traces of chemical weapons. They hastily put together a framework to remove all such weapons within a year.[85] Two implications became clear: that the

United States was not prepared to bomb Syria, and that the Russians would now exert themselves into the conflict with much more force.

THREAT OF THE ISLAMIC STATE

In 2013, an odd sideshow began in northern Syria. The emir of ISIS, al-Baghdadi, took the move to declare a caliphate and to tell al-Nusra that it was merely its franchise. Syria was now a province of the caliphate, and the al-Nusra emir—Abu Mohammed al-Golani—would have to bend his knee to al-Baghdadi. During its yearlong existence, al-Nusra had recruited a great number of Syrians and had embroiled itself in the fight against the Assad government. That was its priority. ISIS had broader goals: to create a caliphate and to expand beyond the mere borders of Syria. Al-Nusra and ISIS began an open fight in northern Syria. ISIS had already seized the northern city of Raqqa in March 2013, asserting its control now along the road from Raqqa to Iraq, maintaining control over the Syrian and Iraqi oil fields. These battles in Syria raised the confidence of the ISIS fighters, drawing in more combatants and groups from Syria, from Iraq, and from the universe of international jihad to their standard and pushed them to make serious inroads to the Turkish border. Al-Baghdadi sent Abu Ali al-Anbari to lead his legions. Al-Anbari, like al-Baghdadi, had been in the Ba'ath and in the Iraqi Army (a major general) before he joined Ansar al-Islam, al-Qaeda, and then ISIS. Al-Golani, on the other hand, came to Iraq in 2003 from Syria to join al-Qaeda. He had none of the military experience of al-Baghdadi and al-Anbari, nor does he have the kind of broader strategic understanding that these former Ba'ath men have. Al-Golani told Al Jazeera in 2015 that Jabhat al-Nusra had no ambition to attack the West. His is a narrower disposition, focused against the Assad government and Alawites. Assistance from Israel is not forbidden by this man, whose nom de guerre refers to the Syrian Golan, occupied by Israel.

Too much, however, was made of the dispute between ISIS and al-Nusra as well as with the Free Syrian Army. In parts of Syria, ISIS, al-Nusra, and the FSA worked together, while in other parts they fought. In November 2013, the pro-rebellion Syrian Observatory of Human Rights's Rami Abdul Rahman said, "ISIS is the strongest group in Northern Syria—100%— and anyone who tells you anything else is lying."[86]

The uprising in Syria afforded the Syrian Kurds an opportunity to create their own autonomous enclave. The Syrian government troops of Bashar al-Assad withdrew to defend Damascus and the heartland cities of Syria. The Syrian Kurds created a militia—the People's Protection Units (YPG)—to defend the three noncontiguous cantons of Syrian Kurdistan, which they called Rojava. Along the Turkish border, the Syrian Kurds controlled Afrin (in the west), Kobane (in the center), and Cizir (in the east). The YPG fighters had been trained by the Kurdish Workers' Party (PKK), a Marxist formation from Turkey, which is considered as a terrorist group in Turkey and by the United States. YPG-PKK fighters—like Hezbollah fighters—had no fear of close combat, which they deployed to good use. The Syrian Kurds first took the city of Kobane on 19 July 2012. It became the main base for Rojava. Cizir and Afrin officially joined the new formation in January 2014. Rojava's constitution carried its audacity, since it claimed to be "founded upon a social contract that reconciles the rich mosaic of Syria through a transitional phase from dictatorship, civil war and destruction, to a new democratic society where civil life and social justice are preserved." Assad had withdrawn a considerable section of his forces from northern Syria, turning the region over to the Kurds. Promises of autonomy were made. This promise is an echo of when Saddam Hussein withdrew from northern Iraq and signed an autonomy agreement in March 1970. (It would last only four years, but it would become the basis for the Kurdish autonomous region that was set up in 1991.)

The YPG had from its earliest days been helped along by the far more sophisticated PKK—with 40 percent of the YPG army made up of the female battalions. Funds had to be collected from the Kurdish population, which gives out of patriotism even though the economic condition in the region has been miserable. Connections to the rest of Syria had been essential for the Syrian Kurds; the surreal state was clear in May 2014 when busloads of Syrian Kurds braved the ISIS front lines to go take school exams in Aleppo. (ISIS fighters kidnapped many of the students on their return journey.) The chaos in Syria has brought economic misery to this newly independent enclave, which nonetheless has financed an army that is supplied by the black market in arms and equipment. They are vastly outgunned by ISIS, which had sophisticated weaponry stolen from the U.S.-supplied Iraqi bases and from the border trade across from Turkey. The Kurds held fast against ISIS, but could not hold them off from all the towns.

Confidence in the Syrian theater sent ISIS back like a pendulum toward Iraq. Bomb blasts in Mosul set the tone. It brought fear to the heart of the garrison. One minute they were holding the fort, and the next minute they had fled. Mosul fell to ISIS—the greatest prize. ISIS then threatened Irbil and Baghdad. Nothing seemed impossible at that moment. Braggadocio from ISIS came in the form of maps that showed its ambitions, from Andalus (the Iberian Peninsula) to the west to Khurasan (South and Central Asia) to the east, from Orobpa (Europe) in the north to the land of Habash (Central Africa) in the south. The ISIS magazine—*Dabiq*—is named for a town in northern Syria where, a hadith has it, the final battle between the Crusaders and the Muslims shall take place. Religious ideas meld with contemporary political challenges; it is as if ISIS wants to taunt the West into this battle so that, as the hadith put it, "the best soldiers of the people of the earth will come from Medina" and prevail. Not only does Dabiq have a religious history. It is also the site of the 1516 battle that established the ascendency of the Ottoman sultans over the Mamluks—the start of Ottoman dominion over Arab lands. The veterans from the Iraqi army and the hardened extremists who came from Chechnya, Libya, and Tunisia modulated the arrogance and fantasies of the true ISIS believers. Set-piece battles continued alongside a public-relations campaign of violence to attract international extremists and goad the West on.

The taking of Mosul was a shock to the West. It is when ISIS became a "threat." Before that it was merely one more player in the dangerous conflict in West Asia. UN High Commissioner for Human Rights Zeid Ra'ad al-Hussein described the adherents of ISIS as *takfiris*—those who want to kill infidels. ISIS, said al-Hussein, reveals "only what a Takfiri state would look like: it would be a harsh, mean-spirited house of blood, where no shade would be offered, nor shelter given, to any non-Takfiri in their midst." This is not an inaccurate description of the Kingdom of Saudi Arabia. Al-Hussein's statement, with some modulation, would not be an inappropriate description of the other Islamist groups—although they do their atrocities in the dark and do not like to confront the West. Shortly after al-Hussein's statement, ISIS released a provocative video with their own view of history and *takfir.* ISIS dates its origin in the fires of the anti-U.S. insurgency in Iraq. Its video reeks of sectarianism and blood—a diatribe against the "unbelievers," who are largely in their eyes the Shia; harsh language against the *rafidi* (he who rejects)—a derogatory word for the Shia—and for the *shirk* (idolatry) that has taken hold in Baghdad. Brutal images of the slaughter of Iraqi and Syrian soldiers—all seen as standards of the Shia—are matched in the video by images of the children killed by Syrian air force barrel bombs. The ISIS video boasts that its soldiers are "hungry lions whose drink is blood and play is carnage." A brutal episode of the beheading of a row of Syrian soldiers suggests that ISIS cannot be built without the mass slaughter of the Shia. It was ingenious of ISIS's leader, Abu Bakr al-Baghdadi, to anoint himself the caliph and to call upon all *salafi* groups to pledge their loyalty to him. No longer staking a claim to mere terrorism (the path of al-Qaeda), ISIS now announced its planetary ambitions—built, however, on the meanness of sectarianism.

None of this drew the approbation of the West. It was the threat to Irbil and the Kurdish oil that awoke the U.S. bombers. Massive oil deposits and the main U.S. ally in the region were within grasp of the caliphate. News reports trickled out in late August 2014 that ISIS had surrounded thousands of Yazidi civilians on Mount Sinjar. Humanitarian intervention to save the Yazidis was the public-relations gesture. "Today, America is coming to help," announced Obama arrogantly. In fact, the YGP and PKK fighters had already fought to build a corridor into Mount Sinjar, to draw out as many Yazidis as possible across the border into Syria. When the first U.S. personnel arrived on Mount Sinjar, they were surprised to be greeted by the "terrorist" PKK fighters. It was these fighters who helped the Yazidis form the Sinjar Resistance Units (YBS), who joined hands with a local Arab militia formed out of the Shammar tribe. They protect their region against ISIS, with immense help from the PKK. The Shammar fighters initially could not fathom the women combatants nor the Kurdish socialism of the YBS, but they took it in their stride. "They are fierce fighters," Abdulkhaleq al-Jarba told Isabel Coles of Reuters. "They have experience in guerrilla warfare."[87] The Yazidis provided the language for the U.S. bombings, but not the real motive. That was more prosaic. U.S. bombers struck hard against ISIS targets, stopping any advance toward Irbil. ISIS remained in Mosul.

Beheadings of Western journalists and aid workers followed—James Foley, Steve Sotloff, and David Haines.[88] These were the stories that the Western media covered. No one paid attention to the seventy-five Syrian soldiers beheaded by ISIS or to the beheading of the Lebanese soldier Ali el-Sayyed. Their deaths meant little to the West. Over 90 percent of the U.S. public believed at that time that ISIS posed a direct threat to their lives. This is an exaggeration built up by the nature of the executions and the spread of the videos. It is precisely what ISIS had wanted—to boost its own notoriety as against the other fighters in the region. Public atrocities by ISIS are a curious business. Brutality by ISIS has been commonplace. They have used YouTube videos of mass executions to cower their enemies into surrender or flight. But the beheadings of the Western journalists and aid workers were of a different quality. These were not to scare the Iraqi troops or the other Syrian rebels. The new killings were a message to the West. Osama bin Laden's attack on the United States on 9/11 had been calculated to draw the West to Afghanistan. That is the reason why al-Qaeda assassinated the Northern Alliance leader Ahmad Shah Massoud two days before the 9/11 attacks. But this time, ISIS knew that the United States would not send massive troop deployments into Syria. ISIS signaled that it simply does not care about international norms and the Western reaction. It recognized that the West has its hands tied. It would bomb from the air, but this was as likely as not to bring recruits to the side of ISIS. Among the *takfiri* fighters, the animosity toward the United States is great. By staking out a position as the preeminent group that stands against the West, ISIS hoped to draw in fighters from other groups. Such prestige might bring it other militant factions that dislike the West on civilizational grounds. ISIS wanted to be the main Islamist outfit in the region. The U.S. reaction to the beheadings allowed it to make that claim.

From August 2014, the United States and its Gulf Arab allies began to bomb ISIS positions in Iraq and Syria. Almost ten thousand bombs fell on Iraq and Syria each month. Raqqa took substantial hits. The pendulum of ISIS swung from Iraq back into Syria. Heavy equipment dashed across the desert to defend Raqqa and to move swiftly to capture new territory. This has been the modus operandi of ISIS—not to hang around and be bombed but to seize the initiative when being hit from the sky. ISIS fighters crossed the Euphrates River at Raqqa and took hold of the Syrian air base at Tabqa. It then went north and encircled Kobane, the central city of Rojava. "We have lost touch with the residents in the villages around Kobane," said Ocalan Iso, deputy head of the Kurdish forces in Kobane.[89] Half a million laid in wait in Kobane. Their fate was fragile. Many tried to sneak across the Turkish border, which was closed to them. Fighters persisted in holding off the city. Reinforcements of Iraqi Kurdish Peshmerga and YPG-PKK fighters alongside U.S. bombing runs on the outskirts of Kobane finally allowed the siege to be lifted. Kobane, meanwhile, had been left a ruin. When Kobane's siege was lifted, ISIS dashed south and took Tadmur and Palmyra. Nothing seemed to stop them. They had the advantage of the ground. American bombers set back ISIS here and there, but did not stop it. The Kurdish forces could only defend their areas. Other extremist groups also went into defensive mode. They were not capable of going after ISIS. Assad would not throw his troops at ISIS unless he received an assurance that the absence of his troops in western Syria would not open the door for the proxies of Saudi Arabia, Turkey, and the West to seize ground. Matters rested in dangerous stasis.

As Western bombers hit ISIS targets, ISIS organized attacks outside its caliphate—whether with direct operational connection to ISIS or conducted in its name. Paris and Brussels were spectacular for being important Western cities, but these terror campaigns have been ongoing in Bangladesh, Egypt, Indonesia, Lebanon, Tunisia, Turkey, and elsewhere. These attacks—particularly in the West—came for several reasons. They brought together disgruntled Muslims whose prospects were weak, and who had been preyed upon by extremist preachers and recruiters. Many of them had been egged on to go fight in Syria—with the full awareness of their intelligence agencies. Belgium sent the highest number of fighters per capita to Syria at a time when the West fully supported their transit home to overthrow Assad. When the West began to bomb ISIS areas, these men fled home. Some had returned to take revenge on their homelands, others to flee the much more dangerous battlefield. It is from among this pool that the recruiters and the leaders of the ISIS cells developed. They brought back the military capacity, and used their own zealotry to encourage demoralized young men to join them in their crusade. As far as ISIS is concerned, the attacks function as a provocation to ask the West to intervene more directly. The expectation of the final combat at Dabiq remains paramount among the ideologues. The foot soldiers who have come from the West want revenge against their feeling of alienation. It is an extreme step, but not unusual. Other attacks took place opportunistically, where local extremists put on the robe of ISIS to have an international angle to what would otherwise have been a minor incident. Inflation of the power of ISIS is part of its appeal. Taliban fighters want to carry its standard, as do those of Boko Haram in Nigeria and al-Shabaab in Somalia. A gruesome video of the Paris attackers called *Kill Them Wherever You Find Them* asks supporters to conduct violent acts wherever they can: fear is the coin.

ISIS OIL

Since ISIS posed such a grave threat, it seemed bewildering that neither did the United States target the ISIS oil infrastructure nor did the Turkish government prevent the entry of ISIS oil into Turkey. From its early entry into Syria, ISIS took control over oil fields in eastern Syria. This was a small cache compared with what it would be able to control once it seized Mosul and its hinterland. How did ISIS get its oil to market? Some of the oil, particularly in Syria, was sold in the domestic market— making its way to urban areas in western Syria. But the Mosul fields produced far more than ISIS could use or sell in its area. Such a lucrative field began to provide millions of dollars in revenue for ISIS.

How did ISIS convert the oil into cash? Older networks created by Iraqi Kurdish business interests in the 1990s came to be useful. Officials at the Iraqi Oil Ministry in Baghdad have long complained about the oil smuggling from northern Iraq through Turkey. This was lost revenue for the Iraqi exchequer. There was no clear evidence that the Iraqi Kurdish autonomous government benefited from the smuggling; but the Kurdish authorities seemed to do little to stop it. Oil from northern Iraq was sold to smugglers who would cart it in tankers to the Turkish border.[90] Primitive refining operations ran along the road to convert the crude oil to partly refined oil. The reason for this is that Turkey requires a license for crude oil's transit across its border; refined oil comes across without papers of provenance. The trucks cross at the Ibrahim Khalil border post and go to Silopi, where they are turned over to mysterious people, such as Uncle Farid or Hajji Farid, an Israeli-Greek dual national. Brokers like Uncle Farid organize the movement of the oil across the length of Turkey to the Mediterranean ports of Mersin, Dortyol, and Ceyhan. On board tankers, the oil then goes to Malta, where some of it is transshipped to destinations such as Ashdod (Israel). This has long been a bone of contention between the Iraqi government, the Kurdish Regional Government, and the Turkish government. The Turkish journalist Tolga Tanis accuses the son-in-law of the Turkish president of involvement in this illegal scheme.[91]

The Russian dossier on ISIS oil, released on 2 December 2015 by Deputy Minister of Defense Anatoly Antonov, went further. The Russians accused the BMZ Group Denizcilik of being a major agent for the transport of the oil. It turns out that one of the owners of BMZ, Bilal Erdoğan, is the son of the president of Turkey. BMZ Group purchased two new tankers in September 2015.[92] The movement of oil through this company has increased in recent months—which might indicate the flow of ISIS oil. Two marine engineers studied the volume of oil passing through the Ceyhan port and ISIS military gains—finding a high correlation between the two.[93] This oil then goes by tanker to the coastline of Malta, where, Iraqi Kurdistan's Minister for Natural Resources Ashti Hawrami alleges, that cargo is transshipped onto other carriers and taken to Israel.[94] This is oil laundering.

Stunningly, the Ceyhan port is a few hours' drive from the Incirlik air base, from where the U.S. jets have been hitting targets in Syria. It is literally under the noses of the U.S. planes that the ISIS oil has been transported. From August 2014—when the United States began to bomb ISIS targets—it has avoided hitting the tanker convoys. U.S. officials say that they did not strike ISIS oil tankers for fear of "collateral damage." In fact, when the United States did hit the oil tankers in December 2015, they did so after warning the drivers by leaflets. This was a very noble gesture, but also out of character. The United States generally does not warn its targets. It began to hit the oil tankers only after Russian jets struck them. Did the United States begin its strike on the tankers so as not to be shown up by the Russians? When I put this question to a U.S. State Department official, she demurred. She said that the United States was merely building up intelligence on the tanker routes and it was now prepared to hit the convoys. That it came after the Russian bombings of the tankers, she said, is mere coincidence. The Turkish government's demand for a "buffer zone" is of interest to the Europeans. They believe it is for refugees. But it could just as well be to protect the tankers from the Russian bombing raids—to protect, in other words, the lucrative ISIS oil trade.

Al-Qaeda and ISIS are not merely part of formations given to terrorist attacks. They also have ambitions of governance. When al-Qaeda was routed from Timbuktu, Mali, in early 2013, among its abandoned piles of papers was a letter by Abu Musab Abdul

Wadud—the nom de guerre of Abdelmalek Droukdel, al-Qaeda's leader in Africa. Droukdel urged his people to behave with care when they took power; otherwise, he said, they would alienate themselves from those whom they ruled. "The current baby is in its first days, crawling on its knees, and has not yet stood on its two legs," he writes about al-Qaeda's state in northern Mali.[95] "If we really want it to stand on its two feet in this world full of enemies waiting to pounce, we must ease its burden, take it by the hand, help it and support it until it stands." Garbage collection was to be a priority, as was security. This is precisely the kind of debate that took place when the Taliban seized Afghanistan in 1996. The balance between provision of basic needs and the obligations of their narrow social agenda had to be managed carefully or else they would alienate everyone. "Every mistake in this important stage of the life of the baby," wrote Droukdel, "will be a heavy burden on his shoulders. The larger the mistake, the heavier the burden on his back and we could end up suffocating him suddenly and causing his death." What Droukdel feared the most was foreign intervention, and weakness to resist intervention if al-Qaeda broke with its Tuareg allies. Precisely both things happened. "The aim of building these bridges is to make it so that our mujahideen are no longer isolated in society," wrote Droukdel. "If we can achieve this positive thing in even a limited amount, then even if the project fails later, it will be just enough that we will have planted the first, good seed in this fertile soil and put pesticides and fertilizer on it, so that the tree will grow more quickly. We look forward to seeing this tree as it will be eventually. Stable and magnificent." Sections in ISIS agree with the kind of position taken by Droukdel. Trash removal, security, orderly traffic—these ordinary conveniences are what attract people who otherwise fear the morass of disorder.

The price to be paid, with al-Qaeda and ISIS, is social and cultural suffocation. Oil money enables not only war but also the creation of social goods. That it is ISIS that manages it means a narrow social world, as can be experienced in the writings of the brave journalists who work at the website *Raqqa Is Being Slaughtered Silently.* One of its writers, Hamoud Almousa, provided a sense of Raqqa in early 2016.[96] Living conditions have declined dramatically, Almousa notes, with the state schools closed and with the hospitals damaged by aerial bombardment as well as a lack of sterilized water. Droukdel's advice is nowhere to be seen, since ISIS has failed to provide basic services. It has shut down local councils and put in place its Islamic Services Authority, often made up of people with little understanding of the localities. Despite no access to water and electricity, the authority collects taxes for it. Meanwhile ISIS imposes its social agenda on the people of Raqqa (such as compulsory "legitimate dress" for women, closure of Internet cafes and satellite television as well as insistence on a *mohram*—male guardian—for women). Raqqa, as the journalists say, is being slaughtered silently. No amount of ISIS oil will stop that.

RUSSIA AND THE END OF REGIME CHANGE

As if from nowhere, Russian military aircraft entered Syria on 30 September 2015. And, as if from nowhere again, the Russians announced on 14 March 2016 that the "main force" would withdraw from Syria.

Through the summer of 2015, the Syrian armed forces faced severe setbacks in several theaters along the western axis of Syria. The newly formed Army of Conquest (Jaysh al-Fateh) seized the crucial town of Jaish al-Shugour, southeast of Idlib—

a city they had taken in March. Momentum swept through Hama Province and toward Damascus. The main elements of the Army of Conquest were Ahrar ash-Sham and Jabhat al-Nusra—both of whom defer to the black banner of al-Qaeda. Saudi Arabia set aside its reservations about the Syrian Muslim Brotherhood and called the leader of the Syrian Coalition, Khaled Khoja, for a conclave in Riyadh. Saudi Arabia's proxy—Jaysh al-Islam—sought an arrangement with Ahrar ash-Sham. Jaysh al-Islam's leader, Zahran Alloush, had been to Turkey in mid-April to meet with the resurgent Ahrar ash-Sham and discuss coordination. Momentum was with the rebels. Tussles between Qatar and Turkey on one side and Saudi Arabia on the other seemed to have slowed down. Money poured in, as did promises from the Americans of various kinds of military aid.

On Martyr's Day, 6 May, Assad said, "Today we are fighting a war, not a battle." The meaning of this statement could simply have been that gains made by the Syrian army over the course of the previous year had now been reversed. "The spread of a spirit of frustration or despair," he said, hung over his forces. His defense minister—Fahd Jaseem al-Freij—had just been to Tehran, seeking more assistance. Iranian aid had been steady but—in the context of negotiations of Iran with the West on its nuclear sanctions—insufficient.[97] Three months later, on 26 July, Bashar al-Assad indicated the declined mood in Damascus. "There is a lack of human resources," he said on television. "Everything is available to the army, but there is a shortfall of human capacity." In other words, the Syrian army had a slump in morale. The sense among his allies was equally bleak. For his al-Quds Day speech on 10 July, Hezbollah's leader, Hassan Nasrallah, warned that if Syria fell, so would Palestine. Palestine—the unifying cause among fractious Arab groups—had been evoked by Nasrallah precisely to bolster the morale of his troops, and to reaffirm the Iranian project. ("If you want to support Palestine, you have to support the Islamic Republic of Iran.") Assad, two weeks later, would not evoke Palestine in this way, nor the importance of Iran. He remained at the level of Syrian nationalism, which has been his calling card since the start of the uprising. "Every inch of Syria is precious," he said. Morale might be low, "but that does not mean we talk about collapse. We will resist." But this resistance needed active help.

Assad is said to have made a plea to both Tehran and Moscow for greater involvement. Tehran dispatched the al-Quds Force leader Qassim Soleimani to Moscow for talks. Plans were laid, and then solidified with a meeting in Tehran of the foreign ministers of Iran, Russia, and Syria. Russian aircraft slipped into Syria and began to bomb the various rebel groups that had put the greatest pressure on the Syrian army. Iran, Iraq, and Russia created a joint operational setup for the campaign against ISIS in Iraq. This was a direct challenge to the U.S. role in providing aerial attacks in Iraq.

The Russian pretext was to fight ISIS, but that was not the full story. The Russians arrived to hit ISIS certainly, but first the proxy armies of Qatar, Saudi Arabia, and Turkey. (Solely U.S.-backed forces had become minimal to nonexistent.) What the Russians did with this intervention was twofold. First, their forces foreclosed the possibility of a Western-backed regime change against the Assad government. No U.S. bomber would fly to attack the Syrian army without risking a serious confrontation with the Russians. Overthrowing the Assad government by force was no longer possible. Most of the major actors, even if grudgingly, had recognized this reality. At the Munich security conference in early February 2016, two Syrian aid workers approached Secretary Kerry at the drinks interval and told him that the

United States had not done enough to protect civilians. Kerry said that the blame for this rests with the Syrian opposition, which did not want to cut a proper deal. Then he said, exasperated, "What do you want me to do? Go to war with Russia? Is that what you want?"[98]

Second, the attacks on the proxy armies made it clear to Qatar, Saudi Arabia, and Turkey that they would eventually come to the table. Their armies—divided among themselves—had not been able to make headway against the Russian-backed onslaught. If not the negotiating table, then the slaughterhouse. It was a harsh choice, more harsh yet in the context of this bloody war. It was undeniable that the Russian entry into Syria had put the Gulf Arabs in a bind, particularly since the United States seemed unwilling to challenge the Russian fait accompli—one that mirrors the situation in Ukraine, where the Russians continue to hold the Crimea.

Of course, the second point is not easy to digest. Turkey shot down a Russian jet in November partly to defend its own proxies—in this case, the Sultan Abdülhamit Brigade, which on pro-government Turkish television was being called "moderate jihadist" (*ilimli cihatcilar*). This brigade is a Turkmen detachment, trained by Turkish Special Forces. It collaborates with the Army of Conquest (Jaysh al-Fateh), one of the umbrella groups of the Syrian opposition fighters, and with Jabhat al-Nusra. Russian air strikes on these groups allowed the Syrian army to advance into their territory. It is what provoked the Turkish attack. Equal to this has been Turkey's attack on the Syrian and Iraqi Kurdish forces, the YPG and the PKK, both of whom have made strides against ISIS. The United States, to sharpen the point, is bombing ISIS, while its NATO ally, Turkey, is bombing those who are fighting ISIS. There is no clearer indication of the muddled nature of global, regional, and local power politics than this confounding situation.

By late October 2015, the various powers came to Vienna to discuss the new realities. Both Iran and Saudi Arabia agreed to participate, and both agreed—surprisingly—on some broad principles for Syria's future. Syria, they agreed in principle, would remain a secular republic with guarantees of minority rights, and would have more robust procedures for internal democracy. This acknowledgment seemed to foreclose the possibilities pushed by Saudi Arabia, whose regime is allergic to secularism and minority rights. There were no Syrians at the table. This meeting was not about the peace *inside* Syria. It was about the peace *around* Syria. But it did not last long. By December, the Saudis had invited sections of the opposition in exile and on the ground that remained insistent on Assad's departure. They formed the High Negotiation Committee. It drew a line around itself, leaving out those who did not insist on Assad's departure as a precondition to talks and those who—like the Kurds—had already gained their objectives (more autonomy for Syrian Kurdistan—or Rojava). Cease-fires come onto the table, and then slip off again.

Under Russian air cover, the Syrian army and its allies took back significant terrain in the south, near the city of Dara'a, cutting off the rebels there from their supply lines into Jordan. That is why some towns decided to give up the fight. Dramatically, the Syrian army took back Palmyra in March 2016. Near Fakhr-al Din al-Maani Castle, toward the city's west, the Russians set up a forward operating base with air defense systems in plain sight. More significantly, Syrian forces—with Iranian Revolutionary Guards at the frontlines—advanced to the Turkish border, with Aleppo's fate in the balance.[99] Bombing of the city has sent thousands of civilians fleeing to the Turkish border. There is much being broken in the heart of the people by this fierce barrage. A cessation of hostilities allowed humanitarian aid to enter besieged cities, where starvation followed bombardment as imminent calamities. Kurdish fighters with the YPG created the Syrian Defense Forces to make alliances with ex-FSA fighters and others to take on ISIS with Russian air support. Groups such as Suqur al-Sahra (Desert Falcons) and al-Usud al-Sarqiya (Lions of the East) formed to batter ISIS, again with Russian and Iranian support. Some of these groups and fighters joined the New Syrian Army, which has an ambiguous relationship with the Syrian Army and with the CIA. Its net objective is to hit ISIS, with air cover from both the Russians and the Americans. Weakened proxy armies and befuddled regional actors emerged out of the shock of the Russian intervention. It turned the tide of the war, bringing the United States around to the view that Assad's departure should no longer be a precondition for dialogue.

Buoyed by the Russian air cover, the Syrian Kurds made a dash to connect their three cantons into one territory. In late March 2016, the Syrian Kurds declared the existence of a Kurdish federation within Syria. Their leadership proposed this as a model for a future Syria, with federations having autonomy with a weakened Damascus. In essence, this is what exists now, but it is not what either the Assad government or the opposition seeks. Both rejected it. That the Syrian Kurds have an office in Moscow now suggests that they are in close contact with at least one of the backers of the Assad government. Federalism might propose a way for reconciliation to begin.[100] It might be a bitter pill for some, but it might also be the only pill on offer.

What little remains of the independent Syrian rebellion had been hidden deep inside Aleppo and other towns. It is unlikely to be able to walk away intact. With the cessation of hostilities, residents of these areas said, the sound of birds could be heard once more. Tentatively, people took to the streets—even to hold signs of protest against the Assad government in the southern town of Saqba and in the heart of Aleppo (where a sign read "We Still Want Freedom"). What terms will be before them is not clear.

The proxy armies of Saudi Arabia and Turkey as well as al-Qaeda do not wish to surrender. They will remain a serious threat to Syria unless a regional accord is reached. In East Ghouta, outside Damascus, two rebel factions—Faylaq al-Rahman (Legions of the Merciful) and the Fustat Army (Army of the Tent, with *Fustat* being the old name for Cairo)—fought a hard-pitched battle. The Fustat Army, which includes Jabhat al-Nusra, and Faylaq al-Rahman compete for the smuggling routes out of their besieged areas. Theirs is a war without logic. Such fissiparousness comes out of exhaustion at the length of the conflict, frustration with the Russian intervention, and the failure of the regional powers to act against it as well as bewilderment at the lack of American air support. Grumbling from Turkey and Saudi Arabia will not alter the power equation in these enclaves of rebellion. The Russian presence—even after its partial withdrawal—is a significant deterrent to any regional intervention.

As this book sits with the printer, the fate of Syria remains unclear. Events move off the page of this book.

· · ·

Responsibility for the emergence of ISIS vests with a number of key actors. The United States's reckless war on Iraq created the reservoir for extremists, as money from the Gulf Arabs came to sustain them in an emerging sectarian clash against an ascendant

Iran. The narrow and suffocating Assad and al-Maliki regimes—
which alienated large sections of their populations—propelled
the disenfranchised to rebellion. In 2007 the cartoonist Ali Ferzat
said of the process called the Damascus Spring, "[E]ither reform
or *le deluge* [the flood]." It was the flood. Alienated people who
measure their alienation in sectarian terms cannot be defeated
only in the battlefield. Ugly sectarian language can be heard even
from decent people, who mask their embarrassment by blaming
their enemies for the slip of their geniality. Political reforms need
to be on the cards. So, too, must an alternative to the economic
agenda pursued in both Iraq and Syria since the mid-2000s.
Under pressure of Western-driven globalization, the Assad and
al-Maliki governments pursued neoliberal policies that increased
inequality and despair. Absent a politics of class, the platforms
against neoliberal corruption took on a harsh sectarian cast. The
various extremists fed on that alienation for their own diabolical
agendas. They can be halted by air strikes and degraded by
ground warfare. But only if the social conditions that produced
extremism—the inequality and the despair—are altered can it
be truly vanquished.

Charles Glass sits with Khaled Khalifa, the Aleppo-born novelist who wrote *In Praise of Hatred* (*Madiha al-karahiya,* 2006), a
novel that considers the conflict between the Syrian state and
the Muslim Brotherhood. His most recent novel, *No Knives in
This City's Kitchens* (*La sakakin fi matabikh hadhini al-madina*), is an
indictment of Ba'ath rule. Khalifa tells Glass, "Stop the war, stop
the blood. The Syrian people are tired now. You can play revolution for some time, but not for a long time."[101] This is a sentiment
that resonates with Ahmed Saadawi, the Iraqi writer, whose
Frankenstein in Baghdad (*Frankenstein fi Baghdad,* 2013) tells the story
of Hadi al-Attag, who lives in al-Batateen—Baghdad's rough

zone. Al-Attag spends his day collecting the body parts of those killed in the season of explosions, and then stitching them together to form Citizen X—the-one-who-does-not-have-a-name, the new crime fighter who seeks revenge against all those who killed the parts of its body. Saadawi sees Citizen X as the composite of Iraq's diversity, the savior of a country in distress, and the "epitome of mass destruction." Citizen X is all these things. This Frankenstein, said Saadawi, "is the fictional representation of the process of everyone killing everyone. This character is the visual representation of the larger crisis, rather than the solution."

Arab futures are not myths of salvation. They are rather dystopias of survival as violence engulfs Arab societies. Hope is on life support. It has often come to mean its opposite. A young Syrian activist tells me that he wants "politics to end." An Egyptian activist asks, "When will it become quiet again?" She does not mean the end of struggle, but the end of violence. The yearning for order has its dangers. It suggests that futures are not possible, and that the unequal and brutal stability of the past and present has merit.

In 2014, journalist Eva Bartlett went to meet Dr. Ali Haidar, leader of the Syrian Social Nationalist Party and a minister of state for national reconciliation. Haidar, a classmate of Assad's from Damascus University, joined the government from the opposition because he wanted to work toward *mussalaha* (reconciliation). This was in June 2012. A few months earlier—in May—Haidar's son, Ismail, was killed by the rebels. It did not sour Haidar. "We have so many martyrs," Haidar said to Bartlett. "There is no one more precious than another. They are all Syrian."[102] His ministry's goal is to rehabilitate fighters back into society. It is a laudable project. How credible it is will have to be seen. At the Andalus rehabilitation center in Homs, ex-fighters try to find a way out of the conflict. Hamzeh al-Reefii tells journalist Maria Finoshina, "I do not want to kill or hurt anybody at all." In his early twenties, al-Reefii wants to live his life, not live in fear of death.

Syria is ground down by the contradictions of great powers and regional powers, and yet Omar Abdulaziz Hallaj—a wise and distinguished architect from Aleppo—persists with his Syrian Initiative. It seeks to build grassroots linkages inside Syria. "Peace in Syria," said Hallaj, "will need sustainable roots. It must be built from the bottom up. The top-down process in the Geneva communiqué can work only if it is supported by transforming the dynamic of the conflict on the ground." He and others like him are hard at work building trust through small gestures. People who live cheek by jowl will have to learn to rely on each other. It takes people like Hallaj to create the basis for this, to speak against the sectarian narrative that has smothered Syrian diversity. But even Hallaj is pessimistic. "The longer the war is prolonged," he says, "the smaller the window of opportunity may become."

A fragile hope rests on the revitalization of Syrian or Arab nationalism as a cord that binds the people across the widened sectarian divides. It is too much to hope for its revival in the midst of this tortured struggle. The politics are bewildering, the human suffering intolerable.

CHAPTER FOUR

Destruction of Countries

A time has passed and another time has not yet come
and will never come.

Ahmad Ibrahim al-Faqih, *Nafaq tudiuhu imra
wahida* (A tunnel lit by one woman), 1991

It takes a hundred years to build a state. It can be destroyed in an
afternoon.

No wonder the Arab nation looks back to *al-Nahda*, the renaissance of the nineteenth century, for the roots of its nationalism.
Out of that national longing came the movements to seize the
old Ottoman and colonial state institutions. These had to be
fashioned—one way or another—into state structures that would
be capable of the imagination of national belonging.

In 2001, the United States and its allies began a major operation against al-Qaeda called the Global War on Terror (GWOT).
That war, which is ongoing, began in Afghanistan but then
expanded to include large swathes of the planet—from the Phil-
ippines to Nigeria. States, built after great sacrifice and difficulty, collapsed under the weight of GWOT—Afghanistan and
Iraq, later Libya and Syria. Somalia had already been destroyed
by GWOT's precursor. It got worse for Somalia during GWOT.

The United States urged the Ethiopians to invade, which was a very poor idea: Ethiopia's society is largely Christian, whose state had claims on the Somali region of Gedo. Its soldiers came in and began a form of killing that locals called "slaughtering like goats."[1] It pushed Somali groups into the arms of the extremists. Al-Shabaab, which had a parochial vision, changed its name in 2009 to Harakat al-Shabaab al-Mujahideen—building up its sensibility with the global Mujahideen networks. It was flung into the arms of al-Qaeda.[2] The War on Terror did not erase the terrorists; it manufactured them.[3]

Fragile states could not withstand the stress of U.S. full-spectrum domination, insurgency, and counterinsurgency. Across the Sahara, states fell as a consequence not only of the GWOT but also of the new trade regime set in place in the 1990s; Libya and Mali had the greatest catastrophes. Four horses of the apocalypse are not sufficient. One of them is GWOT and its twin—terrorism; another is the neoliberal trade regime. But alongside these are poverty, pestilence, illiteracy, ethnic supremacy, misogyny, and resource wars. From the West's point of view, the GWOT has largely prevented any attacks on its own territory. The price for that has been the devastation of the lives of tens of millions of people in the Global South. There are attacks almost daily. They go by without sentiment. They provoke the creation of more distress. They give permission for the GWOT to continue. It is a satanic cycle.

REGIME CHANGE

Five years ago, as NATO prepared to bomb Libya, I asked a senior Western diplomat if he thought that the experience of Iraq would inform this latest adventure. After all, regime change in

Iraq had resulted in chaos—out of which had emerged, in 2006, the parent of ISIS. Regime change produced chaos, which allowed the worst aspects of politics to reveal themselves. The Western diplomat scoffed at my concerns. Libya would be different, he said. What made Libya exceptional? My friend—the diplomat—suggested that in Libya *everyone* hated Muammar Qaddafi. The depth of support for him by 2011 was limited. Once he was toppled, the Libyan people would flock to the National Transitional Council, a weak-kneed group of bankers and lawyers, welcoming them to Tripoli from Benghazi with sweets and flowers. The expectation was that Qaddafi, like Saddam Hussein before him, had limited pockets of support. They were—after all—dictators, and dictators fell as easily as the concrete statues of them in the squares of their cities.

My own experience of Libya did not allow me to be so sanguine. There were large sections that relied upon the patronage of the Libyan state, and even considerable parts of the population that genuinely liked Qaddafi. There was no way to test this because there had been neither elections nor polls, nor indeed any good methodology. It was also true that the Libyan military had barely recovered its morale since its humiliation in the 1987 Chad war. It would not stand by Qaddafi to the end—antithetical to the experience of the bulk of the Syrian Arab Army. However weak the support, there were still pockets of allegiance to Qaddafi. I suggested to the diplomat that perhaps it would be best to push for peace—the objective of the African Union, for instance—rather than push the already centripetal Libya to be torn apart by town and tribe. Western diplomats were not keen on peace. They wanted to burnish their doctrine of humanitarian intervention—tainted by the Iraq experience. A leaked email to U.S. Secretary of State Hillary Clinton from her friend and adviser Sidney

Blumenthal on 2 April 2011 suggested more-base motives for the French government:

1. Gain a greater share of Libya oil production.
2. Increase French influence in North Africa.
3. Improve [Nicolas Sarkozy's] political situation in France.
4. Provide the French military with an opportunity to reassert its position in the world.
5. Address the concerns of [Sarkozy's] advisers over Qaddafi's long-term plans to supplant France as the dominant power in Francophone Africa.

Such aims never touch the public lips of the leaders of the West. They prefer to speak of Responsibility to Protect (R2P), the doctrine of intervention that they pushed through the United Nations in 2005 after the Iraq fiasco. Libya was a good test run for this theory. If anyone had said that the war against Libya occurred because of Qaddafi's attempt to create a new currency union for the African continent that supplanted the CFA franc, the French-denominated currency for Francophone African states, the statement would have been denied immediately. Such imputations were left to the sewer of conspiracy theories. The West acts for only the highest motives. The five points mentioned in Blumenthal's email are too crass for the West.

And yet, some of these points seem logical. France had already intervened in the Ivory Coast in January 2011, and would enter the Mali conflict in 2012. Both cases showed France eager to protect its interests and its influence. Qaddafi had spoken of an African currency union, which would have broken the dependence of France's old African colonies. Most of those former colonies had signed the Abuja Treaty of 1991, which proposed the creation of an African Central Bank with the afriq as the continent's currency—all to come into effect by 2023. An IMF study in 2001 found that the eight Francophone countries of West Africa have benefited only marginally from linkage to the Franc, with low growth and low regional trade.[4] Qaddafi had certainly played a role in pushing for the union, which would have been buoyed by Libyan petro-profits. Sarkozy did have electoral worries of his own, partly because of France's role in Tunisia. Sarkozy's foreign minister and close personal friend of Tunisia's Ben Ali—Michèle Alliot-Marie—said that France had provided the "know-how" that Ben Ali's security used against the protestors.[5] Frédéric Mitterrand, Sarkozy's culture minister, said that Tunisia was not an "unequivocal dictatorship," while Bruno Le Maire, the agriculture minister, praised Ben Ali's reforms. In addition, Qaddafi had already begun to indicate that he would reveal his relationship with Sarkozy—including (what was later shown) that he had financed Sarkozy's electoral run in 2007.[6] All this is utterly circumstantial, and until WikiLeaks breaks into the French state emails, smoking guns will be hidden away. France was the most aggressive power in 2011 for NATO to get a UN Security Council resolution. On 15 March 2011, the U.S. ambassador to the UN, Susan Rice, told her French counterpart at the UN, Gérard Araud, that he would have to persuade powers other than the United States to fight his "shitty war." Immense pressure from U.S. Secretary of State Hillary Clinton on the White House pushed Obama to buy the French narrative. Once the United States backed the French, the UN Security Council resolution came through. With that in hand, French jets first launched strikes on Libya.

Reports from al-Arabiya, a Saudi media outlet with a propensity to say what the regime wants, reported near-genocidal conditions in Libya in early 2011. Obama's adviser Dennis Ross said that Benghazi would be "Srebrenica on steroids," referring to the Bosnian town where a massacre had been committed in July 1995. Ross claimed—according to the *Washington Post*—that "100,000 people might have been slaughtered in Benghazi."[7] Western journalists dashed to Benghazi, filed unverified stories told to them by the rebel commanders, and gloried in the excitement of war. Soberness and doubt are the attributes of war reporting, not excitement and enthusiasm. Based on this fatuous reporting, Obama, Sarkozy, and British Prime Minister David Cameron wrote in a *New York Times* op-ed that Misrata was enduring a "medieval siege."[8] Journalist Alexander Cockburn read that and wrote, "Not yet, surely. A medieval siege was something that usually lasted at least a year, in which the city's inhabitants were reduced to eating rats, then each other, and the besiegers all succumbed to plague."[9] Exaggeration was the order of the day. Analogies to Yugoslavia and medieval Europe functioned to produce a reality that simply did not exist on the ground.

David Kirkpatrick of the *New York Times* wrote with great honesty, "The rebels feel no loyalty to the truth in shaping their propaganda, claiming nonexistent battlefield victories, asserting they were still fighting in a key city days after it fell to Qaddafi forces, and making vastly inflated claims of [Qaddafi's] barbaric behavior."[10] Later, investigations by Human Rights Watch validated what Kirkpatrick wrote—namely, that the death toll was nothing like the rebels had suggested. In the U.S. State Department, lack of information was the norm. "We, the U.S., did not have a particularly good handle on what was going on inside Libya," admitted Derek Chollet, who worked in the National Security Council during the lead-up to the Libya intervention.[11] Yet, the United States went along with the French and British on their latest Libyan adventure. The United Nations passed a Security Council resolution (no. 1973) to protect civilians in the country. Not long after the bombing began, the original intent of the resolution was set aside. Regime change was the name of the game. The first aerial bombardment in world history took place in 1911, when the Italians bombed Libya. A hundred years later, the West returned for a sequel.

NATO took over from France to uphold the UN mandate. Given legitimacy by the UN Human Rights Council and by the International Criminal Court, NATO pummeled Libya with at least ten thousand sorties. Russia and China, as well as India, Brazil, and South Africa (the BRICS states), began to grumble that the NATO operation had far exceeded the mandate. It had run from Responsibility to Protect to regime change. A U.S. military study conducted by the Joint and Coalition Operational Analysis division of the Joint Staff J7 from 2012 shows that the United States bore the burden of the Libyan war, behind the NATO shield. The same study indicates that the U.S. war planners at the African Command "were unsure as to whether 'regime change' was an intended option, or whether operations were to be focused solely on protecting civilian life and providing humanitarian assistance to the refugees."[12] The UN mandate was for the latter, but the confusion allowed the United States and NATO to pursue expanded war aims. This is what angered the BRICS states, who would be reticent to ever allow the West permission under the UN charter to conduct military action anywhere. It is what stalled the possibility of a Western bombardment of Damascus. Libya is the shadow that hung over Syria.

The BRICS states pushed the UN Human Rights Council to investigate the use of UN Resolution 1973. The council did conduct an investigation, and released its report on 2 March 2012.[13] It found that claims that Qaddafi's forces were conducting genocide were grossly exaggerated, and that an investigation of NATO's bombardment was necessary. The authors suggested that all sides—including NATO—had committed war crimes in Libya. When the council tried to investigate the Western bombing, NATO's legal adviser, Peter Olson, wrote a sharp letter to the chair of the Commission of Inquiry on Libya:

> We would be concerned if "NATO incidents" were included in the commission's report as on a par with those which the commission may ultimately conclude did violate law or constitute crimes. We note in this regard that the commission's mandate is to discuss "the facts and circumstance of ... violations [of law] and ... crimes perpetrated." We would accordingly request that, in the event the commission elects to include a discussion of NATO actions in Libya, its report clearly state that NATO did not deliberately target civilians and did not commit war crimes in Libya.[14]

NATO brushed off the investigation. The *New York Times* had found that on 8 August 2011, NATO's bombing of Majer (a village between Tripoli and Misrata) had killed at least thirty-four civilians.[15] One of the *Times's* reporters returned to the story in March 2012, asking why NATO refused to allow an investigation of the Majer incident—one among many. Five days later, the editorial board of the newspaper said that NATO "has shown little interest in investigating credible independent claims of civilian fatalities." The next day, NATO's spokesperson, Oana Lungescu, responded that NATO had already done its investigation and that if the Libyan government asked for an inquiry, "NATO will cooperate."[16] At that time the threadbare Libyan government had no stomach to open an inquiry. In fact, on 2 May in Law no. 38, the government gave amnesty to all rebels, which implicitly extended to NATO.

On 14 May 2012, Human Rights Watch (HRW) released a report that revisited the question of civilian casualties in NATO's air war. HRW looked at eight sites (out of ten thousand sorties), and in these sites found that NATO bombs killed seventy-two civilians—half of them under the age of eighteen. HRW concluded, "NATO has failed to acknowledge these casualties or to examine how and why they occurred."[17] HRW had contacted NATO for assistance. Deputy Secretary of Operations for NATO Richard Froh wrote on 1 March to say that NATO had already cooperated with the UN inquiry (which it had not) and that HRW should see those "detailed comments to the Commission, which we understand will be published in full as part of that report." Nothing in that report would have helped HRW in their specific investigation. NATO merely said it was not interested in civilian oversight. The UN and human-rights groups were useful in the lead-up to the war, but not so important in the aftermath of regime change.

NATO had done its deed, whether for France's base reasons or otherwise. A fractured Libyan population saw the state institutions destroyed, Qaddafi lynched on the streets of his hometown, Sirte, and the various factions of the rebels take the spoils without concern for the well-being of the nation. This was a free-for-all. Regional powers pushed forward their own proxies, who took charge of parts of the country. Oil spluttered at the pumps. An enormous number of civilians fled either the country or their homes—a million displaced out of a population of just over six million.[18] Qaddafi followers took the lead in the caravans out of the country, while those who remained went either underground or into prison. Thousands of Qaddafi followers remain in prison, held without trial. The chief of the UN Support Mission in Libya (UNSMIL), Ian Martin, told the UN Security Council on 1 May 2012 that "cases of mistreatment and torture of detainees continue." HRW's Joe Stork amplified these reports of torture, which "propagates a culture of selective justice that Libyans fought so hard to overcome." An Amnesty International report found that at least twenty-four hundred detainees had been held without charge.[19] A UN report from May 2012 suggested that the number of Qaddafi supporters held without charge was seven thousand. Many more might have become "ghost prisoners." Victor's justice was the code. International law had been sidelined.

Regime change's lessons had not been learned from Iraq.[20] There the U.S. occupation fired all Ba'ath Party members, a misjudgment that contributed to the insurgency. The Libyan regime put in place by NATO passed a Political Isolation Law, which disenfranchised anyone with ties to the Qaddafi establishment. Law no. 37 of 2012 allowed the government to arrest and imprison anyone who "glorifies" Qaddafi or who denigrates the February 17 revolution. The civil court in Zawiya heard the case against five alleged supporters of Qaddafi, who were said to have planned "terrorist acts" against the new regime. The charge sheet was garbled, yet the head of the court—Ali Ashaab Mohammed—said that the men "confessed that they took part in fighting battles in some areas." Such nebulous trials began the persecution of those who had been part of the Qaddafi establishment and state. Among them was Saif al-Islam Qaddafi, who was held by a militia, which refused to turn him over to the Libyan government or to the International Criminal Court, whose warrant had been part of the justification for the war.

Five years after the regime-change intervention, the West prefers to blame the Libyans for the collapse of the country rather than their war. Gérard Araud, France's ambassador to the United States, who pushed for the intervention, said in 2016 that the problem was that the West rushed with elections too soon after the fall of the regime. "You organize elections in a country with no experience of compromise or political parties. So you have an election, and you think that everything is solved. But eventually tribal realities come back to haunt the country."[21] The West, smug with its liberalism, walks away briskly, sniffing the air for "tribal realities."

My Libyan friends often say, wryly, "if NATO acts without investigation, why not the *thuwar* [rebels]?" It is a fair question.

ASSASSINATIONS

With regime change accomplished, the West and its chosen Libyan liberals went hastily toward the framing of laws and the holding of elections. They formed political parties and sat back hoping to win power easily. In April 2012, the Libyan liberals and their western advisers banned parties "based on religion or ethnicity or tribe." Ambassador Araud's reflections on "tribal realities" did not mention this constraint on democracy, insisted upon by the West. The Muslim Brotherhood, backed by Qatar and Turkey, found this puzzling. "We don't understand the law," their statement read. "It could mean nothing or it could mean that none of us could participate in the elections." The Brotherhood's leader, Alamin Belhaj, was not going to be set aside. He knew that his people could win the elections.[22] Meanwhile, the emir of Tripoli's *thuwar*, Abdel Hakim Belhaj, took off his rebel garb and founded the Hizb al-Watan party. This sent shudders through Washington, since Belhaj—a founder of the Libyan Islamic Fighting Group—had cut his teeth in the Afghan wars and had been returned to Libyan prisons by the West as part of the extraordinary rendition program of the War on Terror. He was not a Western ally. Indeed, by American standards, Belhaj should have been in Guantánamo. Yet he was on the threshold of political power in the new Libya, far more popular than the Libyan liberals.

Belhaj might not have been the most dangerous situation in Libya those days. Far more worrisome was the unknown violence that made itself apparent. On 3 June, the commander of the Awfeya battalion from the town of Tarhuna—Abu Ajilah Habshi—was arrested. One can write only in passive voice because the details remain unclear: was he kidnapped on the road to Tripoli airport or arrested by some government authority? The Awefya battalion, angry at the arrest of their leader, seized the airport and demanded his release. The seizure of the airport had become a tactic in the first few months after the killing of Qaddafi; General Khalifa Hifter's men took control of it after someone shot at his car in December 2011. The airport had oscillated between militias from Zintan and Tripoli. Now the Awfeya battalion held it for a few hours, before they withdrew home without their commander. He vanished into the pit of Libya's prisons.

Tarhuna is a quiet town forty miles southeast of Tripoli and on the road to Bani Walid. It is known for its production of what used to be Libya's main export before oil: esparto grass (*halfa*). Qaddafi favored a section of the town's elite and had close ties to the Tarhuna tribal leadership. From among that leadership, Abu Ajilah Habshi broke with the Qaddafi regime in the first weeks of the rebellion. Pressured by his kinsmen, he left for Tunisia and then returned to Libya via Egypt. In Benghazi, the epicenter of the uprising, he formed the Awfeya battalion and fought along the Mediterranean Road. He returned to Tarhuna with the victor's smile on his face. But the town remained divided, with a large section still loyal to Qaddafi—but with no space to develop those attachments. Sections of this population tried to assassinate the deputy head of the Tarhuna Military Council, Colonel Abdullah Hussein, and his colleague Colonel Salim Souissi. In May 2012, when the Misrata *thuwar* tried to go to Bani Walid to flush out Qaddafi loyalists, the Tarhuna armed forces blocked the road.

These pro-Qaddafi sections held tighter to their guns as they began to feel like strangers in their own land. Many fled across the border into Tunisia and Egypt. In Cairo, Qaddafi's close friend Khuwaildi al-Hamidi set up the Libyan Popular National Movement. Al-Hamidi was banned from the 2012 elections. He was eager to run pro-Qaddafi candidates to show that what he called "the lies of the West" could be revealed. Libya's people, he told me, would provide al-Hamidi's movement with a mandate against the NATO war and the liberals. But the rules cast them out. This "green movement" did go into the shadows, as al-Hamidi said in his Cairo exile. It lay in silence till his death in July 2015, after which it emerged on the fourth anniversary of Qaddafi's death on 20 October from Bani Walid to Benghazi. Their chant on the streets of Tripoli is revelatory: "*Inshallah ashra Saddam, ashra Muammar*" ("May God send ten Saddams, ten Muammars").

Fractured Libya now had to deal with rebels who felt that the country had been delivered to them. In the western part of the country, the militias from Misrata—al-Nimer (Tiger Brigade), al-Isnad (Support Brigade), al-Fahad (Jaguar Brigade), al-Asad (Lion Brigade), al-Qasba (Citadel Brigade), Ussoud al Walid (Lions of the Valley Brigade)—dashed about with abandon. They moved on Tripoli and Sirte, killing Qaddafi along the way. The Misrata militias went into the town of Tawergha, south of their city, and forcibly ejected its population of thirty thousand dark-skinned Libyans. Cell-phone images from the violence show the Misrata militiamen using racist epithets ("black snakes") against their prisoners who were being accused of loyalty to Qaddafi. On the road out of Tawergha, the Misrata Brigade painted a slogan calling itself "the brigade for purging slaves and black skin."[23] The Tawergha residents went into concentration camps or fled. The local council of Tawergha tried to find a way for them to return home, to no avail. The West watched with little commentary as this racist ethnic cleansing happened in broad daylight.

Equal to this was the Misrata militias' violence against the people of Bani Walid, again accused of ties to Qaddafi. It was said that a group in Bani Walid had killed Omar bin Shaaban, the twenty-two-year-old Misratan who had killed Qaddafi. The government passed Resolution no. 7, which gave anyone the right to take revenge for the murder of bin Shaaban. On the basis of this, Misrata's fighters entered Bani Walid after a protracted siege. "If we win this fight," said their spokesperson, Mohammed el-Gandus, "Libya will finally be free." The actual outcome was that the Misrata militia saw itself as untouchable, gangsters in a gangsters' paradise. It was these Misrata groups—led by Salah Badi, a man damaged by posttraumatic stress disorder—that fashioned itself as Libyan Dawn. In 2012, a U.S. Defense Department official said that these groups—armed by Qatar—were "more antidemocratic, more hard-line, closer to an extreme version of Islam," than the people the United States was funding (although even this is hard to establish).[24] Combatants from the Libyan Islamic Fighting Group (with older links to al-Qaeda), wizened leaders from the Muslim Brotherhood, Misrata rebel factions, and Tripoli-based rebel groups formed Libyan Dawn (Fajr) and seized Tripoli as well as several other towns in western Libya. Their control in these areas remains intact today.

The elections of July 2012 displeased the political Islamists, who felt that the West and their chosen liberals had cheated them of victory. Some of these groups would ally with Libyan Dawn and refuse to honor the constitutional process. In Benghazi, disgruntled sections formed a variety of groups—including Ansar al-Sharia. Assassinations against military personnel and the liberals—particularly women—defined the politics of the city that started the revolt. In one week of 2013, three military men were assassinated—Colonel Fathi el-Emami of the Derna Air Force; Colonel Aqila al-Dukali Ubaidi, commander of the Derna Air Force; and Colonel Abdel Latif Amdawi el-Mazeeni, who, at age seventy, was largely retired. Ubaidi had been on the staff of Major General Abdel-Fattah Younis, who had taken charge of the rebel force against Qaddafi and then was assassinated—most likely by the Obaida ibn Jarrah Brigade, a group of Islamists who had been prisoners in Qaddafi's Abu Salim jail. Retribution defined their horizon. It is likely that they went after these men in green.

But it was the liberals who suffered the most strategic attacks. As the human-rights lawyer Abdel Salam al-Mismari left his mosque in Benghazi on 27 June 2013, a sniper shot him dead. Al-Mismari had been a key player in the early uprising against Qaddafi—one whose character was defined neither by NATO nor by the Islamists. He, along with his kinsman the novelist Idris al-Mismari, the lawyer Fateh Terbil, and others, went to Maidan al Shajara for the early Benghazi protests in February 2011. People like al-Mismari and Jamal Bilnour were in front of the Benghazi courthouse, demanding more reforms that they hoped would open political space in Libya. Revolution was not on their mind. Unable to move Qaddafi's emissary to Benghazi, Abdullah Senussi, the activists escalated their struggle. It was al-Mismari who convinced Major General Abdul-Fattah Younis to send out the *sa'aiqa,* the crack troops, to take on the bulk of the government's forces. Al-Mismari no longer was merely a protestor. He had effectively become a party to war. It was Major General Younis's defection that removed Benghazi from Tripoli's control. This was the spur for Qaddafi's great frustration and anger in his speeches. After the fall of Qaddafi, as it turned out, Abdel Salam al-Mismari's kind of politics before he went to seek out Major General Younis was not to be allowed. It was more than poetic that the bullet found his heart.

The killings did not end with al-Mismari. The year after, Benghazi's senior lawyer, Salwa Bugaighis, was killed when hooded men wearing military uniforms assassinated her in her house. She had just returned home from voting in the ill-starred 2014 elections. She was a classical liberal, eager to create a society where people could be seen as individual citizens. Bugaighis joined the National Transitional Council in March 2011, but left four months later out of frustration with its corrupt leadership. She believed in women's rights, which was not something shared by other liberals. It was they who in January 2012 cut the clause that provided a 10 percent quota for women in the national constituent assembly. "I know the society is not ready yet because of the tribal mentality, the stereotypes of women. We have to work hard to change the mentality of society," Bugaighis said. Magdulien Abaida of the Hakki movement had been part of a national campaign to push for this quota. "In our society," Abaida said factually, "people will not vote for women." She later told me that it was women such as herself—of all ages, all backgrounds—who had fought for the quota. In fact, Bugaighis had said that nothing less than 30 percent would do. Abaida and Bugaighis felt betrayed by the parliament. Women had been pushed out of the political domain; Health Minister Fatima Hamroush, Hakki movement leader Magdulien Abaida, Benghazi's councilor Najat al-Kikhia,

Bani Walid's parliamentarian Amina Mahmoud Takhtakh are only a few of the names. Other liberals fell to the guns—the editor of *Burniq*, Miftah Bouzeid; cultural activist Entissar al-Hasaari; youth activists Tawfiq Ben Saud and Sami Elawafi. None of them ever had a chance.

Hundreds of people fell to the assassins' guns over these five years. Among the dead are names of people of great integrity and experience as well as young people who were fueled by the most deceitful but necessary emotion—hope. One of the tragedies of the liberals is that they sought a politics of the shortcut, believing that they would be able to ride the tiger of NATO and the Islamist fighters to leadership of their country. But neither the West nor the Islamists took them seriously. For the West, the liberals provided them with Libyan cover, while for the Islamists, the liberals' apparent leadership hoodwinked the West. Without power of their own, the liberals had been disposable for everyone. The few liberals that remained fled Tripoli and Benghazi and took up residence in the eastern cities of Tobruk and Bayda. There, with backing from the West and the Saudis, they formed their own government. Libya had two governments by 2014—the Libyan Dawn one in Tripoli and the liberal-dominated one in Tobruk-Bayda.

On the road between Tobruk and Benghazi is the town of Derna. Well known in the redoubts of Islamic extremism, Derna sent hundreds of fighters to Afghanistan and Syria as part of the Libyan Islamic Fighting Group. It had become common to find an *al-Libi*—someone from Libya—in these places as Libya began to provide the highest number of recruits for al-Qaeda and its associated bodies. Many of these men returned to Libya in 2011 to fight against their old adversary, Qaddafi. Those *thuwar* who went off with their guns on board pick-up trucks from

Benghazi toward Tripoli carried their experience and their ideology with them. They had not come to deliver Libya to the liberals. After the war ended, these groups formed Ansar al-Sharia in Benghazi and Ajdabiya, while in Derna the fighters created their own version of Ansar al-Sharia and, later in 2014, the Shura Council of Islamic Youth.

Derna's leader is Abu Sufian bin Qumu, a former Libyan military man who went to Afghanistan to fight the Soviets. Trained into al-Qaeda, he went to Sudan and then joined the Libyan Islamic Fighting Group. Blocked from any movement in Libya, he returned to Afghanistan to join the Taliban. Picked up by the United States, he was sent to Guantánamo, from where he was released to Libya in 2007. Quiet for a few years, Abu Sufian was enthused by the 2011 uprising, which he led in Derna.

If Abu Sufian came to the rebellion with a long and dangerous history, Wissam bin Hamid had the opposite story. He was a car mechanic in Benghazi, who dropped his tools in 2012 and took up the gun. He joined the newly created Ansar al-Sharia, being part of those who would drive around town in cars decorated with his group's emblem—Kalashnikovs, a Quran, the black flag of al-Qaeda. In an Ansar al-Sharia video, bin Hamid welcomes others like him—salt of the earth—to become fighters, saying, "We will not stop until we establish the rule of God." It was likely this group that attacked the U.S. consulate in Benghazi—killing U.S. Ambassador Chris Stevens and firing at the convoy of the French consul general. Between Abu Sufian and bin Hamid is the range of the fiercer extremists.

By late 2012, it had become clear that the destruction of the Libyan state would create not a "Kuwait on the Mediterranean," as Saif al-Islam Qaddafi used to brag in the 2000s, but a "Somalia on the Mediterranean." The new governments in Tripoli spent their time cutting oil deals and trying to stabilize the currency. They had little time to create a central security apparatus or to whittle away at the growing assertions of the extremists. The September 2012 attack on the U.S. consulate came amid a slew of attacks in Benghazi against ordinary people and against the oil installations. There was no grand gesture from the new government. Flashy Libyans from the diaspora appeared on the streets of Tripoli and Benghazi, coming to reclaim their inheritance lost in the 1969 coup. Those who fought on the front lines against the Libyan army—the urban militias and the Islamists—began to assert their right to the new state, and to do so with the one coin that they had: violence. The liberals, who understood oil contracts better than their own society, made hasty deals with the old social classes, the urban militias, and the Islamists. Women's rights could be sacrificed to the pressures from the orthodoxy. Salwa Bugaighis's agenda was set aside. The Muslim Brotherhood and the Islamist militias claimed the new Libya, handed to them by NATO's war.

In early March 2016, the UN special representative to Libya, Martin Kobler, went to the Security Council. He talked about the state of Libya, where about half the health facilities are broken, where a third of the population—about two million people—is in urgent need of humanitarian assistance, and where almost one and a half million people are food insecure. The death toll mounts, and refugees sit along the coastline waiting for the weather to improve. When it does, these regime-change refugees will risk the transit across the Mediterranean Sea to Europe. A few days before Kobler went to New York to present his report, Mahmud Shammam, the former chief spokesman of the interim government in 2011–12, said, "Nobody will say it's too late. No one wants to say it. But I'm afraid there is very little time left for Libya."[25]

ARTERIES OF PETROLEUM

In April 2012, an IMF team arrived in Libya. It found that the unemployment rate—arrived at by the Libyan Ministry of Labor and Capacity Building—had doubled since 2010 to 26 percent. This seemed an estimate of what was a far worse situation. The study team's report looked forward to the creation of a "vibrant private sector"—this for a country in the midst of uncertainty and one that relied heavily upon the state-run oil sector. Libya, wrote the IMF visitors, is "overly dependent on hydrocarbons." While it is necessary to "expand hydrocarbon production," they noted, the industry is "capital intensive and therefore can only make a very limited contribution to employment growth." The nonhydrocarbon sector accounted for less than 30 percent of measured economic activity. What the IMF recommended was to enhance Libya's tourism potential "in light of Libya's rich archeological sites, Mediterranean climate, and proximity to European markets." To get there, Libya needed to slough off its public sector. "The size of the civil service will need to be reduced, and public sector wages contained to limit growth in the reservation wage," noted the IMF. "The transition will not be easy: it will be important to strengthen social safety nets to support those in need while allowing the labor market to operate freely and effectively."[26] Everything in this report had been the plan of Saif al-Islam Qaddafi in the years before 2011. He had imagined a Kuwait on the Mediterranean. It had been implemented by his advisers, such as Mahmud Jibril, who had become Qaddafi's main adversary in 2011. History is cruel. NATO's war broke Libya, and then the IMF returned to Tripoli with the same agenda as before the war.

No doubt the Libyan liberals took the IMF seriously. Before they had control over security, talk went in the direction of cuts and oil contracts. On 19 March 2011, while the war in central Libya was ongoing, the liberals in Benghazi formed a new central bank and a new oil company. This is perhaps the first time in world history that a rebel leadership has created new bank and oil institutions while in the middle of a civil war. This was their priority—money before stability. From 24 April to 9 May 2012, the oil workers of the Arabian Gulf Oil Company (Agoco) went on strike. They occupied the gates outside Agoco's oil company in Benghazi. Fifty workers and unemployed youth sat around the gate, angry at the new Libya that had promised so much and had yet to deliver anything for them. The oil began to flow during the conflict, but its revenues were not properly accountable. Things were in such bad shape that the Libyan interim finance minister, Hassan Ziglam, often threatened to resign. "I will resign," he said on 11 May. "I can't keep working in these circumstances. There is a wastage of public money because nobody fears God." The strike hurt Agoco, a subsidiary of the National Oil Company. It had already cut oil production by almost one hundred thousand barrels per day. The company indicated that if the strike did not end, Agoco would shut down all production. Fortunately for the management, the workers stood down. Nothing went their way. Oil production did slow down; European markets did suffer the cutbacks.[27]

Qaddafi had moved the National Oil Company headquarters away from Tripoli to Benghazi in 1970. It was part of his approach to diversify the centers of power in the country. Early in the uprising, the Agoco leadership went over to the rebels and began to use the oil money against Qaddafi. When the workers went on strike, many said that they had fought in the uprising but benefited little from it. Unemployed youth and exploited labor believed that their blood had won the new Libya, and so they deserved to be paid for their sacrifices. That is why on 8 May rebels from the Nafusa Mountains broke into Prime Minister Abdulrahim al-Keib's office in Tripoli. "These militias made the revolution but they don't get paid," a hotel worker, Moatasem Sotni, said.[28] While the Agoco strike went on, the workers at the Libyan Cement Company in two cement factories in Benghazi went on strike. They formed a Workers' Solidarity Group, which tried to entice the workers of cement plants in al-Fataiah, Derna, and Tajourah (the main working-class district in Tripoli) to join their struggles. They were not successful. These *thuwar* are an earthy lot, hailing from the shadowy class that works in the oil sector but is linked by family ties to those who work in the informal sector. They thought that the uprising was a revolution of the poor, when in fact it was regime change by the West to benefit the liberals. Those liberals were not going to sit on the floor and eat *z'ummeeta*. It is not their world. In that sense, Qaddafi's saltiness was closer to the cultural sensibility of the ordinary people.

On 10 May, the day the Agoco strike ended, the Revolutionaries' National Supreme Council held its second conference in Sabratha, not far from Tripoli. The council represents about two hundred of these *thuwar* brigades. They demanded several things, but most importantly improvement of the livelihood of the fighters, amnesty for these fighters, and criminal penalties for the Qaddafi-era beneficiaries. There was harshness in their tone, but also need. The new regime paid out 1.8 billion Libyan dinars (U.S. $1.4 billion) to the fighters, and would continue to do so—but this vanished into consumption. All that the regime would do was to encourage the ruthlessness by going after anyone associated with Qaddafi. It was severity that won the day over concern for the well-being of the fighters.

What this callousness did was to dishearten and anger the rebels. There was no experienced trade union or left party to carry forward the animosity that brewed rapidly. Tribal and regional ties operated with ease, but even here the tenor of the anger exceeded the capacity of the elders. Oil workers and their kinsmen periodically seized oil fields and oil-processing units. One of the leaders that emerged in this struggle was Ibrahim Jadhran of Ajdabiya. Jadhran became leader of the Petroleum Defense Guards, a position supposedly for the protection of the oil and its channels. Instead, this young man of Barqa—the eastern part of Libya—broke with western Libya, spouted secessionist views, and adopted the occupations as his own. His people seized oil installations along the Gulf of Sidra—in Zueitina here, Ras Lanuf there. Oil production is at about 20 percent of capacity, with a great deal of smuggling depriving the oil ministry of money. Jadhran claims about twenty thousand supporters in arms, and the naval capacity to ship oil to the oil laundries of the Mediterranean. Matters are so grave that the two governments— in Tripoli and in Tobruk—warned ships that they would be bombed if they carry smuggled oil. One of his ships—M.V. *Morning Glory*—was seized by U.S. forces in 2014. It pushed Jadhran to a fiercer tone.

ISIS

ISIS announced its presence in Libya to the world with a horrid video shot north of Sirte, of its fighters killing twenty-one Coptic Christians. This was released in February 2015. But ISIS had taken Sirte, Qaddafi's hometown, in May 2014. They came as the Zawiya Martyrs' Brigade withdrew from the city. The black flag flew confidently from Sirte's high buildings. Not four hundred miles south of Europe sat this branch of the caliphate. It was not to be easily dislodged. Hardened ISIS fighters crossed over the Tunisia–Libya border, while fighters from the eastern provinces of Libya who had lost faith in their own emirs drifted toward Sirte. These fighters were drawn to ISIS by its audacity. Their message—with the video and the photo spread in *Dabiq*—was simple: "We will conquer Rome, by Allah's permission," said one of the killers, his knife lazily pointed toward Europe.

Egyptian and Libyan bombers targeted ISIS bases in Sirte, but also extremist camps in Derna. It was a mark of frustration. Nothing more could be done. ISIS had inserted itself as it had in Mosul, Ramadi, Fallujah, and Raqqa. If it would lose one of those cities, as it would, others would fall into its net.

Older extremist groups in Libya now seemed petty compared with the grand designs of ISIS. In Derna, entrenched extremism would have had to be uprooted for ISIS to establish itself, whereas in Sirte, matters seemed easier to manage. Authority figures, such as the Salafi cleric Khaled Ferjani, were killed. When his followers rose up in August 2015, ISIS crushed them. Ferjani's mosque was renamed after Abu Musab al-Zarqawi—the founder of al-Qaeda in Iraq, ancestor of ISIS. In taking out Ferjani's people, ISIS also either killed or sidelined others who would threaten its presence. A source in the city told me that some of Qaddafi's followers joined ISIS as a way to break out of their isolation. (This mimics the move of Ba'athists in Iraq into what became ISIS.) ISIS has many Tunisians and some Algerians, but there are also many Libyans—including its outspoken leader, Hassan al-Karami, who comes from Benghazi and was involved there with Ansar al-Sharia.

During the last months of 2015, ISIS pushed out the Misrata militia from the roadways south of the city and made a dash along the Libyan coastline to seize various oil installations, from Es Sider to Ras Lanauf. Libya's National Oil Corporation (NOC) released a desperate message: "We are helpless and are not able to do anything against this deliberate destruction to the oil installations. NOC urges all faithful and honorable people of this homeland to hurry to rescue what is left of our resources before it is too late." This message was addressed to none in particular. There are few who can do anything about it. NOC officials watched as ISIS pushed against strategic towns along the desert fringe southeast of Sirte, opening a clear path for them to seize the main ports. The taking of Bin Jawad in early January 2016 sent the signal that ISIS was ready to move toward the oil towns. Security for these fields has dispersed. It is worth mentioning that one of Ibrahim Jadhran's brothers joined ISIS. What this means for the relationship between Ibrahim Jadhran and ISIS is not clear. They had tried to come to an agreement earlier to no avail. Forty-eight billion barrels of oil are at stake. So is the future of Libya.

Here and there word comes of Western bombings of this or that town in Libya, and then rumors spread of Western special forces. None of this is of any consequence. There was no attempt to disarm the fighters in 2012—apart from Mustafa el-Sagezli's Warriors Affairs Commission, which was not taken seriously. In fact, the West encouraged the payment of money to commanders, who would then deepen their patronage networks among their fighters. Guns from the Qaddafi armories and from the Gulf Arabs remained in the hands of these militia groups, many of whom ran protection rackets and become purveyors of the illegal goods that travel across the Sahara (including human trafficking). There is no comprehensive understanding of what to do when regime change breaks a country. The best option is to declare victory, walk away, and pretend that the problem has nothing to do with you. That has been the attitude of the West and the Gulf Arab states.

Chaos in Libya spread rapidly across northern Africa. Al-Qaeda in the Islamic Maghreb (AQIM) had been bogged down between the tribulations of its ideological commitments and the pragmatic lure of smuggling. Libyan military arms caches opened up to these groups, which also welcomed the opportunity to send their fighters to gain battlefield experience in Libya. Abu Yahya al-Libi, a Libyan leader of al-Qaeda, announced in August 2011 that his fighters had a choice: "You either choose a secular regime that pleases the greedy crocodiles of the West and is for them to use it as a means to fulfill their goals, or you take a strong position and establish the religion of Allah." They rushed in from Algeria and Tunisia. By 2012, these fighters returned to their homelands—bringing with them arms and experience as well as renewed confidence. In March, Qaddafi had warned, "If al-Qaeda manages to seize Libya, then the entire region, up to Israel, will be at the prey of chaos." In this he was correct. But these fighters began to see al-Qaeda as too moderate. Hamada Ould Mohammed Kheirou created the Monotheism and Jihad Movement in West Africa in 2011, which morphed—in alliance with the charismatic "Afghan Arab" Mokhtar Belmokhtar two years later—to form al-Mourabitoun (The Sentinels). These groups operated from Algeria to Côte d'Ivoire, from Mali to Libya. Kidnappings, attacks on hotels and beaches, and seizure of oil installations became routine. AQIM and al-Mourabitoun reunited in 2015.[29] North African fighters and Libyan arms found their way to Syria, where they joined up with ISIS and Jabhat al-Nusra. It was the circularity between North Africa and northern Syria that brought ISIS to Libya.

Under the flag of a united Libya, the militias of Misrata and other parts pushed hard against the ISIS base of Sirte in June— scattering the ISIS fighters to the small towns of North Africa from Tunisia to Egypt. This is less a victory than a premonition of more violence to come.

Strikingly in the Global War on Terror, it is not always the armies of states that are capable of the fight against the terrorists. In Syria, the most competent outfit is the Lebanese militia Hezbollah, helped along by newly created Syrian militias (such as the Shabiha, the ghost soldiers). It fights militias of their own— Jabhat al-Nusra or ISIS, Ahrar al-Sham or the Free Syrian Army. Libya provides another example: here is Libya Dawn, there is ISIS; here is Jadhran's Petroleum Guards, there is Khalifa Hifter's Operation Dignity. It is the age of the nonstate actors fighting the nonstate actors, this militia against that one. Charles Tilly's aphoristic claim that modern states are a product of the institutions of violence could be turned on its head:[30] states are being destroyed by war, and nonstate militias are creating fiefs of their own rather than states with a broader, less sectarian aspiration.

Fear of ISIS and the conduit of refugees brought Libya back to European attention in 2015. Pressure on the United Nations to push for a unified government intensified. Attempts to foist one or another political force to the front seized up the process. When it turned out that the UN envoy, Bernardino León, had financial ties to the United Arab Emirates, suspicions fell on advantages given by the UN toward UAE's proxies in Libya. León's successor, Martin Kobler, managed to create the semblance of unity, with a descendent of one of Tripoli's grand families—Fayez al-Sarraj—intended to sit in the prime minister's chair. European countries gathered together to pledge funds toward this effort. Stability for Libya is a high priority not only for them, but also for neighboring Tunisia and Egypt. Al-Sarraj's government hangs by a fine thread. There is no easy road. The creation of a presidential guard to defend government buildings is a sign that al-Sarraj's team is at least realistic. It does not worry about the banks before it worries about its security. Ahmad Maiteeq, the vice chair of Libya's Presidential Council, said in May that the new government would likely call upon Russia to help with the war against ISIS and to build a strong Libyan army. Washington must shudder at such sentiments.

Was there an alternative to the regime-change strategy that has destroyed countries and created chaos? It is important to remember that the African Union had wanted to insert itself in the early months of 2011 to mediate inside the complexity of the Libyan civil war—before the French bombers began to destroy the state. The union was set aside.[31] When Saddam Hussein was arrested in Tikrit, he said, "I am Saddam Hussein, president of Iraq, and I want to negotiate." The U.S. troops humiliated him and threw him in prison, where he underwent a farcical trial and was executed. No doubt Saddam Hussein was responsible for all manner of atrocities—most notably the use of Western-supplied chemical weapons against the Kurdish people of Hallabja in 1988.[32] But that moment was essential for Iraq: "I want to negotiate." Negotiations are the antidote to regime change. Saddam Hussein might have been able to bring his Fedayeen Saddam to the table, asking for a truce and a new dispensation to save Iraq from destruction. Was he a credible force? Not for *all* of Iraq, but certainly for parts of it. In 2011, a NATO missile hit Qaddafi's convoy as it left Sirte. The Misrata militia seized Qaddafi, humiliated him as well, and then lynched him. He, too, should have been allowed to surrender, and then to bring his political bloc to the table. In fact, in the early days of the Libyan revolt, Qaddafi sent emissaries—such as the retired U.S. rear admiral Charles Kubic and General Wesley Clark—to say that he wanted a deal.[33] The African Union's delegation sat in an aircraft ready to broker a deal. It was sidelined. Brazil's president, Lula de Silva, offered to go to Libya and mediate a deal—backed by the African Union, Latin American states, and even the Arab League.[34] The West wanted a war.

Instead, in both cases the West and its allies prosecuted a complete victory—which ends in complete disaster if other political blocs remain intact. There was no appetite for negotiations in Iraq, in Libya, or in Syria. It seemed acceptable to allow the old guard to return in Egypt and even in Tunisia. These countries had been made pliable by other means. It seemed even more acceptable to allow the monarchies complete freedom to crack down on their regimes. But the old Arab nationalists—in Iraq, Libya, and Syria—could have no quarter. Despite their own drift from their earlier commitments, these political forces had to be fully destroyed. The lessons of Iraq were not learned. They were repeated in Libya, and they fly—like a famished vulture—over Syria. These countries hang by a thread. Their people suffer painfully. They have been sacrificed to a theory that is arrogant and erroneous. It is a liberal religion that seeks to save the lower orders and make them darker reflections of a Western fantasy that no longer exists even in the West. That theory—regime change—deserves a place in the dustbin of history.

CHAPTER FIVE

Turkey and the Camp of the Counterrevolution

Turkey is the living sore of European legitimacy.

Karl Marx, 1853

Danger lurks in Turkey. On 28 November 2015, gunmen brazenly shot and killed Tahir Elçi, prominent human-rights advocate and president of the Diyarbakir Bar Association. Elçi had bravely spoken out against the atrocities in Turkey, including against the Kurds—his own community. Perhaps the most dangerous statement he made was that the banned Kurdistan Workers' Party (PKK) is "not a terrorist organization." With that, Elçi brought the wrath of the fascistic nationalists on his head. A bullet followed.

Elçi's is not the first political murder in Turkey. His death comes in the context of harsh repression in the majority Kurdish region of eastern Turkey. Major cities in that part of the country—Cizre, Nusaybin, and Sur—are under curfew. The Turkish state has reopened its war against the PKK and its fraternal Syrian group, the People's Protection Units (YPG). Rather than tackle the growth of ISIS on its borders, Turkey has decided to attack the only proven force capable of beating back ISIS. The death of Elçi is part of the new and vicious assault on the Kurds inside Turkey. Gone is the peace process inaugurated a few years ago. Turkey is embroiled in a major civil war.

Two days before Elçi's murder, on 26 November, the ruling government of the Justice and Development Party (AKP) arrested two prominent Turkish journalists: the editor of *Cumhuriyet Gazetesi,* Can Dündar; and its Ankara bureau chief, Erdem Gül. What was the reason for their arrest? Dündar and Gül had exposed the Turkish government's logistical assistance to Syrian rebels in January 2014. The paper had video and photographs of trucks that belonged to Turkish intelligence (MIT) ready to ferry arms and ammunition into Syria. Turkish President Recip Tayyip Erdoğan said then that "the individual who has reported this will pay a high price." The price to be paid was extracted with ninety-two days in prison. When Dündar went to court in May 2016 to defend himself against the charge of treason, he was shot at by Murat Sahin, who was overpowered by a bystander and by Dündar's wife. It was a close call.

On 24 November, Turkish aircraft shot down a Russian jet that had been bombing extremist forces along the Turkish–Syrian border. Among those who had been bombed was the Sultan Abdülhamit Brigade—a group of Turkmen extremists who have been one of the proxy armies of Turkey inside Syria. It is because of the presence of these proxy armies, which Turkey supports, that the pro-AKP media has begun to talk of them as "moderate jihadis" *(ilimli cihatcilar)*. The brigade closely collaborates with Jaysh al-Fatah (the Army of Conquest) and the al-Qaeda proxy, Jabhat al-Nusra. Turkey has been playing with fire. It knew early in 2011 that the removal of Syrian President Bashar al-Assad would require Western bombardment, but it also knew—as a former Turkish military official told me—that such a Western intervention at the necessary scale would not be forthcoming. In the absence of such an intervention, Turkey has fired up its proxies to create a situation where the West will feel obliged to intervene. Turkey's stature as a NATO power allows it (under Article V of the NATO Charter) to call for Western help if it is attacked. Perhaps the reckless shooting down of the Russian jet was intended to draw the West more forcefully into this conflict. It did not work.

Meanwhile, the entry of Russian and Iranian forces into Syria near the Turkish border has complicated matters for Turkey. Salih Muslim, the leader of the Syrian Kurdish political party— the PYD—said that this troop buildup made it impossible for Turkey to intervene in Syria. Muslim's party opened an office in Moscow. It was a clear message to Turkey of its own geopolitical alignments. Erdoğan's "zero problems with neighbors" policy has been upended. So has the image of Turkey as a democratic state. Images of the crackdown on the Gezi Park protestors and on the Soma miners are vivid. They have corroded the reputation of Erdoğan. The AKP is firmly in power, cemented by its victory in the November 2015 election, but its authority is dented. No longer does it carry the name of "moderate Islamism"; a more accurate sense of its politics is "authoritarian populism."

ORIGINS OF THE AKP

The AKP emerged on the Turkish political scene in 2001. It picked up the mantle of narrower Islamist political parties such as Refah (Welfare), Doğru Yol Partisi (True Path), and Fazilet (Virtue). These parties drew support from about a fifth of the population at most—people who believed that religious piety and practice must be allowed to have a place in Turkish political life. For them the epitome of politics was to pray in public. Turkey's long-time ruling party—the Cumhuriyet Halk Partisi (Republican People's Party or the CHP)—and the military had disallowed any public religious symbolism. The state's militant secularism led the Constitutional Court to shut down Refah and Fazilet because they were accused of trying to "redefine the secular nature of the republic." The AKP grew out of the ashes of Fazilet, but it pushed aside the more extravagant religious aspects of their traditions (which would be harnessed by the Saadet [Felicity] party, which has a marginal presence in Turkish politics). Rather, the AKP accepted the legacy of its religious heritage (signaled by the word *justice* in its name) but pushed for "development" as its main theme. The leaders of the AKP, Erdoğan and Abdullah Gül, dressed like midlevel Anatolian businessmen, with nondescript suits and ties as their uniform. Erdoğan (as mayor of Istanbul from 1994 to 1998) joined his party leaders in winning local government seats, where they proved their ability to govern. It was where the AKP established its reputation as a "moderate Islamist" force.

In 2002, the AKP won the parliamentary election with a majority: 34 percent of the vote translated—because of Turkish electoral rules—to 60 percent of the seats in the parliament. Erdoğan became the prime minister. That he had been in jail briefly in 1998 for "inciting hatred based on religious difference" did not seem to matter. He had what counted as a popular mandate. The AKP and Erdoğan rightly feared a military coup to oust them. Their political vision was outside that of the consensus between the CHP and the military. In many ways, Erdoğan's push for Turkey to join the European Union was a way to insulate his party from military action; the EU's rules forbid military governments. Early indications of liberalism from Erdoğan came not because of benevolence or "moderate Islamism," but because of fears of the military. The AKP had to tread carefully.

AKP IN POWER

Erdoğan inherited a Turkish economy spluttering along on fumes. Policies to protect the old Istanbul elite's chokehold on the economy had run their course. The debt crisis that hit the Global South in the 1980s had an impact on Turkey as well. The business sector needed foreign investment, and it—with slack domestic demand— needed access to foreign markets. The classic IMF goal to draw in foreign direct investment and to design the industrial sector toward export-oriented growth dominated. In Anatolia, the vast landmass of Turkey in Asia, small industrial units and business houses bristled with the desire to break the dominance of Istanbul's large tycoons and enter both Europe and the Arab world to sell their goods. These Anatolian businessmen formed the backbone of the AKP's support base. They watched as Turkey's economy shrank by 6 percent between 1994 and 1999, then by 9 percent in 2001.[1] High debt rates and unimaginative policy slates swept coalition government upon government out of power, as their leaders—Akbulut, Yilmaz, Demirel, Çiller, Yilmaz, Erbakan, Yilmaz, and Ecevit—took the oath and then crumbled. Anatolia's businessmen did not like the instability. They threw in their chips with the AKP, which swept to power. The AKP's business supporters' commitment to Europe was equal parts desire for access to the European Union's Customs Union and for curtailment of the monopoly power of the old guard.[2]

A soft touch by the AKP toward its own programmatic commitment to Islamism did not stop its supporters from their own enthusiasm. In 1994, when Erdoğan won the race to become mayor of Istanbul, his supporters cheered, "The other Turkey has come to power." What they meant was clear. Those who wanted to display their personal piety had long felt like second-class citizens in Turkey. It was Erdoğan's gesture toward the piety of the poor and the lower middle class that drew mass support for the AKP. Erdoğan condensed the entire spectrum of beliefs, from piety to business, in his defense of the family. He argued that the family is the main subject of the nation, and said—in 2013—"Nation and state exist only if family exists." Politics, he noted, must be "a servant of family." Development would follow only if the family was strong. What does Erdoğan mean by family? He means that traditional values—with the wife being subordinate to the husband—must be upheld, that women must have at least three children, and that the spiritual idea of the family must be reiterated in social life so that Western-style individualism does not get free rein.[3] Social-welfare politics of the government and Islamic charity work focused attention on the family as the atom of the new Turkey. Politics returned to reproductive issues (such as abortion rights) and to ideas of gender relations. Such a suffocating agenda appealed to sections of the lower middle class that saw their futures blocked by the westernized elite of Istanbul. The AKP camouflaged its neoliberal policy direction by turning rhetorical attention to the behavior of the Turkish people.

Ideas of "Islamic reformism" and "Muslim democracy" allowed the AKP to showcase its commitment to neoliberal capitalism and to the politics of piety, with the latter couched firmly in the domain of the family. What was the character of this "Islamic reformism"? It was precisely that Turkey was a Muslim democracy, which was not in the camp of monarchy or dictatorship—

the other examples in the Middle East. The bar was low for Erdoğan's purposes. What made the AKP even more "moderate" in the early 2000s was that it welcomed an IMF plan to cut public expenditure and privatize public institutions and lands. The AKP's fealty to IMF-style neoliberal policy classified it on the global stage as moderate or reformist. That it was elected by the ballot box and was a Muslim-oriented party gave it the patina of "Islamic reformism."

Being a member of NATO meant that Turkey had close links to the West. This went back to the post–World War II era, when Turkey threw itself into the West's camp and became a forward post against the Soviet Union. Turkey's army was allowed considerable latitude with its coups (1960, 1971, 1980) as long as it allowed its soil to base NATO surveillance and military aircraft and PGM-19 Jupiter missiles. By the 1990s, the West had begun to slough off its association with military governments. These had become a post–Cold War embarrassment. A muted coup in 1997 (also known as the postmodern coup) saw the military use a memorandum rather than tanks to oust the Refah party's Erbakan from his short tenure as head of a coalition government. Erdoğan was right to be anxious in 2002, worried that the military would move against the AKP government.[4] But the AKP's eagerness to join the European Union and its willingness to work with NATO neutralized any threat from the military. This kind of "moderate Islamism" had no problem with NATO and its wars.

The test for the AKP came in 2003, when the United States was ready to attack Iraq. Almost all of Turkey's citizens opposed the war. In February 2003, the AKP deputies voted to allow the U.S. military to modernize their bases in Turkey. The next month, the parliament was to vote on allowing the United States to use these bases in its war on Iraq. The AKP leadership told their deputies to vote for the use of these bases, despite popular opinion. Nearly half the AKP deputies broke with their leadership to join the opposition and voted to prevent the use of Turkish soil for America's war. Erdoğan held a third vote, where he whipped his deputies into shape and delivered a mandate for the United States to use the bases. It turned out that the Iraqi Kurdish leadership did not want the United States to use Turkey as a launchpad, invalidating the need for the bases.[5] What Erdoğan showed NATO, however, was that he could deliver his land for Western interests against the will of his population. That vote did not dent Erdoğan's popularity within Turkey. Mosques, which would have been expected to erupt in anti-Western chatter, remained silent. A few minor protests by the Left and the by-now-mute Saadet party made no impact. Erdoğan had taken Turkey's Islamist tradition and delivered it to NATO. This is the true definition of "moderate Islamism." What was allowed—as a safety valve—were public protests in 2006 against the Danish cartoon controversy and demonstrations in 2009 against the Israeli bombing of Gaza. These became the authorized forms of protest for the Islamists. Criticism of Erdoğan was forbidden.

Erdoğan's close associate Foreign Minister Ahmet Davutoğlu defined his foreign-policy terrain as "zero problems with neighbors."[6] Despite the AKP's association with NATO and desire for entry into the European markets, there was a clear understanding that the opportunities posed in West Asia and North Africa should not be underestimated. With the downturn in the Western economies by 2007, this strategy of looking south paid off handsome dividends. In 2010, the Turks signed a four-country free trade zone agreement—the Close Neighbors Economic and Trade Association Council—which included Jordan, Lebanon, and Syria. Massive Turkish finance went into the real-estate boom in Syria, which had opened its economy to neoliberal policies under Bashar al-Assad's government. Turkish exports drove across the border to inundate the markets of these three countries.[7] Turkey's economic intervention in Syria, writes Cihan Tuğal, "had helped to worsen the plight of youth in the country's run-down agricultural towns, from Daraa in the south to Homs, Hama and Idlib, which would be the center of the revolt, while a tiny elite had grown spectacularly rich."[8] Economic ties with Israel also flourished, with Turkish goods entering Israel at exponential speed.

Turkey's GDP expanded from $230 billion in 2002 to $788 billion in 2014. The fruits of its economic policy paid off dividends for the Istanbul-based oligopoly and the Anatolian businessmen alike. Confidence in the AKP rose. It had "solved" the economic crisis for the wealthy, and it had silenced the military in the barracks. Restive forces among the informal sector and the working class had to be contained. By 2005, the AKP opened up a full-scale attack on workers' rights and threatened constitutional changes to put more draconian power in the hands of Erdoğan. The full force of the state went after those who would question Erdoğan's authority—tax inspections of dissidents, legal shenanigans to silence critics.[9] The AKP would lash out at its various opponents—the tentacular Islamist movement of Fethullah Gülen, the establishment in the military, the trade unions, and of course the various national minorities (the Alevis, the Armenians, the Kurds). From the shadows emerged the fascistic Grey Wolves to do the dirty work—assassinating this leader of that community and threatening violence when it best suited them. The AKP—in their suits—would sit back and watch the thugs of the Grey Wolves and their own shock troops take their views to their logical conclusion. The AKP bared its teeth through the

Grey Wolves and its own thugs, who would return periodically to draw blood.

In 2010, the AKP won a referendum that would allow the rewriting of the Turkish constitution. What the AKP wanted was to create a presidential system of governance with Erdoğan at its head. In early 2016, Erdoğan bizarrely cited Hitler's Germany as an example of a successful presidential system. One of the main ambitions of the AKP is to abolish the parliament, which is—to its eyes—fractious, and turn the Turkish state over to presidential rule. The AKP's demographic advantage in Anatolia allows it to imagine that its candidate—whether Erdoğan or not—would win presidential elections for many decades to come. It would cement power in the hands of the AKP for as long as it would take to legislate Turkey into its image. To recast the 1980 constitution, the AKP had to win a two-thirds majority in the parliament. By 2010, the republican opposition had been tethered. It found no avenues to grow. The Left was marginal, and the Kurdish political parties were threatened with violence. Neither alone would be able to break the 10 percent vote barrier and enter parliament with a sufficient bloc to stymie Erdoğan. Nothing seemed in the way of the AKP and Erdoğan. When the Arab Spring broke out, the arrogance of the AKP spilled over its borders before it had consolidated its power internally.

TURKEY'S AUTUMN

The Arab Spring of 2011 turned Davutoğlu's calculations of "zero problems with neighbors" upside down. The AKP has a temperamental connection with the Muslim Brotherhood around the Mediterranean. When the uprisings took place, it—along with Qatar—reached out to its contacts, from Tunisia's

Ennahda to Syria's Muslim Brotherhood. But this association with the Muslim Brotherhood brought the AKP's government out of line with the West's reaction to the uprisings. When the West was wary, the AKP was jubilant. The fall of Mubarak in Egypt brought Erdoğan to Cairo, where—at a major public address—he put the AKP forward as the model for the Egyptian Muslim Brotherhood. Erdoğan went to Assad as mediator and urged him to declare the Syrian Muslim Brotherhood to be legal. The West, particularly the United States, and the Saudis were not comfortable with the arrival of the Muslim Brotherhood. They had other irons in the fire. But this gap between Turkey and the West would not last long. Turkey backed the Saudi invasion of Bahrain to smash the peaceful protestors, and soon Turkey would be alongside Saudi Arabia in its support for proxy armies in Syria and the demolition of the Libyan state. Gaps would open up when the Saudis went all out to destroy the Muslim Brotherhood in Egypt and Libya. The Turks did not do anything material to counter them. The association with the West was too powerful for the AKP to break with NATO and the Saudis on their emergent narrative of the Arab Spring. Syria was the touchstone.

All the contradictions that had been muted by the AKP since 2002 unraveled as the Syrian war continued. Erdoğan had expected that the Assad regime would fall quickly and that his preferred Brotherhood leaders would ride into Damascus, turning Syria into an extension of Turkish authority. He also hoped that his Syrian Turkmen proxies on the border would allow older nationalist claims on that territory to the fore: Turkey has long wanted to claim parts of northern Syria as its own. Erdoğan openly gestured toward an end to any Kurdish aspirations on the borderlands. But Assad's rule did not end, and Turkey's maximum position against him made a climb down almost impossible. There was no room for a rapprochement. Turkey had opened its doors to the Syrian opposition to set up their offices in Istanbul, and it had allowed Syrian rebels of all stripes to set up bases on the Turkish side of the border. It was here that Western governments had their best entrée into Syria, with the diplomats in close contact with the political leadership in Istanbul as their intelligence services massaged the rebels on the border. By June 2011, the Free Syrian Army formed its main base in the southern Turkish province of Hatay. The Turks had been enthusiastic about the NATO attack on Libya (despite the fact that Erdoğan had been a close associate of Muammar Qaddafi, having received the 2010 al-Qaddafi Human Rights Prize in Tripoli). There was an expectation that NATO would now shift its aircraft to bomb Damascus and to remove Assad speedily. The Free Syrian Army—egged on by Turkey—called for a no-fly zone over Syria. This did not happen, largely because the Russian and Chinese would not permit any kind of United Nations resolution to effect regime change in Damascus. Erdoğan and Davutoğlu saw their plans come unstuck. Syria became a quagmire for their ambitions—even as the Turkish army did not directly involve itself in the war.

The war in Syria forced the Syrian Arab Army to move away from its northern border and consolidate the main population centers to the west of the country. Assad delivered to the Syrian Kurds their long-demanded autonomy. Turkey's experienced (and banned) political party—the Kurdish Workers Party (PKK)—came across the Iraqi and Turkish border to assist their Syrian compatriots in their allied party—the PYD—to form an army, the YPG. This army fought off other rebels (and later ISIS) to create Rojava, a Kurdish enclave in northern Syria. The presence of a Kurdish enclave was seen—north of the border—

as a major political victory for the Kurds. Iraqi Kurds had their own autonomous region, and now so did Syrian Kurds. Turkey's Kurds, meanwhile, remained in the midst of a cease-fire with the Turkish state and were in a peace process that seemed close to being completed. The PKK's leader, Abdullah Öcalan, was in Imrali Prison, where he had been in the midst of the Imrali Process with Erdoğan's government—a peace negotiation between the PKK and the Turkish state that began in late 2012. All this would collapse as the Syrian war continued, as the YPG and PKK established themselves on the border, and as Erdoğan's obstinacy over Syria began to suck Turkey into its morass.

An indication that the long dialogue with the PKK would unravel came at the end of 2011, when Turkish aircraft killed thirty-four Kurdish smugglers in the Turkey–Iraq borderlands. This was the high point of Erdoğan's Syria policy. Why did the Turkish armed forces bomb these men and boys as well as their mules? The government did not offer a clear answer at that time, and the government's report—published in 2013—did not clarify anything. It insinuated that the smugglers had nefarious motives— to infiltrate PKK commanders Cudi Gui, Kazim, and Fehman Hüseyin into Turkey. No evidence was offered. Dutch journalist Fréderike Geerdink went to Gülyazi, the village from which the men and boys had gone on their fateful journey. An enormous plastic banner greeted her with the faces of the victims: "Erdoğan's thirty-three bullets. Dersim, Zilan, Agri, today Qilaban. Erdoğan murdered." It is a powerful statement, which links the massacre of the Kurds to that of the Armenians. Poverty in Gülyazi is striking, with smuggling being the main supplement to meager incomes. Geerdink shows that there is little PKK activity here—a view shared by Levent Gök of the Republican People's Party (CHP) and Ertuğrul Kürkçü of the People's Democratic Party (HDP).[10]

These politicians dissented in the official inquiry. No one listened to them. When the Turkish jets fired at the Kurdish smugglers, these men did not scatter as combatants would, but huddled with each other as ordinary people do. The impunity for this action—which came to be known as the Roboski Massacre—emboldened the state. It also suggested that the Kurds would be easily pacified once Assad was defeated.

The Syrian war opened the door to the rise of sectarianism in the region. Saudi Arabia's proxy Jaysh al-Islam and al-Qaeda's proxy Jabhat al-Nusra, as well as Turkey's proxies such as the Sultan Abdülhamit Brigade, reframed the Syrian conflict from a civil dispute into a sectarian one. It was now to be a war between the Sunni and the Shia. The Turkish Islamist press took this opportunity to drill into the long-dormant traditions of sectarianism and Sunni communalism.[11] The Grey Wolves took to the streets—drawing chalk marks on the doors of the Turkish Alevis. Even more dangerous are the JÖH (Gendarme Special Operations) and the PÖH (Police Special Operations)—outfits with closer ties to the AKP and with a more religious bent. Grey Wolf cadres have found new homes here, and greater license to use paramilitary violence against their enemies. Animosity over Kurdish autonomy in northern Syria rankled the conservatives among the Islamists, the fascist-nationalists, and the republican nationalists. None wanted to see their long-hated enemy gain political power. Turkey would do everything to sideline Kurdish autonomy and to destroy the Assad government, even if it meant giving leeway to the most hard-line Islamist radicals.

In 2014, a senior Kurdish commander of the YPG told me, with a smile, that Turkey was to Syria as Pakistan was to Afghanistan. What he meant was that, like Pakistan, Turkey had allowed itself to become a base for foreign extremists eager to go across the border and destabilize its neighbor. Airports along the rib of Anatolia—particularly at Mardin—welcomed extremists from Libya and Europe, who then went along to shore up first the assortment of groups in the western parts of Syria, but then—after 2012—to the more audacious ISIS. In 2014, Press TV's Serena Shim reported that ISIS fighters and supplies seemed to have no problem crossing the border. Her team took footage of trucks with World Food Organization logos carrying fighters into Syria. Syrian Kurdish journalist Barzan Iso reported that Qatari charities had sent aid and assistance to Carablus, under ISIS control. Dündar's *Cumhuriyet* published photographs of trucks believed to be from Turkish intelligence carrying arms into Syria. Wounded ISIS fighters crossed into Turkey at the border town of Akçakale and went to Urfa's Balıklıgöl State Hospital for treatment—in plain sight. The Turkish government became belligerent toward journalists who tried to cover stories of ISIS recruiters inside Turkey. Erdoğan called reports of recruitment centers "shameless, sordid and vile." He went after the *New York Times*'s Ceylan Yeginsu. Dündar did a stint in prison. Shim died when a cement truck hit her car en route to Suruç a day after she filed her story, and days after she had been threatened by Turkish intelligence. Turkey's border became the main lifeline for various kinds of extremists.

When the Kurdish town of Kobanî came under ISIS siege within hundreds of meters from Turkey, the Turkish authorities prevented Kurdish fighters from crossing the border to reinforce the town. Instead, the Turkish military sat back, garrisoned the border, and allowed ISIS to seize the town. While this was going on, in October 2014 Turkish aircraft bombed Kurdish positions on the Iraq–Syria border. With great reluctance and under immense pressure, the Turkish government finally allowed Kurdish forces in Kobanî to be resupplied by the Iraqi Kurdish government. Kobanî was retaken in January 2015, but only after it had been destroyed. Turkey's involvement with ISIS is a mystery. It has certainly not closed its border to them. When it allowed U.S. aircraft to use Turkish bases to bomb ISIS targets, the price it extracted from the United States was the allowance for it to bomb PKK bases in Iraq and to open up a small war against the Kurds once more. Since October 2015, the Turkish armed forces have hit not only the Kurdish cities in southeastern Turkey but also PKK and YPG combatants inside Syria. PKK leader Cemil Bayik accused the Turkish state of attacking the PKK to "stop the Kurdish advance against ISIS."[12]

A massive bomb went off on 12 January in Istanbul's Sultanahmet Square. This is the heart of the city's monuments—in sight of the Blue Mosque and Hagia Sophia. Erdoğan suggested that the bomber—from ISIS—was of Syrian origin.[13] In March 2016, a car bomb in Ankara killed dozens of people. Fingers pointed in all directions. The government accused the PKK, who in turn denied responsibility. A splinter Kurdish group—the Kurdistan Freedom Falcons—said they had done some of these bombings. None of this can be ascertained. Turkey is in serious crisis. There is the government's war against the Kurds in the southeast; there is the war in Syria and Iraq on the border, with ISIS breathing into Turkey. Turkey is as vulnerable as the driest tinder.

THE TURKISH LEFT

Why did the Turkish government go after the Kurds again and not after ISIS? The question resolves around the AKP's collapsing domestic agenda as much as its geopolitical expectations. In the parliamentary elections of June 2015, the AKP was unable to win the decisive victory Erdoğan needed to revise the constitution. His path was blocked by the People's Democratic Party, the HDP, which won more than 10 percent of the popular vote and so earned seats in parliament. The HDP is not strictly speaking a Kurdish party, although that is how it is often described in the media. It was formed in 2012 when a group of left-leaning political organizations—all with firm pro-Kurdish views—formed an electoral coalition. The similarity with Greece's Syriza and Spain's Podemos would not be unkind. The HDP holds fairly conventional leftist positions—against nuclear power, for LGBT rights, against discrimination of minorities, for women's equality, against neoliberalism, for workers' power.

The HDP nonetheless has a strong current that is close to the PKK and that reveres its jailed leader, Öcalan (known as Apo). At HDP rallies leading up to the parliamentary election, PKK flags and pictures of Öcalan did not appear. The HDP was careful to distance itself from those connections. Nonetheless, people from the crowd would cry out, "*Biji serok Apo*" ("Long live Apo!"). The HDP held together currents that are pro-cease-fire and pro-PKK, although the former clearly dominate the leadership. It says a great deal that the two leaders of the HDP are Selahattin Demirtaş, who comes from the Kurdish heartland and its main political parties (Democratic Society Party and Peace and Democracy Party), and Figen Yüksekdağ, who comes from a Marxist-Leninist tradition in the Socialist Party of the Oppressed. The unity of these two strands—Kurdish and leftist—is not new. In the 1990s, the People's Labor Party (HEP) and the Social Democratic People's Party (SHP)—one Kurdish, the other leftist—fought the general election of 1991 together. An alphabet soup of parties followed along these lines as the Turkish state banned them and arrested their leaders. The objective conditions for a Left–Kurdish united political force have existed at least since the 1980s.

Turkey's Left has struggled to chart a path out of Young Turk nationalism (Kemalism). Plagued by sectarian splits and violence, the Left went into disarray. On May Day 1977, two hundred thousand people gathered at Taksim Square in Istanbul. Violence took the lives of thirty-nine people and scattered the Left into its fragments. Classical neoliberal policies that followed disarmed the working class as an informal sector grew outside the trade-union movement. Rural-to-urban migration expanded the population in the cities, and contributed to the pool of the informal sector. The reservoirs of the Turkish Left had been emptied. New opportunities had to be seized, but the Left was not prepared for the challenge. When thousands of people descended to protect Gezi Park in Istanbul from the neoliberal bulldozer in 2013, the Left found itself made vital again. It is the Gezi dynamic that poked a hole in the AKP's narrative of being the sole representative of the Turkish people, and drew disenfranchised and alienated Turks (including the Kurds) to pin their hopes on an alternative.

Among those who migrated to the cities over the past several decades were a large number of Kurds. Half of the Kurdish population now lives in the western part of Turkey, away from their older Kurdish homeland in the east. Over a million Kurds live in Istanbul, making it the largest Kurdish city in the country. It had been clear for decades, therefore, that in Turkey the Kurdish question could not be solved as it had in Iraq and then in Syria. In Iraq, the Kurds live—by and large—in the country's north. They have a contiguous homeland that became—after 1991—their autonomous region. In Syria, the Kurds have pockets of concentration on the northern border with Turkey. It is these areas that became Rojava during the civil war. Nothing like this is possible in Turkey. The Kurdish parties had to pivot from calls for secession of a Kurdish homeland to the transformation of Turkey into a country of multiple nationalities. This is why the PKK ended its call for an independent homeland in 1993 and sued for peace. This is precisely why the Kurdish parties, since the 1990s, have sought a wide alliance with the Left.

TWO ELECTIONS OF 2015

The HDP's ability to secure 10 percent in the June parliamentary elections stymied the AKP. Erdoğan wanted to break the HDP so as to secure a complete mandate in the second election of November—after his party was not able to form a government in June. To clear the way for the AKP, Erdoğan had to do two things: he had to break the HDP and to take votes away from the fascistic Nationalist Movement Party (MHP). Both birds would be killed with one stone—namely, a frontal attack on the Kurdish and other minority populations.

Rather than accept the HDP victory as a sign of life in Turkish democracy, the AKP opened a direct attack on this legitimate political force. Syrian Kurdish gains against ISIS combined with the HDP's 13 percent in the Turkish election rankled the anti-Kurdish forces that slumber within Turkey. They went ballistic on 8 September, burning down HDP offices and attacking Kurdish shops and homes. A few hours before the attack on the HDP headquarters, the Turkish air force and special forces units struck PKK bases in Avashin, Bazyan, Qandil, and Zap—in Iraq. The virulent attack took place after PKK units ambushed a Turkish military convoy in Dağlıca, killing fifteen soldiers. The death of these soldiers provided Erdoğan with the opportunity he needed. The Turkish troops opened a full-scale assault on the PKK positions. Retaliations have come on both sides, leading Turkey toward the worst period of the conflict that ran from 1984 to 2012 (with a lull between 1999 and 2004). It is difficult to imagine how Turkey or the PKK can walk away from the intensification of this war or return to the negotiation table.

In the run-up to the parliamentary elections of 1 November, a bomb blast in Ankara at an HDP rally killed over a hundred (mostly young) activists. Shock waves went through the HDP support base. Was this a message from the AKP, whose government had neglected to provide the most basic security for the rally? It was feared that liberals who had voted for the HDP would now rethink their votes and cast their ballot for stability. This violence took a toll on the electorate. It allowed the AKP to put itself forward as the party of order. Sections of traditionalist Kurds, who had already been uneasy with the HDP's radical political platform (socialism, gay rights, women's rights), went for the AKP this election cycle. Between intimidation and a call for traditionalism, the AKP was able to make inroads into the Kurdish heartland. "Unfortunately, it was a difficult and troubled period of election campaigning. Lives were lost," said Selahattin Demirtaş, the leader of the HDP.

The alliance between Kurdish nationalists and the Left has moved the Kurdish parties to step away from the separatist ambitions of Kurdish nationalism. The new language was for human rights and dignity within Turkey, not departure from Turkey. A section of (mainly younger) Kurds who have seen their livelihood collapse and an increase in the security pressure from the army and Turkish intelligence are not prepared to accept the Turkish bargain. The violence visited upon Turkey's southeast by the Erdoğan government put a great deal of stress on these communities, whose youth broke their allegiance for the HDP and voted for the marginal—but firmly Kurdish separatist—Rights and Freedoms Party (Hakpar). Among the Left there is also a lack of unity, with the Patriotic Party (Vatan), the People's Liberation Party (HKP), and the Communist Party (KP, founded in 2014) standing outside the HDP. Each of these parties took votes away from the HDP.

Winks and nods toward Turkish supremacy over the minorities—including public statements by Erdoğan denying the Armenian genocide and denying the existence of the Kurdish problem—drew voters of the fascistic MHP to the AKP. Why would they vote for the MHP when the AKP—much more likely to win—had adopted much of the vision of the MHP? The MHP support collapsed. In November, they lost half the seats they won in the June elections to the AKP. The MHP voters went to the AKP, as did disaffected traditionalist Kurds. Erdoğan's gambit succeeded—although the HDP did succeed in getting over 10 percent and securing seats in parliament.

What can the HDP do to prevent Turkey's spiral into civil conflict? The violence against the Kurdish majority areas has depressed the ability of the HDP to provide any kind of moderation to the AKP regime. An assassination attempt against HDP leader Demirtaş came just before the murder of Tahir Elçi. At Elçi's funeral, Demirtaş said coldly, "What killed Tahir was not the state, but statelessness." This is a small indication that the idea of Kurdish nationalism remains intact. Pushed to the wall, even Demirtaş, centerpiece of the Kurdish–Left alliance, might seek shelter in Kurdish nationalism. But the HDP has greater tasks ahead. It is the only force that would be able to guide the country toward peace negotiations and insist upon a more reasonable position vis-à-vis Syria. The AKP is in a bind—caught between its commitments to NATO and its own Islamist ambitions for West Asia. It is not capable of breaking out of this contradiction. Turkey will have to suffer that blockage. No alternative force is as yet capable of defeating the AKP. Only the HDP can prevent it from total power, but it cannot come close to taking power itself.

One limited opportunity is for a split in the AKP. The resignation by Prime Minister Davutoğlu in early May, not six months after the AKP won a mandate, is a consequence of Erdoğan's predatory claim on power. The Turkish press called this a "palace coup," although a neutered Davutoğlu downplayed his disappointment with Erdoğan. "His family's honor is mine," said Davutoğlu. Davutoğlu followed his mentor into the prime minister's office, he filled his office with Erdoğan's choices, and he governed on his behalf. There was no cause for his removal. On 1 May, an anonymous document—the Pelican Brief—appeared on the Internet. It suggested that Davutoğlu did not agree with Erdoğan's attack on journalists, and it carved out minor but sensible positions that separated Davutoğlu from the presidential palace. The brief was written by someone "who would sacrifice his soul for the CHIEF"—a reference to Erdoğan. Davutoğlu tried to push back, but it was futile. He had to go. Currents in the AKP suggest disappointment with this outcome. Whether the restive currents in the AKP will act against Erdoğan is hard to predict.

Erdoğan has cemented his power and might be able to change the constitution. But what will he inherit? A country with many fewer democratic rights, with an opposition that has been weakened to anger and an insurgency that claimed forty thousand lives and might yet claim many thousand more. Hardly the empire of Mehmed II, Erdoğan's hero.

WAR ON THE KURDS

The Turkish state opened up terrible violence against the Kurdish southeast. Tanks shelled the town of Cirze, near the Syrian border, and military operations in Diyarbakir and Silopi escalated with each day. The region—say local journalists—resembles a war zone. These journalists—such as Deniz Babir of *Azadiya Welat*, Zeki Karakuş of *Nusaybin Haber*, and Beritan Canözer of JINHA—were hastily arrested and detained away for their reportage. Erdoğan called the violence a "fight against separatist terror organizations," framing his war as part of the Global War on Terror. Diyarbakir's mayor, Gultan Kisanak, said, "Tanks and heavy weaponry, which are only used in conventional warfare, are being used by the Turkish armed forces, in areas where hundreds of thousands of civilians live." Kisanak, a former political prisoner and very popular politician, bravely stood up—as an MP—against the Roboski Massacre. She does not mince words, nor exaggerate them.

Nor does Demirtaş, who has a calm and careful political demeanor. From great desperation, Demirtaş backed a resolution from the Kurdish Democratic Society Congress (DTK), passed on 3 January 2016, reiterating the old demand for the creation of Kurdish autonomous regions and self-governance bodies. Erdoğan called Demirtaş's action "treason," tying the HDP to the PKK. When the HDP responded that it had no "organic ties" to the PKK, Erdoğan scoffed at his Ramazan speech at a mosque in Istanbul's suburban Ataşehir district. He said that the HDP and the PKK have an "inorganic tie." Erdoğan wanted war against not only the PKK (which is an armed force) but also the HDP (which is a respected parliamentary party). Both had to be dented. The Turkish government believes it can score a military victory against the PKK, which is why it has been striking PKK camps inside Turkey, in Iraq, and in Syria. Before the PKK can be destroyed, the Turkish forces will have to raze the cities and towns of southeastern Turkey. They are on the road to doing this—with little international condemnation of their actions.

On 4 January 2016, three campaigners of the HDP were killed in the town of Sirnak (near Silopi). Who were they? Seve Demir was a member of parliament of the Democratic Regions Party (DBP), affiliated with the HDP in parliament. Fatma Uyar was a member of the Free Women Congress. Pakize Nayir was the cochair of the Silopi People's Assembly. They are the second trio of Kurdish feminist socialists killed together. The other three—Sakine Cansız, Leyla Şaylemez, and Fidan Doğan— were killed in Paris in January 2013. They died in passive voice. No one will be prosecuted for these deaths. No one will be held accountable. The next assassins will be emboldened to repeat the feat. This is the temptation of impunity. It is the fate of the Kurdish people. It is increasingly the fate of the Turks as well.

Yemen and Palestine

Have the Barbarians already arrived?
Mahmoud Darwish, 1987

If attention is focused on Syria and Iraq, with a glance on occasion toward Libya, there is no question that the bombing of Yemen and the strangulation of Palestine play a role in the wider turmoil of the region.

As 2015 wound down, ISIS leader Abu Bakr al-Baghdadi shrugged off the loss of Ramadi and the bombing raids on Raqqa with a turn to Palestine. "The Jews thought we forgot Palestine," he said, "and that they had distracted us from it. Not at all, Jews. We did not forget Palestine for a moment. With the help of Allah, we will not forget it." It is common for Arab leaders to turn to the cause of the liberation of Palestine as a way to revive support for their ambitions. Evidence for any ISIS activity against Israel is slim. Hamas political chief Khaled Meshal warns that if the status quo of the Israeli occupation continues, in the alleyways of Gaza forces far worse than anything imaginable would emerge. Such forces—which would likely ally with ISIS—are the product of disillusionment in the political process. Jabhat al-Nusra, cousin to

ISIS, sits near the Israeli border at the occupied Golan Heights. Its wounded fighters cross into Israel for treatment, as Israeli jets pound Hezbollah forces in Syria that threaten Jabhat al-Nusra. A suspicious mind would say that al-Qaeda has an understanding with Israel rather than displays any hostility toward it. The confusion around Jabhat al-Nusra's activities and the threats from ISIS reflect the complexities of the current moment in West Asia. Nothing is simple.

Israel's endless occupation of the Palestinians comes with no exit. Frustration percolates across Palestine, from the West Bank to Gaza. Knife attacks by Palestinian teenagers are met with harsh retribution from Israeli forces. Lives lived encaged by the occupation produce—says UN Secretary General Ban Ki-moon—"fear, humiliation, frustration and mistrust. It has been fed by the wounds of decades of bloody conflict, which will take a long time to heal. Palestinian youth in particular are tired of broken promises and they see no light at the end of the tunnel." Secretary Ban blamed the "settlement enterprise" for the tension in the region. Frustration is the order of the day. I meet some young men from a camp near Ramallah. They see no outlet for their anger. Every day they see their families and friends humiliated by the occupation. This situation drives them to desperation. "We have to do something," says one young man. His eyes are tired. He looks older than his teenage years. He has lost his friends to Israeli violence. "We marched to Qalandiya [checkpoint] last year," he says, "in a peaceful protest. They fired on us. My friend died."[1] Colonial violence bears down on his spirit. Around him young children are eliminated by the Israeli military. His body twitches with anxiety and fear.

Highly charged rhetoric leads to dangerous outcomes. No exit from the Israeli occupation suggests perilous times ahead. The two-state solution has been largely invalidated by the Israeli settlement policy. Israeli settlers have seized most of the best land in the Jordan Valley—given to Palestine under the Oslo agreement. U.S. charitable money (namely, tax free) goes to underwrite these illegal settlements. The one-state solution is anathema to the Israeli political consensus, which would like to move toward the open declaration of the country as a Jewish state. A sizable Palestinian population would dilute this ethno-nationalist claim. In 2014, Israel's justice minister, Ayelet Shaked, declared that the "entire Palestinian people is the enemy." She called Palestinian children "little snakes." Such language is echoed by Rabbi Ovadia Yosef, who said of the Palestinians, "You must send missiles to them and annihilate them. They are evil and damnable." What remains is endless occupation and frustration. It is the cause of the silent murder of Palestinian children. What will germinate among the survivors is hard to anticipate. It is what Khaled Meshal fears.

It is a testament to the Palestinians that they have concentrated their own fight on their national aims. Even Hamas has not been sucked into the wider conflict. It exited Syria during the rebellion, largely in keeping with its Muslim Brotherhood orientation; its local affiliate led the rebellion, and its paymasters in the Gulf required some display of fealty to their anti-Assad line. But Hamas remained largely silent on Syria, focusing its objectives on the Israeli occupation. This is an error that PLO leader Yasser Arafat made in 1990, when he backed Saddam Hussein's invasion of Kuwait against the Saudis and the West. That weakened the Palestinian position and sent them to the Oslo accords of 1994—the "Palestinian Versailles," as Edward Said characterized it.[2] Not for Khaled Meshal this kind of error.

Twice during the aftermath of the Arab Spring has Israel conducted its punctual bombing of Gaza—2012 and 2014. These were brutal assaults on the livelihood of the Palestinian population. Gaza had not yet recovered from the 2009 bombardment, and will likely not recover from these, either. Oxfam says it will take Gaza a hundred years to recover from the 2014 assault. The United Nations Relief and Works Agency (UNRWA), which is tasked with the provision of relief to the Palestinian refugees, complained that "people are literally sleeping amongst the rubble; children have died of hypothermia." Of the two and a half thousand Palestinians who died in the 2014 attack, over five hundred were children.

South of Saudi Arabia, in Yemen, the Saudis and Emiratis have been bombing that country since March 2015.[3] Hospitals, schools, and residential neighborhoods—nothing is sacrosanct. The bombing resembles in every respect Israel's punctual bombardment of Gaza. There is no care for human life, no regard for international law. When the ordinance runs low, the West comes in to resupply these powers.[4] Neither Israel nor Saudi Arabia has to worry about censure or sanctions. They are comfortable in their various continuous wars.

One of the most dangerous outcomes of the war in Yemen has been the deepened sectarian tension. In March 2015, the International Crisis Group noted, "Previously absent Shite-Sunni narrative is creeping into how Yemenis describe their fight."[5] The earlier war in Yemen between the Houthis and the government from 2004 to 2010 pitted the former against a president who was himself—like the Houthis—a Zaydi (Shia). Sectarianism did not define that war. The new battlefield has become—in a short time—rapidly sectarian. Saudi claims that the Houthis are an Iranian proxy seek to make this conflict part of the wider geopolitical tussle. In no time at all, the complex political problems of Yemen that have plagued the country since unification in 1990 have been reduced to the inexplicable language of sectarianism. So much more has been at stake, but now so little is considered on the table.

Meanwhile, two horses of the apocalypse stalk Yemen.

On the one side is famine—with the UN agencies in constant distress about the deterioration of living standards for the population. The World Food Programme said in early January 2016 that Yemen was one step away from half the population being in famine conditions. More than fourteen million of the twenty-three million Yemenis are "food insecure." Julien Harneis, UNICEF chief in Yemen, laid out some of the data that the agency has collected. More than a million children have been displaced from their homes; more than a million children under five risk acute malnutrition and acute respiratory-tract infections. Two million children cannot go to school. "The longer-term consequences of all this for Yemen—which was already the Middle East's poorest nation even before the conflict—can only be guessed at," said Harneis.[6]

The other horse of the apocalypse is extremism. Al-Qaeda in the Arabian Peninsula (AQAP) and the Islamic State group, says the Crisis Group, "are arguably the war's principal beneficiaries."[7] AQAP not only now holds some towns of the Hadramout region, such as Mukalla, but has been active in this war alongside the Southern Resistance in Taiz and elsewhere. It has found the Saudi air cover salutary and has made major gains as a consequence. In August 2015, Ansar al-Sharia's Jalal Baleidi called upon all Yemeni Sunnis to fight the Houthis—bringing the geopolitical sectarianism right into Yemen's political war. That Baleidi had been touted as a potential ISIS leader is now moot. Neither AQAP nor Ansar al-Sharia seems interested in any internecine battles; they are focused on pushing their sectarian agenda—with Saudi air cover—and winning adherents among the general population. A sign of the times is the turn by Dammaj Salafis, as distant from AQAP in normal times as even the Houthis, who have now made common cause with AQAP. Meanwhile, a breakaway group from AQAP has fashioned itself as a new ISIS franchise. On 20 March 2015, it announced its existence with a massive attack that killed more than 140 people who were in or near Zaydi mosques in Sanaa.

"In the Middle East's convulsions," the Crisis Group notes, "the Yemen war is relatively unnoticed, but over 2,800 civilians have been killed, the majority from airstrikes, and the country is suffering an acute humanitarian crisis that could trigger catastrophic famine and refugee flows that would further destabilize the region."[8] The World Health Organization puts the death toll at over sixty-five hundred. Yemen is Saudi Arabia's Gaza.

Seriousness about peace is hard to find. Even as a Yemeni delegation sat in Saudi Arabia in March 2016 to find agreement on a cessation of hostilities, Saudi jets bombed a market in the province of Haja. Over forty civilians died in that bombing of 15 March 2016. Peace talks in Kuwait took place to the sound of Saudi bombing raids. At 3 A.M. on 10 May, my friend Haykal Bafana, who lives in Sanaa, wrote, "Saudi jets scream over the city, like enraged Wahhabi clerics who've spotted an unmarried couple holding hands." Humor provides a way to survive the madness. It is hard to imagine peace in this context. Cease-fires are on the horizon. The wreck of Yemen would need the guns to go silent and then for its own history to begin again.

I recall how, many years ago, ordinary Afghans would say that they welcomed the Taliban since these fighters provided a respite from the bloody era of warlord battles of the 1990s. The Taliban's rough justice allowed for calm compared with the erratic violence of the warlord era. A survey of Syrians from ORB International in late 2015 showed that a fifth of the population said that ISIS has a "positive influence" on the country. It is likely that they judge ISIS rule just as the Afghans judged the Taliban between 1994 and 2001: far better than war and chaos. It is a very low standard. The conflict in Yemen—with no outcome in sight—will possibly draw ordinary Yemeni Sunnis to consider AQAP a positive influence on the country. This is the danger of sectarian wars that have no endgame. They will not end with a utopian outcome. They can end only where life becomes evil.

Tucked away in Beirut's Verdun neighborhood is the Institute for Palestine Studies. The Lebanese author Elias Khoury is the editor of the institute's Arabic-language journal, *Majallat-al-dirasat-al-filastiniyah*. In late 2013, Khoury tells me—joyfully—about a protest in East Jerusalem. For some years Israel has laid claim to land just east of Jerusalem in a parcel named E1. Even the United States, Israel's steadfast advocate, has cautioned Israel not to build settlements on this land, which by most accounts should be part of the future Palestinian state. In January 2013, three hundred Palestinians set up tents on the land to form the village of Bab Al-Shams, the Gate of the Sun. The name of the village refers to Elias Khoury's most famous novel (*Bab al-Shams*, published in 1998), which tells the story of a Palestinian couple, Younis and Nahila, one a fighter in Lebanon and the other a defender of their home in the Galilee (Israel). The couple meet secretly in a cave called Bab Al-Shams, their haven. The activists who created their village called Bab Al-Shams the "gate to our freedom and steadfastness."

The Israeli authorities destroyed the camp three times, even though the activists had broken no Israeli laws. (They used tents, which do not require permits.) The activists kept rebuilding their camp till Israeli Prime Minister Benjamin Netanyahu ordered that this be designated a closed military zone. The young activists came out of the popular resistance committees. Their politics reflected their frustration with the strategy of negotiation and conciliation. "For decades," said the organizers of the village, "Israel has established facts on the ground as the international community has remained silent in response to these violations. The time has come to change the rules of the game, for us to establish facts on the ground—our own land." At one of their village evenings, the occupants heard from Khoury, who was on the phone from Beirut. "I was so moved by the experience," Khoury recounts. This was a glimmer of the "different way" that he hopes will open up for the Palestinian cause.

The day after their encampment was first put up, Khoury sent the citizens of Bab Al-Shams a letter. "I see in your village all the faces of the loved ones who departed on the way to the land of our Palestinian promise," he wrote. "Palestine is the promise of the strangers who were expelled from their land and continue to be expelled every day from their homes. I see in your eyes a nation born from the rubble of the *nakba* that has gone on for sixty-four years. I see you and in my heart the words grow. I see the words and you grow in my heart, rise high and burst into the sky."

Much the same letter could be written to the Arab nation. It is a promise. It will have to be redeemed with struggle and tenacity.

ACKNOWLEDGMENTS

I am not an expert in either North Africa or West Asia. But I have lived and traveled in the region for many years, and tried my utmost to learn about dynamics and events from friends and colleagues who know the area much better than I. My expertise—if there is any—might be measured by my two-volume work that provides a panorama of the history of Africa, Asia, and Latin America from the early twentieth century to the present: *The Darker Nations* (2007) and *The Poorer Nations* (2013). In this book, I draw deeply from the broad narrative that appears in those accounts.

What you have here is not a historian's book, although, being trained as a historian, I find it impossible not to fall into that style. It is more properly the work of a journalist, which is what I have been for almost thirty years. My first report from the region was on the Turkish government's incursion into northern Iraq in 1996 to attack PKK bases in the mountains of the border region.[1] Since then I have covered the region off and on, but largely off—with my focus drifting to the Americas (with Latin America being a main focus for several years). In the mid-2000s, I began to cover developments from Iran to Lebanon—largely driven by a fascination with the rapid changes in the area produced by the Iraq War. It was that war that drew me back to the region, allowing me to learn about Iraq and Syria, Iran and the Gulf. When the Arab Spring broke out, I was lucky to be able to cover developments there on a sporadic basis. Moving to Beirut in 2013 allowed me to deepen my understanding of the region, and begin—more frequently—to write about it for *Frontline* (thank to my longstanding editor R. Vijayashankar) and for the *Hindu* (starting with Siddharth Varadarajan, then Malini Parthasharti, and now Suresh Nambath, Srinivas Ramani, and Mini Kapoor). Weekly columns formerly for *al-Araby al-Jadeed* (thanks to Lamis Andoni and Ibrahim Halawi) and currently for *BirGün* (thanks to Ömür Keyif and Can Ugur) have allowed me to broaden my horizons as I write for audiences not only in India but elsewhere. In the United States, I have been very lucky to write for *Counterpunch* (under the keen eye of my dear friend—now gone—Alexander Cockburn, and Jeffery St. Clair) and for *Alternet* (thanks to my editor, Jan Frel). I am very grateful to *Democracy Now*'s Amy Goodman; *The Real News Network*'s Paul Jay, Sharmini Peres, and Jessica Devereaux; and *TeleSur*'s Chris Hedges and Abby Martin for allowing me to test out my ideas on their television programs. Several of these essays—in a much shorter form—were first published in the *Marxist*, thanks to Prakash Karat.

Could I have written this slim book without holding the hands of highly knowledgeable and wise people? Unlikely. Six people read the entire manuscript and offered me pointed and sharp criticisms and suggestions—Aijaz Ahmad, Kifah Hanna, Mark LeVine, Mayssoun Sukarieh, Omar Dahi, and Richard Falk. I couldn't have done this without them. Close reporting companions—such as Radwan Mortada, Salwa Bugaighis, and two who shall remain unknown for now—made the journey to the story possible.

There are others, so here they are (in alphabetical order of first name): Adam Hanieh, Ahmad Dallal, Ahmet Tonak, Akram Mohammed Ismail, Alex Lubin, Ali Issa, Ali Wick, Ali Osserian, Ambassador Anita Nair, Anne Barnard, Antoun Issa, Arianne Shahvisi, Ambassador Asoke Kumar Mukerji, Basileus Zeno, Bassam Haddad, Bilal-El Amin, Brinda Karat, Brooke Atherton El-Amin, Can Ertuna, Can Semercioglu, Coralie Hindawi, Dahlia Gubara, Dina Hussein, Elias Khoury, Fatima Hamroush, Fawwaz Trabulsi, High Commissioner Filippo Grandi, Githa Hariharan, Ghiwa Sayegh, Haifa Zangana, Hala Dimechkie, Haneen Zoabi, Hans von Sponeck, Ambassador Hardeep Singh Puri, Hassan Awad, Haykal Bafana, Horace Campbell, Ibrahim Fraihat, Ira Dworkin, Jamal Juma, Jana Nakhal, Jean Said Makdisi, Jeff Bachman, Jodie Evans, Juan Cole, Karim Makdisi, Karine Walther, Katty Alhayek, Kevork Almassian, Khair el-din Haseeb, Khaled Almaeena, K.P. Fabian, Lina Atallah, Linda Tabar, Madawi Al-Rasheed, Magdulien Abaida, Maha el-Said, Mahmood Mamdani, Mansour A, Mariam Said, Marwan Osman, Masha Refka, Mather Mather, Medea Benjamin, Miriyam Aouragh, Mounira Soliman, Muna Khalidi, Munira Khayyat, Mustafa Said, Nabil Abdo, Nader el-Bizri, Nadera Shalhoub-Kevorkian, Ambassador Navdeep Suri, Neil Singh, Ambassador Nirupama Rao, Ambassador Nirupam Sen, Nour Samaha, Noura Erakat, Nouri Gana, Omar Nashabe, Omar Robert Hamilton, Patrick Cockburn, Paul Amar, Pernille Ironside, Phyllis Bennis, Prabir Purkayastha, Philip Khoury, Rabi Bashour, Rabia Nasser, Rafia Zakaria, Raja Khalidi, Rami Khouri, Rania Masri, Rashid Khalidi, Rayan El-Amin, Raymond Baker,

Rida Hamdan, Rima Khalaf, Rima Rassi Harfouche, Rosemary Sayegh, Roy Singham, Rumla Khalidi, Sabine Hamdan, Safia Antoun Saadeh, Sahar Mandour, Samar Ghanem, Samer Abboud, Samir Makdisi, Sari Kassis, Sasha Ammar, Shaden Khalaf, Shadi Rachid, Sharmine Narwani, Sherene Seikaly, Stanly Johny, Tania El K, Tania Saleh, Tariq Ali, Tariq Tell, Thanassis Cambanis, Wael Eskander, Wael Gamal, Walid Hamdan, High Commissioner Y.K. Sinha, Yasmine Moataz, Yazan al-Saadi, Zayde Antrim, and Ziad Abu Rish.

Sudhanva Deshpande, my comrade at arms in LeftWord Books, and Niels Hooper at UC Press believed in this book enough to make me write it. Carl Walesa did the line-edits, Sudhanva did the index, Jessica Ling saw the book through and Tania Saleh—the Bulbul of the Levant—did the cover: immeasurable thanks.

Thanks to my family—particularly Lisa Armstrong, Zalia Maya, and Rosa Maya—for your love and joy. This book is for Soni Prashad—my wonderful mother.

May 2016

NOTES

INTRODUCTION

1. Mahmoud Darwish, *Journal of an Ordinary Grief* (Brooklyn, NY: Archipelago, 2010), 172.

CHAPTER ONE

1. Vijay Prashad, *Arab Spring, Libyan Winter* (New Delhi: LeftWord; Oakland, CA: AK Press, 2012).

2. Sinan Antoon, "The Arab Spring and Adunis's Autumn," *Jadaliyya,* July 11, 2011, http://www.jadaliyya.com/pages/index/2047/the-arab-spring-and-aduniss-autumn. In September 2011, Syrian opposition intellectual Michel Kilo gave a seminar in Beirut, where he worried—like Adunis—about how the armed struggle had "put the leadership of the insurrection in the hands of extremist Islamist centres of power." He envisaged the descent of Syria into sectarianism. "Syria, in the aftermath of such an eventuality," he said, "will not be as it was before." Michel Kilo, "Syria ... The Road to Where?" in *The Arab Spring: Critical Analyses,* ed. Khair El-Din Haseeb (New York: Routledge, 2013), 169.

3. Leon Trotsky, *The History of the Russian Revolution* (London: Sphere, 1967), 3:322–23.

4. Karen Pfeifer, "Rebels, Reformers and Empire: Alternative Economic Programs for Egypt and Tunisia," *Middle East Report,* no. 274 (Spring 2015).

5. The most important book on this strand is Philip S. Khoury, *Urban Notables and Arab Nationalism: The Politics of Damascus, 1860–1920* (Cambridge: Cambridge University Press, 1983). Also see Ralph Coury, *The Making of an Egyptian Arab Nationalist: The Early Years of Azzam Pasha, 1893–1936* (Ithaca, NY: Cornell University Press, 1998).

6. Douglas Boyd, *Broadcasting in the Arab World* (Philadelphia: Temple University Press, 1982).

7. Salah Badreddin, *The Kurdish National Movement in Syria: A Critical Approach from Inside* (Berlin: Kurdish Kawa Cultural Center, 2003).

8. Quoted in Douglas Little, *American Orientalism* (Chapel Hill: University of North Carolina Press, 2004) 79.

9. James Risen, "Secrets of History: The CIA in Iran—A Special Report," *New York Times,* 16 April 2000; Ervand Abrahamian, *The Coup: 1953, the CIA and the Roots of Modern US–Iranian Relations* (New York: New Press, 2013).

10. Irene Gendzier, *Notes from the Minefield: United States Intervention in Lebanon, 1945–1958* (New York: Columbia University Press, 2006), 34.

11. Robert Vitalis, *America's Kingdom: Mythmaking on the Saudi Oil Frontier* (London: Verso, 2009), 164.

12. Tahia Gamal Abdel Nasser, *Nasser: My Husband* (Cairo: AUC Press, 2013), 96ff.

13. Mohamed Heikal, *The Sphinx and the Commissar* (New York: Harper & Row, 1978), 261–62.

14. Vijay Prashad, *The Poorer Nations: A Possible History of the Global South* (London: Verso; New Delhi: LeftWord, 2013), chap. 1.

15. Vijay Prashad, *India's Iran Policy: Between US Primacy and Regionalism,* Issam Fares Institute for Public Policy and International Affairs Working Paper Series no. 19 (Beirut: American University of Beirut, 2013).

16. Ambassador Richard Olson, "Abu Dhabi Crown Prince Warns DOE DEPSEC Poneman about Iran," US State Department Cable, no. 09ABUDHABI1151_a, 17 December 2009, WikiLeaks cache.

17. Hillary Clinton, "Secretary Clinton's April 7, 2009 Meeting with UAE Foreign Minister Sheikh Abdullah Bin Zayed," US State Department Cable, no. 09STATE34688_a, 9 April 2009, WikiLeaks cache.

18. For more on this sensibility, see Sami Hermez, "'The War Is Going to Ignite': On the Anticipation of Violence in Lebanon," *Political and Legal Anthropology Review* 35, no. 2 (2012).

19. Sahar Mandour, *32*, trans. Nicole Fares (Syracuse, NY: Syracuse University Press, 2016).

20. Sahar Mandour, "Yesterday's Story," trans. Maia Tabet, *Orient-Institut Studies* 2 (2013).

CHAPTER TWO

1. "Arab Spring Is 'Strongest Answer' to 9/11," *al-Ahram*, 9 September 2011.

2. For excellent introductions, see Alison Pargeter, *Muslim Brotherhood: From Opposition to Power* (London: Saqi Books, 2013); and Raymond Baker, *Islam without Fear: Egypt and the New Islamists* (Cambridge: Harvard University Press, 2006).

3. For a flavor of that era, see Beth Baron, *The Orphan Scandal: Christian Missionaries and the Rise of the Muslim Brotherhood* (Palo Alto, CA: Stanford University Press, 2014).

4. Mark Curtis, *Secret Affairs: Britain's Collusion with Radical Islam* (London: Serpent's Tail, 2010), 109.

5. Hanna Batatu, "Syria's Muslim Brothers," *MERIP Reports* (November–December 1992), is the sharpest essay on the Syrian branch of the Muslim Brotherhood.

6. Mayssoun Sukarieh and Stuart Tannock, *Youth Rising? The Politics of Youth in the Global Economy* (London: Routledge, 2015), chap. 4.

7. For an excellent analysis of the class use of "youth," see Mayssoun Sukarieh, "From Terrorists to Revolutionaries: The Emergence of 'Youth' in the Arab World and the Discourse of Globalization," *Interface* 4, no. 2 (November 2012).

8. Samia Mehrez, ed., *Translating Egypt's Revolution: The Language of Tahrir* (Cairo: American University of Cairo Press, 2012).

9. For example, Hossam El Hamalawy, "Comrades and Brothers," *Middle East Reports,* no. 242 (Spring 2007); and Tarek Osman, *Egypt on the Brink* (New Haven, CT: Yale University Press, 2013).

10. Thanassis Cambanis, *Once upon a Revolution: An Egyptian Story* (New York: Simon and Schuster, 2015), 70.

11. Olivier Lavinal, "Upheaval in the Middle East and Syria's Refugee Crisis," (seminar presentation, Hampshire College, Amherst, MA, 3 March 2016).

12. *Youth Unemployment, Existing Politics and Way Forward: Evidence from Egypt and Tunisia* (Washington, DC: World Bank, 2008), 2.

13. "Maya Jribi: I nostri giovani, senza speranza né future," *Il Manifesto,* 29 January 2009.

14. For a discussion of the workers' role in the 2011 revolution, see Joel Beinin, "Workers and Egypt's January 25 Revolution," *International Labour and Working-Class History* 80 (Fall 2011); and for an update, see Heba F. El-Shazli, "Where Were the Egyptian Workers in the June 2013 People's Coup Revolution?" *Jadaliyya,* July 23, 2013, http://www.jadaliyya.com/pages/index/13125/where-were-the-egyptian-workers-in-the-june-2013-p.

15. Samer Soliman, *The Autumn of Dictatorship: Fiscal Crisis and Social Change in Egypt under Mubarak* (Palo Alto, CA: Stanford University Press, 2011), 150.

16. Osman el-Sharnoubi, "Revolutionary History Relived," *al-Ahram,* 6 April 2013.

17. Laryssa Chomiak, "The Making of a Revolution in Tunisia," *Middle East Law & Governance* 3 (2011); Amin Allal, "L'autoritarisme participative: Politiques de développement et protestations dans la région minière de Gafsa en Tunisie 2006–2010," *Les Cahiers d'EMAM: Études sur le Monde Arabe et la Méditerranée* 22 (2013).

18. Walid Hamdan, "The ILO and Worker's Rights in the Arab Region: The Need to Return to the Basics," in *The Land of Blue Helmets: The UN in the Arab World,* ed. Karim Makdisi and Vijay Prashad (Berkeley: University of California Press, 2016).

19. I make this argument in chapter 4 of *The Poorer Nations: A Possible History of the Global South* (London: Verso; New Delhi: LeftWord, 2013).

20. For a parallel analysis, see Sami Zemni, Brecht De Smet, and Koenraad Bogaert, "Luxemburg on Tahrir Square: Reading the Arab Revolutions with Rosa Luxemburg's *The Mass Strike*," *Antipode* 45, no. 4 (2013).

21. More detailed country studies are available in Paul Amar and Vijay Prashad, eds., *Dispatches from the Arab Spring* (Minneapolis: University of Minnesota Press; New Delhi: LeftWord, 2013).

22. The term *deep state* comes from Turkish—*derin devlet*. The term has now traveled; see, for example, Eckart Woertz, "Egypt: Return of the Deep State," *openDemocracy*, January 20, 2014, https://www.opendemocracy.net/arab-awakening/eckart-woertz/egypt-return-of-deep-state.

23. This was one of the main arguments of my *Arab Spring, Libyan Winter* (New Delhi: LeftWord; Oakland, CA: AK Press, 2012).

24. For details, see the essays in Karim Makdisi and Vijay Prashad, eds., *The Land of Blue Helmets: The United Nations in the Arab World* (Berkeley: University of California Press, 2016).

25. United Nations Economic and Social Commission for West Asia, *Institutional Development and Transition: Decentralization in the Course of Political Transformation* (Beirut: ESCAW, 2013).

26. Padamja Khandelwal and Agustin Roitman, "The Economics of Political Transitions: Implications for the Arab Spring," *IMF Working Paper* 13, no. 69 (March 2013): 10, http://www.imf.org/external/pubs/ft/wp/2013/wp1369.pdf.

27. *Economic and Social Inclusion for Peace and Stability in the Middle East and North Africa: A New Strategy for the World Bank Group* (Washington, DC: World Bank, 2015).

28. Katerina Dalacoura, "Islamism and Neoliberalism in the Aftermath of the 2011 Arab Uprisings: The Freedom and Justice Party in Egypt and Nahda in Tunisia," in *Neoliberal Governmentality and the Future of the State in the Middle East and North Africa,* ed. Emel Akçali (London: Palgrave Macmillan, 2016).

29. Anne Brockmeyer, Maha Khatrouch, and Gaël Raballand, *Public Sector Size and Performance Management: A Case Study of Post-Revolution Tunisia,* Policy Research Working Paper, no. 7159, Governance Global Practice Group (Washington, DC: World Bank, January 2015).

30. Karen Pfeifer, interview with the author, 19 March 2016, Smith College, Northampton, MA.

31. Mayssoun Sukarieh, "Egyptian Revolts," *Counterpunch,* 26 November 2012, http://www.counterpunch.org/2012/11/26/egyptian-revolts/.

32. "All According to Plan: The Rab'a Massacre and Mass Killings of Protestors in Egypt," *Human Rights Watch,* 12 August 2014, https://www.hrw.org/report/2014/08/12/all-according-plan/raba-massacre-and-mass-killings-protesters-egypt.

33. Abdullah Al-Arian, *From the Ashes of Rabaa: History and the Future of Egypt's Muslim Brotherhood,* University of Denver, Center for Middle East Studies Occasional Paper Series, Paper no. 4, November 2015, http://www.du.edu/korbel/middleeast/media/documents/occasionalpaper4.pdf.

34. Passant Rabie, "He Who Has Lost Something, Does Not Give It," *Mada Masr,* 7 March 2014, http://www.madamasr.com/sections/politics/he-who-has-lost-something-does-not-give-it.

35. Vijay Prashad, "Cairo's Quest," *Frontline,* 4 April 2014.

36. Nadine Abdalla, "Neoliberal Policies and the Egyptian Trade Union Movement: Politics of Containment and the Limits of Resistance," in *Neoliberal Governmentality and the Future of the State in the Middle East and North Africa,* ed. Emel Akçali (London: Palgrave Macmillan, 2016).

37. Quoted in Salah al-Din al-Jorashi, "Tunisian President: Arab World Is Marching to the Abyss," *New Arab,* 21 February 2016, https://www.alaraby.co.uk/english/indepth/2016/2/22/tunisian-president-arab-world-is-marching-to-the-abyss.

CHAPTER THREE

1. Darryl Li, "A Jihadism Anti-Primer," *MERIP,* no. 276 (Fall 2015).

2. For a full assessment, see Sameer Abboud, *Syria* (London: Polity, 2015), chap. 3.

3. Charles Lister, *The Syrian Jihad: Al-Qaeda, the Islamic State and the Evolution of the Insurgency* (New York: Oxford University Press, 2015), 187.

4. Essential reading for the timeline of the conflict is Omar Dahi, "Some Days before the Day After," *Middle East Report,* no. 274 (Spring 2015).

5. Syrian Centre for Policy Research, *Syria: Confronting Fragmentation; Impact of Syrian Crisis Report* (Damascus: SCPR, 2016), 64.

6. United Nations Assistance Mission for Iraq—Human Rights Office, *Report on the Protection of Civilians in the Armed Conflict in Iraq: 1 May–31 October 2015,* 1, http://www.ohchr.org/Documents/Countries/IQ/UNAMIReport1May31October2015.pdf.

7. Amy Hagopian, Abraham D. Flaxman, Tim K. Takaro, Sahar A. Esa Al Shatari, Julie Rajaratnam, Stan Becker, Alison Levin-Rector, Lindsay Galway, Berq J. Hadi Al-Yasseri, William M. Weiss, Christopher J. Murray, and Gilbert Burnham, "Mortality in Iraq Associated with the 2003- 2011 War and Occupation: Findings from a National Cluster Sample Survey by the University Collaborative Iraq Mortality Study," *PLOS Medicine* 10, no. 10 (October 2013).

8. Gilbert Burnham, Shannon Doocy, Riyadh Lafta, and Les Roberts, "Mortality after the 2003 Invasion of Iraq: A Cross-Sectional Cluster Sample Survey," *Lancet,* 13 October 2006.

9. Physicians for Social Responsibility, *Body Count* (Washington, DC: PSR, 2015), 15.

10. It is worth reading the leaked "Taguba Report" on atrocities at Abu Ghraib: *Article 15–6 Investigation of the 800th Military Police Brigade,* May 2004, http://www.npr.org/iraq/2004/prison_abuse_report.pdf.

11. Michael S. Schmidt, "Junkyard Gives Up Secret Accounts of Massacre in Iraq," *New York Times,* 14 December 2011.

12. On Blackwater, see Jeremy Scahill, *Blackwater: The Rise of the World's Most Powerful Mercenary Army* (New York: Nation Books, 2007).

13. Ambassador Joe Wilson to Secretary of State Hillary Clinton, personal letter, 13 September 2010. Unclassified. US Department of State case no. F-2014–20439, doc no. C05772428, released 29 February 2016.

14. Amnesty International, *Escape from Hell: Torture and Sexual Slavery in Islamic State Captivity in Iraq* (London: Amnesty International, 2014), https://www.amnesty.org.uk/sites/default/files/escape

_from_hell_-_torture_and_sexual_slavery_in_islamic_state_captivity_in_iraq_-_english_2.pdf, has an extensive investigation by Donatella Rovera of the crimes against the Yazidis.

15. Quoted in Daniel Williams, *Forsaken: The Persecution of Christians in Today's Middle East* (New York: OR Books, 2016), 49.

16. Vijay Prashad, "Sadrist Strategems," *New Left Review,* no. 53 (September–October 2008).

17. Vijay Prashad, "The Arab Gramsci," *Frontline,* 21 March 2014; Rula Jurdi Abisaab and Malek Abisaab, *The Shi'ites of Lebanon: Modernism, Communism and Hizbullah's Islamists* (Syracuse, NY: Syracuse University Press, 2014).

18. The most important book to assess the tensions between the Arab nationalists and the Communists is Hanna Batatu, *The Old Social Classes and the Revolutionary Movements of Iraq* (Princeton, NJ: Princeton University Press, 1978).

19. Tareq Y. Ismael, *The Communist Movement in the Arab World* (New York: Routledge, 2005), 17–20.

20. Vitalis, *America's Kingdom,* 152.

21. Vijay Prashad, *The Darker Nations* (New York: New Press; New Delhi: LeftWord, 2007), 270–85.

22. Vitalis, *America's Kingdom,* 237.

23. Two books by Madawi al-Rasheed have been essential for my understanding of Saudi society and politics: *A History of Saudi Arabia* (Cambridge: Cambridge University Press, 2010) and *Muted Modernists: The Struggle over Divine Politics in Saudi Arabia* (London: Hurst, 2015).

24. Timothy Mitchell, *Carbon Democracy: Political Power in the Age of Oil* (London: Verso, 2011).

25. Fred Halliday, *Arabia without Sultans* (London: Penguin, 1974).

26. Patty Paine, Jeff Lodge, and Samia Touati, eds., *Gathering the Tide: An Anthology of Contemporary Arabic Gulf Poetry* (Reading, UK: Ithaca Press, 2011), 172.

27. Vijay Prashad, "Contract Slavery," *Frontline,* 10 January 2014; Vijay Prashad, "Work Woes," *Frontline,* 28 June 2013.

28. Quoted in Fouad Ajami, *The Dream Palace of the Arabs* (New York: Vintage, 1999), 126.

29. Lutz Kleveman, *The New Great Game: Blood and Oil in Central Asia* (New York: Grove Press, 2004), 239–40; Robert G. Wirsing, *Pakistan's Security under Zia, 1977–1998* (New York: Macmillan, 1992), 75. Wirsing suggests that the CIA had been funding these men since 1973—six years *before* the Soviet intervention.

30. Patrick Seale, *Asad: The Struggle for the Middle East* (Berkeley: University of California Press, 1990).

31. Jubin Goodarzi, "Syria and Iran: Alliance Cooperation in a Changing Regional Environment," *Ortadoğu Etütleri* 4, no. 2 (January 2013): 39.

32. Pierre Razoux's formidable history of that war ignores this meeting and produces a narrative that suggests that the war was entirely Saddam Hussein's idea—with the hope of Saudi support once Iraq's Falcons took off to bomb Iran's air force; see Pierre Razoux, *The Iran-Iraq War* (Cambridge, MA: Harvard University Press, 2015), 70. In 1991, Iraq's ambassador to India—Dr. Abdul Wadood el Shekhly—told me that the reason Iraq invaded Kuwait was to collect on the debts for the war that, he claimed, Iraq had fought at the behest of the Gulf Arabs.

33. Dilip Hero, *The Longest War: The Iran-Iraq Military Conflict* (London: Grafton, 1989), 78.

34. For more on the sectarian tensions, see Paulo Pinto, "Syria," in *Dispatches from the Arab Revolt*, ed. Paul Amar and Vijay Prashad (New Delhi: LeftWord, 2013).

35. William Roebuck, "Influencing the SARG in the End of 2006," US State Department cable no. 06DAMASCUS5399_a, 13 December 2006, WikiLeaks Archive.

36. Ambassador Talcott Seelye, "Prospects for Assad's Survival," US State Department cable no. 1979DAMASC06042, 16 September 1979.

37. Patrick Cockburn, *The Rise of Islamic State* (New Delhi: Left-Word, 2015); Patrick Cockburn, *Chaos & Caliphate: Jihadis and the West in the Struggle for the Middle East* (New York: OR Books, 2016), pts. 5 and 6.

38. Haifa Zangana, *Dreaming of Baghdad* (New York: Feminist Press, 2009), 15.

39. Vijay Prashad, "Polling in the Time of Bombs," *Frontline*, 16 May 2014.

40. Thomas Ricks, *Fiasco: The American Military Adventure in Iraq* (New York: Penguin, 2006), 96–100.

41. Nesir Khadim, "Militants Taking Control of Baquba," *ICR*, no. 207 (June 2007).

42. Patrick Cockburn, *Muqtada: Muqtada al-Sadr, the Shia Revival, and the Struggle for Iraq* (New York: Scribner, 2008), 149.

43. Tony Karon, "Learning from Fallujah," *Time,* 12 April 2004.

44. Zaki Chehab, *Inside the Resistance: The Iraqi Insurgency and the Future of the Middle East* (New York: Nation Books, 2005), 180.

45. Osama Bin Laden to Abu al-Abbas, April 2007, Office of the Director of National Intelligence.

46. Agresto quoted in Zaid al-Ali, *The Struggle for Iraq's Future* (New Haven, CT: Yale University Press, 2014), 64–65. For more on Agresto, see Rajiv Chandrasekaran, *Imperial Life in the Emerald City: Inside Iraq's Green Zone* (New York: Knopf, 2006), chap. 16; and for the general looting of Iraq, see Pratap Chatterjee, *Iraq, Inc.: A Profitable Occupation* (New York: Seven Stories Press, 2004).

47. A good primer on these struggles is in Ali Issa, *Against All Odds: Voices of Popular Struggle in Iraq* (Washington, DC: Tadween, 2015).

48. Vijay Prashad, "Polling in the Time of Bombs," *Frontline,* 16 May 2014.

49. On the attack on minorities, see Williams, *Forsaken;* and, from an evangelical perspective, see Mindy Belz, *They Say We Are Infidels: On the Run from ISIS with Persecuted Christians in the Middle East* (Carol Stream, IL: Tyndale, 2016).

50. See, for example, Human Rights Watch, "Iraqi Kurdistan: Arabs Displaced, Cordoned Off, Detained," 25 February 2015, https://www.hrw.org/news/2015/02/25/iraqi-kurdistan-arabs-displaced-cordoned-detained; and Amnesty International, "A Deadly Spiral of Sectarian Violence—a Year On from IS Onslaught on Iraq," 10 June 2015, https://www.amnesty.org/en/latest/news/2015/06/a-deadly-spiral-of-sectarian-violence-a-year-on-from-is-onslaught-on-iraq/.

51. The exceptions here are the Iraqi Kurdish president, Massoud Barzani, who welcomed them as part of his own conflict with the Kurdistan Workers' Party (PKK), and Atheel al-Nujaifi, former governor of Ninevah Province, whose family had been Ottoman grandees in Mosul

and who is now desperate to find an armed force capable of reviving his declining fortunes in the province.

52. *Asharq al-Awsat,* 7 September 2015.

53. A serving diplomat in the Iraqi foreign ministry told me this in a private conversation.

54. Robert Spencer, "Scores Die As Baghdad Hit by Three Bombings in One Day," *Telegraph,* 11 May 2016.

55. *Rethinking Economic Growth: Towards Productive and Inclusive Arab Societies* (Geneva: International Labour Organization, 2013), 52.

56. Syrian Center for Policy Research, *Confronting Fragmentation,* 52, http://scpr-syria.org/publications/policy-reports/confronting-fragmentation/.

57. Charles Glass, *Syria Burning: ISIS and the Death of the Arab Spring* (New York: OR Books, 2015), 48.

58. Basileus Zeno, interview with the author, 15 March 2016.

59. Pinto, "Syria," 235–38.

60. Jared Cohen of Google wrote to Clinton's team about this on 25 July 2012:

> Please keep close hold, but my team is planning to launch a tool on Sunday that will publicly track and map the defections in Syria and which parts of the government they are coming from. Our logic behind this is that while many people are tracking the atrocities, nobody is visually representing and mapping the defections, which we believe are important in encouraging more to defect and giving confidence to the opposition. Given how hard it is to get information into Syria right now, we are partnering with Al-Jazeera who will take primary ownership over the tool we have built, track the data, verify it, and broadcast it back into Syria. I've attached a few visuals that show what the tool will look like. Please keep this very close hold and let me know if there is anything else you think we need to account for or think about before we launch. We believe this can have an important impact.

Part of the Hillary Clinton email tranche release, unclassified, US Department of State, case no. F-2014–20439, doc no. C05795577, 7 January 2016, part B6.

61. Glass, *Syria Burning,* 123. The essential book on the emergence on this class is Bassam Haddad, *Business Networks in Syria: The Political*

Economy of Authoritarian Resilience (Palo Alto, CA: Stanford University Press, 2011).

62. Quoted in Reese Erlich, *Inside Syria* (Amherst, MA: Prometheus Books, 2015), 129.

63. Evidence of the drought is available in Benjamin I. Cook, Kevin Anchukaitis, Ramzi Touchan, David Meko, and Edward Cook, "Spatiotemporal Drought Variability in the Mediterranean over the Last 900 Years," *Journal of Geophysical Research: Atmospheres* 121, no. 5 (16 March 2016), http://onlinelibrary.wiley.com/doi/10.1002/2015JD023929 /full.

64. Quoted in Erlich, *Inside Syria,* 130.

65. *Al-Araby TV,* 28 September 2015.

66. Glass, *Syria Burning,* 17.

67. Patrick Seale, *The Struggle for Syria: A Study of Post-War Arab Politics, 1945–1958* (Oxford: Oxford University Press, 1965).

68. Vijay Prashad, "Syria, Libya and the Security Council," *Frontline,* 10–23 March 2012.

69. Mark Mazzetti and Matt Apuzzo, "Saudis, the CIA and the Arming of Syrian Rebels," *New York Times,* 24 January 2016, 6.

70. Vijay Prashad, "A Nation of Pain and Suffering (Part 3)," *Jadaliyya,* 13 December 2012, http://www.jadaliyya.com/pages/index/8994/a-nation-of-pain-and-suffering_syria-(part-3).

71. Dahi, "Some Days before the Day After," 20–21.

72. Raphaël Lefèvre, *Ashes of Hama: The Perilous History of Syria's Muslim Brotherhood* (New York: Oxford University Press, 2013), 164 (on Tayfour's role).

73. International Crisis Group, *Tentative Jihad: Syria's Fundamentalist Opposition,* Middle East Report no. 131 (12 October 2012), crisisgroup.org, i, http://www.crisisgroup.org/~/media/Files/Middle%20East%20North %20Africa/Iraq%20Syria%20Lebanon/Syria/131-tentative-jihad-syrias -fundamentalist-opposition.pdf. By December, the *New York Times* recognized that "radical Islamists were playing a growing role"; see Mark Landler, Michael R. Gordon, and Anne Barnard, "US Will Grant Recognition to Syrian Rebels, Obama Says," *New York Times,* 11 December 2012. This was by now in plain sight.

74. International Crisis Group, *Tentative Jihad,* ii.

75. Glass, *Syria Burning,* 49.

76. Vijay Prashad, "Khoury's Talismans," *Frontline,* 11 November 2013.

77. "Please Take Care of Syria," *Religion & Ethics,* PBS, 31 July 2012.

78. Roy Gutman and Mousab Alhamadee, "Tense Relations Between the U. S. and Anti-Assad Syrian Rebels," McClatchy, 1 September 2014. http://www.mcclatchydc.com/news/nation-world/world /article24772522.html.

79. Hillary Clinton, "Terrorist Finance: Action Request for Senior Level Engagement on Terrorism Finance," US State Department cable no. 09STATE131801_a, 30 December 2009, WikiLeaks Archive.

80. Asli Bali and Aziz Rana, "The Wrong Kind of Intervention in Syria," in *The Land of Blue Helmets: The UN in the Arab World,* ed. Karim Makdisi and Vijay Prashad (Berkeley: University of California Press, 2016).

81. Vijay Prashad, "The Mystery of the Syria Contact Group," *Asia Times,* 22 September 2012; Vijay Prashad, "Barbarians Arrive As UN Judges Syria," *Asia Times,* 26 September 2012.

82. Vijay Prashad, "Obama's Syria Dilemma," *Hindu,* 17 September 2014.

83. Ben Hubbard and Mayy el-Sheikh, "WikiLeaks Shows a Saudi Obsession with Iran," *New York Times,* 16 July 2015.

84. Seymour Hersh, "The Red Line and the Rat Line," *London Review of Books* 36, no. 8 (17 April 2014). Hersh's essay was widely attacked in many forums for its reliance upon anonymous sources and for its claims that the Assad forces might not have fired the chemical weapons. Hersh had already tried to muddy the waters around the Sarin gas story in "Whose Sarin?" (*London Review of Books* 35, no. 24 [19 December 2013]). Human Rights Watch comes to the opposite conclusion in its report *Attacks on Ghouta: Analysis of Alleged Use of Chemical Weapons in Syria,* 10 September 2013, https://www.hrw.org/report/2013/09/10 /attacks-ghouta/analysis-alleged-use-chemical-weapons-syria. For a sense of the complexity of the issue based on interviews in Damascus and in the UN, see Karim Makdisi, "Chemical Weapons and Cease-fires: Reflections on a Trip to Damascus, Syria," *Counterpunch,*

18 September 2015, http://www.counterpunch.org/2015/09/18/chemical-weapons-and-ceasefires-reflections-on-a-trip-to-damascus-syria/.

85. Karim Makdisi, Coralie Hindawi, Samar Ghanem, and Majd Nassan, *Creative Diplomacy amidst a Brutal Conflict: Analyzing the OPCW-UN Joint Mission for the Elimination of the Syrian Chemical Weapons Program, 2016* (Beirut: Issam Fares Institute for Public Policy and International Affairs, AUB, 2016).

86. Gul Tuysuz, Raja Razek, and Nick Paton Walsh, "Al Qaeda-Linked Group Strengthens Hold in Northern Syria," *CNN*, 6 November 2013.

87. Isabel Coles, "In remote corner of Iraq, an unlikely alliance forms against Islamic State," *Reuters*, 11 May 2016.

88. Al-Zarqawi's group had beheaded at least two U.S. nationals in 2004—Nicholas Berg and Owen Armstrong—as well as several other nationals (from Bulgaria, Japan, Nepal, South Korea, Turkey, and the United Kingdom).

89. Vijay Prashad, "Siege of Kobane," *Frontline*, 17 October 2014.

90. Vijay Prashad, "ISIS Oil," *Counterpunch*, 2 December 2015; "Raqqa's Rockefellers: How Islamic State Oil Flows to Israel," *al-Araby al-Jadeed*, 26 November 2015. Also see Erika Solomon, Robin Kwong, and Steven Bernard, "Inside ISIS, Inc.: The Journey of a Barrel of Oil," *Financial Times*, 11 December 2015. The Israeli defense minister, Moshe Ya'alon, joined the chorus in January; see Herb Keinon, "Ya'alon: ISIS Has 'Enjoyed Turkish Money for Oil' for a Long Time," *Jerusalem Post*, 26 January 2016. From inside Raqqa comes a report on the oil transit: Abu Mohammed, "ISIS, Financing and Developing," *Raqqa Is Being Slaughtered Silently*, 15 November 2015, http://www.raqqa-sl.co/en/?p=1546.

91. Tolga Tanis, *Potus ve Beyefendi* (Istanbul: Doğan Kitap, 2015).

92. "Bilal Erdoğan's Firm Purchases Two New Tankers at Cost of $36 Million," *Daily Zaman*, 15 September 2015.

93. George Kiourktsoglou and Alec Coutroubis, "ISIS Export Gateway to Global Crude Oil Markets," *Marine Security Review*, March 2015.

94. "Kurdish Oil 'Being Sold off the Coast of Malta,'" *Times of Malta*, 17 November 2015.

95. Rukmini Callimachi, "In Timbuktu, al-Qaida Left Behind a Manifesto," *Associated Press*, 14 February 2013.

96. Hamoud Almousa, "Two Years on the Control of ISIS over Raqqa Province," *Raqqa Is Being Slaughtered Silently,* 13 January 2016, http://www.raqqa-sl.co/en/?p=1635.

97. Vijay Prashad, "Manoeuvres on the Syrian Chessboard," *Hindu,* 15 May 2015.

98. Dania Akkad, "Kerry 'Blames Opposition' for Continued Syria Bombing," *Middle East Eye,* 7 February 2016.

99. Robert Fisk, "Syria Civil War: On the Frontline with the Iranian Revolutionary Guards Battling outside Aleppo," *Independent,* 23 February 2016.

100. Vijay Prashad, "How the Kurds Will Save Syria," *Alternet,* 24 March 2016, http://www.alternet.org/world/how-kurds-will-save-syria.

101. Glass, *Syria Burning,* 22.

102. Eva Bartlett, "As Foreign Insurgents Continue to Terrorize Syria, the Reconciliation Trend Grows," *Dissident Voice,* 22 August 2014,http://dissidentvoice.org/2014/08/as-foreign-insurgents-continue-to-terrorize-syria-the-reconciliation-trend-grows/.

CHAPTER FOUR

1. Amnesty International, *Routinely Targeted: Attacks on Civilians in Somalia* (London: Amnesty International, 2008), 8.

2. International Crisis Group, *Somalia's Divided Islamists,* Africa Briefing no. 74 (Nairobi/Brussels, 18 May 2010), 7–8, http://www.crisisgroup.org/~/media/Files/africa/horn-of-africa/somalia/B74%20Somalias%20Divided%20Islamists.pdf.

3. Debora Valentina Malito, "Building Terror while Fighting Enemies: How the Global War on Terror Deepened the Crisis in Somalia," *Third World Quarterly* 36, no. 10 (2015).

4. Paul Masson and Catherine Pattillo, *Monetary Union in West Africa (ECOWAS): Is It Desirable and How Could It Be Achieved?* (Washington, DC: IMF, 2001).

5. On Alliot-Marie's friendship with Ben Ali, see Vijay Prashad, *Arab Spring, Libyan Winter* (New Delhi: LeftWord; Oakland, CA: AK Press, 2012), 161.

6. Farbrice Arte and Karl Laske, "Sarkozy–Kadhafi: La preuve du financement," *Mediapart,* 28 April 2012, https://www.mediapart.fr/journal/international/280412/sarkozy-kadhafi-la-preuve-du-financement; https://histoireetsociete.wordpress.com/2012/04/28/sarkozy-kadhafi-la-preuve-du-financement-par-fabrice-arfi-et-karl-laske/.

7. Gary J. Bass, "Why Humanitarian Wars Can Go So Wrong," *Washington Post,* 8 April 2011.

8. Barack Obama, David Cameron, and Nicolas Sarkozy, "Libya's Pathway to Peace," *New York Times,* 14 April 2011.

9. Alexander Cockburn, *A Colossal Wreck* (London: Verso, 2013), 494.

10. David Kirkpatrick, "Hopes for a Qaddafi Exit, and Worries of What Comes Next," *New York Times,* 21 March 2011.

11. Quoted in Jo Becker and Scott Shane, "Clinton, 'Smart Power' and a Dictator's Fall," *New York Times,* 28 February 2016.

12. Joe Quartararo, Michael Rovenolt, and Randy White, "Libya's Operation Odyssey Dawn: Command and Control," *Prism* 3, no. 2 (March 2012): 150.

13. UN Human Rights Council, *Report of the International Commission of Inquiry on Libya,* no. A/HRC/19/68 (Geneva: Human Rights Council, 2012).

14. Peter Olson to Judge Philippe Kirsch, 15 February 2012; UN Human Rights Council, *Report of the International Commission,* 39.

15. C.J. Chivers and Eric Schmitt, "In Strikes on Libya by NATO, an Unspoken Civilian Toll," *New York Times,* 17 December 2011.

16. C.J. Chivers, "NATO's Secrecy Stance," *New York Times,* 25 March 2012; Editorial Board, "NATO's Duty," *New York Times,* 29 March 2012; Oana Lungescu, "NATO and Libya Deaths," *New York Times,* 30 March 2012.

17. Human Rights Watch, *Unacknowledged Deaths: Civilian Casualties in NATO's Air Campaign in Libya* (New York: Human Rights Watch, 2012).

18. Megan Bradley, Ibrahim Fraihat, and Houda Mzioudet, *Libya's Displacement Crisis: Uprooted by Revolution and Civil War* (Washington, DC: Georgetown University Press, 2016).

19. Amnesty International, *Militias Threaten Hopes for a New Libya,* 15 February 2012, http://www.amnestyusa.org/research/reports/militias-threaten-hope-for-new-libya.

20. Mahmood Mamdani, "Libya: Behind the Politics of Humanitarian Intervention," in *African Awakening: The Emerging Revolutions,* ed. Firoze Manji and Sokari Ekine (Nairobi: Fahamu, 2012).

21. Quoted in Scott Shane and Jo Becker, "After Revolt, a New Libya 'With Very Little Time Left,'" *New York Times,* 29 February 2016.

22. For an excellent window into the Libyan Brotherhood, see Mary Fitzgerald, "Finding Their Place: Libya's Islamists during and after the Revolution," in *The Libyan Revolution and Its Aftermath,* ed. Peter Cole and Brian McQuinn (London: Hurst, 2015).

23. Andrew Gilligan, "Gaddafi's Ghost Town after the Loyalists Retreat," *Telegraph,* 11 September 2011.

24. James Risen, Mark Mazzetti, and Michael Schmidt, "US Approved Arms for Libya Rebels Fell into Jihadis' Hands," *New York Times,* 5 December 2012.

25. Quoted in Shane and Becker, "After Revolt, a New Libya."

26. IMF, *Libya beyond the Revolution: Challenges and Opportunities* (Washington, DC: IMF, 2012).

27. Ajay Makan, "Libya and International Oil Groups Pay the Price for Unrest," *Financial Times,* 16 September 2013.

28. Quoted in Christ Stephen, "Libyan Rebels Storm Prime Minister's Office," *Guardian,* 8 May 2012.

29. Dionne Searcey, Eric Schmitt, and Rukmini Callimachi, "Qaeda Branch Extends Reach in West Africa," *New York Times,* 16 March 2016.

30. Charles Tilly, *Coercion, Capital and European States, AD 990–1990* (Oxford: Basil Blackwell, 1990).

31. This is the central part of the argument in Horace Campbell, *Global NATO and the Catastrophic Failure in Libya* (New York: Monthly Review Press, 2013).

32. Human Rights Watch, *Genocide in Iraq: The Anfal Campaign against the Kurds* (New York: Human Rights Watch, 1993). For the U.S. role, see Shane Harris and Matthew Aid, "CIA Files Prove America Helped Saddam As He Gassed Iran," *Foreign Policy,* 26 August 2013.

33. Becker and Shane, "Clinton, 'Smart Power' and a Dictator's Fall."

34. Charles Abugre, "Libya: The True Costs of War," in *African Awakening: The Emerging Revolutions,* ed. Firoze Manji and Sokari Ekine (Nairobi: Fahamu, 2012), 301.

CHAPTER FIVE

1. Ahmet Ertuğrul and Faruk Selçuk, "A Brief Account of the Turkish Economy, 1980–2000," *Russian & East European Finance and Trade* 37, no. 6 (November–December 2001).

2. Çağlar Keyder, "The Turkish Bell Jar," *New Left Review,* no. 28 (July–August 2004); Ziya Öniş and Umut Türem, "Business, Globalization and Democracy: A Comparative Analysis of Turkish Business Associations," *Turkish Studies* 2, no. 2 (2001).

3. Zafer Yilmaz, "'Strengthening the Family' Policies in Turkey: Managing the Social Question and Armoring Conservative-Neoliberal Populism," *Turkish Studies* 16, no. 3 (2015); Berna Yazici, "A Return to Family: Welfare, State and the Politics of the Family in Turkey," *Anthropological Quarterly* 85, no. 1 (2012).

4. Reşat Kasaba and Sibel Bozdoğan, "Turkey at a Crossroad," *Journal of International Affairs* 54, no. 1 (2000).

5. Cihan Tuğal, "NATO's Islamists," *New Left Review,* no. 44 (March–April 2007).

6. Ahmet Davutoğlu, "Turkey's Zero-Problems Foreign Policy," *Foreign Policy,* May 20, 2010.

7. See the essays in Raymond Hinnebusch and Özlem Tür, eds., *Turkey–Syria Relations: Between Enmity and Amity* (Farnham, Surrey, UK: Ashgate, 2013); also see Tarık Oğuzlu, "Middle Easternization of Turkey's Foreign Policy," *Turkish Studies* 9, no. 1 (2008).

8. Cihan Tuğal, *The Fall of the Turkish Model: How the Arab Uprisings Brought Down Islamic Liberalism* (London: Verso, 2016), 182.

9. Ayşe Buğra and Osman Savaşkan, *New Capitalism in Turkey: The Relationship between Politics, Religion and Business* (Cheltenham, UK: Edward Elgar, 2014); İsmet Akça, Ahmet Bekmen, and Barış Alp Özden, eds., *Turkey Reframed: Constituting Neoliberal Hegemony* (London: Pluto, 2014).

10. Fréderike Geerdink, *The Boys Are Dead: The Roboski Massacre and the Kurdish Question in Turkey* (London: Gomidas, 2015), 134–41.

11. Cihan Tuğal, "Democratic Janissaries? Turkey's Role in the Arab Spring," *New Left Review,* no. 76 (July–August 2012), 19; Tuğal, *Fall of the Turkish Model*, 184.

12. Vijay Prashad, "Turkey's War on the Kurds," *Hindu, 5* January 2016.

13. Vijay Prashad, "From Roboski to Sultanahmet: Turkey Dry as Tinder," *New Arab,* 13 January 2016, http://www.alaraby.co.uk/english /Comment/2016/1/13/ From-Roboski-to-Sultanahmet-Turkey-as-dry-as-tinder.

EPILOGUE

1. Vijay Prashad, "Palestinian Lives Matter!" *New Arab,* 27 December 2015, https://www.alaraby.co.uk/english/comment/2015/12/28/palestinian-lives-matter; Nadera Shalhoub-Kevorkian, "Clowns in Palestine Cry: The Occupied Bodies and Lives of Jerusalem's Children," *Journal of Palestine Studies* 45 (Winter 2016): 13–22.

2. Edward Said, "The Morning After," *London Review of Books,* 20–21 October 1993.

3. For a historical overview, see the essays in Sheila Carapico, ed., *Arabia Incognita: Dispatches from Yemen and the Gulf* (Charlottesville, VA: Just World Books, 2016).

4. Human Rights Watch, *Yemen: Cluster Munitions Wounding Civilians; US Supplied Weapon Banned by 2008 Treaty,* hrw.org, 14 February 2016,https://www.hrw.org/news/2016/02/14/yemen-cluster-munitions-wounding-civilians.

5. International Crisis Group, *Yemen at War,* Crisis Group Middle East Briefing no. 45 (Sanaa/Brussels, 27 March 2015), 5, http://www .crisisgroup.org/~/media/Files/Middle%20East%20North%20Africa /Iran%20Gulf/Yemen/b045-yemen-at-war.pdf.

6. Vijay Prashad, "The Tragedy of Yemen Is Not a Marginal One," *New Arab,* 10 February 2016, https://www.alaraby.co.uk/english /Comment/2016/2/10/The-tragedy-of-Yemen-is-not-a-marginal-one.

7. International Crisis Group, *Yemen: Is Peace Possible?* Middle East Report no. 167 (9 February 2016), 17, http://www.crisisgroup.org /~/media/Files/Middle%20East%20North%20Africa/Iran%20 Gulf/Yemen/167-yemen-is-peace-possible.pdf.

8. International Crisis Group, *Yemen: Is Peace Possible?* p. 31.

ACKNOWLEDGMENTS

1. Vijay Prashad, "Hot Turkey: US Authorised Kurdish Massacre," *Economic and Political Weekly,* 12 October 1996.

INDEX